Theologising with the Sacred 'Prostitutes' of South India

CW00821464

Currents of Encounter

STUDIES IN INTERRELIGIOUS AND INTERCULTURAL RELATIONS

VOLUME 65

The titles published in this series are listed at *brill.com/coe*

Theologising with the Sacred 'Prostitutes' of South India

Towards an Indecent Dalit Theology

By

Eve Rebecca Parker

BRILL

LEIDEN | BOSTON

Cover illustration: "The Dalit Woman's Cross "by W. Jebasingh Samuvel, Dalit Christian artist and ordained minister of Jaffna Diocese, Church of South India in Sri Lanka. He migrated to Sri Lanka in 2017 and currently serves as a presbyter in CSI Church, Colombo.

All chapters in this book have undergone peer review.

Library of Congress Cataloging-in-Publication Data

Names: Parker, Eve Rebecca, author.
Title: Theologising with the sacred 'prostitutes' of South India : towards an Indecent Dalit theology / by Eve Rebecca Parker.
Description: Leiden ; Boston : Brill, Rodopi, [2021] | Series: Currents of encounter, 0923-6201 ; volume 65 | Revision of the author's thesis (doctoral)–University of St. Andrews, 2016. | Includes bibliographical references and index.
Identifiers: LCCN 2021001660 (print) | LCCN 2021001661 (ebook) | ISBN 9789004450073 (paperback) | ISBN 9789004450080 (ebook)
Subjects: LCSH: Devadāsīs–India, South. | Devadāsīs–Religious life. | Marginality, Social–Religious aspects–Christianity. | Marginality, Social–India, South. | Liberation theology–India, South.
Classification: LCC BL1237.58.D48 P37 2021 (print) | LCC BL1237.58.D48 (ebook) | DDC 294.5/22–dc23
LC record available at https://lccn.loc.gov/2021001660
LC ebook record available at https://lccn.loc.gov/2021001661

Typeface for the Latin, Greek, and Cyrillic scripts: "Brill". See and download: brill.com/brill-typeface.

ISSN 0923-6201
ISBN 978-90-04-45007-3 (paperback)
ISBN 978-90-04-45008-0 (e-book)

Printed by Printforce, United Kingdom

Contents

Acknowledgements

I am extremely grateful to Tamil Nadu Theological Seminary (TTS), to the students, staff and wider community of Madurai. My first visit to TTS was in October 2010, when I was working for the Council for World Mission (CWM), and responsible for the Training in Mission programme that was being held at the college. I am very grateful for this opportunity that sparked my passion for India and where I first met John Samuel Ponnusamy, M. Gnanavaram, Jayachitra Lalitha, and the many other faculty members and college students who inspired me and taught me a great deal about Indian Christian Theology, the history of Christianity in India, and the contextual difficulties faced by the Church and in particular Dalit Christians.

I returned to India in January 2011, this time to Aizawl Theological Seminary in Mizoram, where I am thankful in particular for meeting Lalrindiki Ralte, who introduced me to the tribal justice issues experienced by Mizo people and the battle for gender justice in the region. I left Mizoram to visit Bishop's College, Kolkata, as part of my role in being responsible for the theology programmes of CWM, where I will be forever grateful for meeting Isaac Devadoss and the wonderful Dalit rights activist and theologian, Philip Vinod Peacock – who has since become one of my greatest friends.

In March 2011, I returned to Madurai, this time to the slums of Chennai, where students of TTS were placed for a semester of practical theology. In the slums, unlike in the comfort of the colleges, there were no flushing toilets, or running water, and no air conditioning. I also witnessed slum segregation based upon caste discrimination and how Christian Dalits were further marginalised for their 'strange' beliefs, and further, how life and religion for people in the slums was shaped around their daily struggles. I am extremely grateful to TTS for this experience, it took me out of my comfort zone and challenged me to further grapple with the socio-economic realities of the people I stayed with, it was here that I began to learn the true meaning of practical theology in the South Indian context.

The following year I was reunited with Philip Peacock in Sao Paulo, Brazil, for a World Council of Churches (WCC) conference on 'International Financial Transformation for the Economy of Life', held between 29 September to 5 October. This opportunity enabled me to re-connect with Philip whilst writing the Sao Paulo statement together; fuelled by coffee we bonded over a shared love of Marcella Althaus-Reid. In December 2012, I was asked by Philip and the Dalit theologian Satianathan Clarke to participate in a conference of Dalit theologians in New Delhi and deliver a paper on the future of Dalit Theology. I will be forever grateful for this experience, where I was introduced to the Dalit theologians – Peniel Rajkumar, Elizabeth Anderson-Rajkumar, Ashley Tellis, Deenabandhu Manchala, Joseph Prabhakar Dayam, and Geevarghese Mor Coorilos. The feedback, conversations and continued friendships have been of great help throughout my research.

On the final evening of the conference we were joined by Asha Kowtal, the General Secretary of the *All India Dalit Women's Right Forum*, over dinner she gave us a greater insight into the plight of Dalit women. The narratives she told were of women who had been gang-raped, violently beaten and sexually assaulted by their Landlords and neighbours. Dalit women whose children had been killed, whose land had been stolen, and who had been raped by their husbands. I am deeply indebted to Asha for challenging me to focus on the reality of such narratives and calling on us all to join the fight for justice.

It was based upon these combined experiences that I made the decision to move back to Scotland in 2013 to study for my PhD and focus on the plight of Dalit women – I am extremely grateful to the University of St Andrews for awarding me with the 600th Anniversary Scholarship that made this possible.

In November 2013, I returned to Madurai to conduct fieldwork for my PhD – on this occasion I spent one month there. I entered the field as a white, British, northern, socialist, feminist and Anglican, with a commitment to Dalit justice issues, in particular Dalit women, and aware of the need to keep all presuppositions aside from my research. My knowledge of Dalits was limited to what I had learnt from my time at CWM – therefore through the lens of the Church of South India and Church of North India, and the Dalit theologians and activists who I had, had the privilege of meeting along the way. When travelling to India on previous occasions I had been somewhat 'protected' whilst being part of CWM and working with the colleges and churches it was very easy to get around, find translators, and have places to stay. Travelling on my own proved more difficult.

For the first week, I stayed at the campus of TTS, with thanks to John Samuel and his wife Sheila who invited me to their home for dinner every evening, John Samuel introduced me to people who were working with *devadāsī* communities in Karnataka, Andhra Pradesh and Tamil Nadu. He made it possible for me to have access to the Dalit Resource Centre at TTS, and other libraries and resource centres in Madurai that were significantly helpful in my research. John Samuel also introduced me to Precilla Jayakumari who was my translator for a significant amount of my fieldwork.

I am deeply indebted to Precilla, together we travelled from Chennai to the Chittoor district of Andhra Pradesh, she sat through numerous interviews and patiently translated everything for me from Telugu to English. We shared meals together, train journeys, moped rides, and beds. Without Precilla and John Samuel this field research would not have been possible.

Most importantly I am eternally grateful to the dedicated women who I met during my time in Andhra Pradesh and Tamil Nadu. During the time that I spent in the Chittoor district of Andhra Pradesh, I offer a special thanks to Mathamma Kanaganithian who is a truly amazing individual – I was a complete stranger and yet she opened up to me, to offer me an insight in to her life and that of her families. Thank you to the many other women who I had the great pleasure of meeting, some of whom, will by their choice remain anonymous and have therefore had their names changed in this book. Thank you also to the *devadāsī* community who I met in Holagallu, Karnataka who taught me a great deal about Dalit village religiosity.

I am also grateful to the Church of South India, for enabling me to meet their partner organisations that have been working with the young girls who have been dedicated to village goddesses and focusing their mission efforts on giving these young people access to an education.

In December 2013, I was asked by the Dalit theologian, Joseph Prabhakar Dayam, to participate in a workshop on the future of Christian mission in India at the United Theological College, Bangalore – I am grateful for this experience and to the students of the college whose questions and passion for Dalit justice aided my research greatly.

Following this, I journeyed to Madras Christian College, Chennai, where I had been invited to attend the Tambaram Platinum Jubilee Conference – organised by the WCC and National Council of Churches in India and the Church of South India. I am grateful for this opportunity where I met Raj Bharath Patta, who was then responsible for the Student Christian Movement in India and a vital voice of the Dalit youth movement. As well as the feminist theologian, Aruna Gnanadason, whose style of questioning and positive spirit has been of a great benefit to me throughout my research.

Prior to my fieldwork, I had experienced Christianity in India, and the experiences of Dalits and *devadāsīs* in South India from a mostly etic perspective – my theologising was therefore limited to what I had learnt from text books, Dalit theologians, the narratives of the church and NGOs. Upon returning to South India for my fieldwork, my time spent in Andhra Pradesh and Tamil Nadu enabled me to take an emic approach to my research – by allowing the voices of the Dalit women to speak for themselves. My views and understandings were transformed as a result. By the time my fieldwork had come to an end I had been attacked in a back street in Chennai, I had, had dengue fever, and severe food poisoning, and yet I will be forever grateful for every aspect of this journey.

I would also like to thank the Dalit theologian, Peniel Rajkumar, for inviting me to speak at the NIFCON conference on Diaspora Hindus and Anglican-Lutheran relations, in Birmingham, in October 2014 – and the World Council of Churches and United Church of Christ conference on Multiple Religious Belonging in Cleveland, Ohio in April 2015, the opportunity to apply my research to these subject areas was of great benefit, particularly in relation to the feedback received and I am grateful that the papers presented were included in publications.

My gratitude also goes to the Methodist Women in Britain, for focusing their mission agenda on Dalit women in India and for asking me to speak at their national conference in 2014 on the social realities faced by Dalit Women in India. This experience enabled me to connect with the Dalit Solidarity Network in the UK and meet with Dalit theologians in the UK including Elizabeth Joy.

And of course a huge thank you to my supervisor, Prof Mario Aguilar – for being a constant inspiration, I thank him for his ongoing support, his great wisdom, his passion for justice, Liberation Theology and world religions. Most importantly I thank him for never letting me give up and never doubting me, even when I found out I was having a baby midway through my research, his calmness kept me calm. I am also grateful to him for introducing me to the works of Marcella Althaus-Reid, Ernesto Cardenal, Elsa Tamez and many other liberation theologians during my undergraduate years at St Andrews, these lessons came at a time in my life when I needed them the most.

I am very grateful to everyone at St Mary's College at the University of St Andrews, I have spent the last ten years being part of the college family and along the way have had the opportunity to be taught by many great people. A special thank you to those who influenced me the most, Eric Stoddart, Grant Macaskill, and Ian Bradley.

I would also like to thank the members of the Centre for the Study of Religion and Politics at St Andrews who I have not already mentioned, in particular Dan O'Connor – a fantastic human being, who sent me many encouraging emails and whose vast knowledge of Christianity in India was greatly appreciated. My thanks also to Kabir Babu and James Morris for their thoughts and friendship.

I am also very thankful to the Council for World Mission for giving me a job when I graduated from St Andrews and where my journey in South India began. Thanks to CWM I had the opportunity to work on theology and intercultural programmes in India, Zambia, Jamaica, Fiji, South Africa, Samoa and Guyana. I am particularly grateful to the theological colleges that I had the opportunity to work with, including the Pacific Theological Seminary, Fiji; United Theological College, Zambia; Bishop's College, Kolkata; Tamil Nadu Theological Seminary, Chennai; United Theological Seminary, Bangalore; and Aizawl Theological College, Mizoram. I met so many amazing people and learnt a great deal about contextual, liberation, and postcolonial theologies around the world.

To the many others I have forgotten, my thanks and apologies.

Thank you to my partner in life, James for all his love and support and our amazing children Minerva and Iris. Thank you also to my family – my mother and Dan, my sisters, Kim and Boo, and my brother, Alex – for all their love, support and laughter. Thank you to my father – who I miss every day and who continues to inspire me in all I do, although he never got to see me graduate from St Andrews, I hope he will be proud of me and I pray that I one day get to see him again at the table of *Christa*. I thank him for everything he did for his family, for teaching me and my siblings to challenge all injustices and to never give up fighting for what we believe in. I dedicate this book to him.

Figures

Introduction

Oh, Mother, my life has been only pain and sorrow.
Death is far better than this wretched life.
With beads and nose rings and arms full of green bangles,
They make me believe that God is my husband.
Oh, Mother, pain and sorrow burn my life![1]

• • •

Renukaa, Jagadambaa; Renukaa, Jagadambaa;
Renuka, mother of the world; Renuka, mother of the world;
Your name is very sacred,
Your feet are very sacred.
Daily for you seve, leaves and flowers are needed;
rose-water for your bath, pujaris for your seve.
I, thinking you were mine, went about trusting them,
but my people were not for me a refuge.
We gather in devotion, make pilgrimage to you,
Seek boons, seek compassion from you...
Living among seven lakes, born in Nandipur,
Protect us, we pray. I remember you, I sing your praises...[2]

• •
•

It took three different trains from Chennai, a two-hour bus journey and a long moped ride through the stunning rice fields and swamp lands of the Chittoor district of Andhra Pradesh, before I reached the rural village of Nagalpurum.

---

1   The song is written by a *devadāsī* who suggests that her life as a dedicated woman is embedded in a state of humiliation and oppression. See, Catherine Rubin Kermorgant, *Servants of the Goddess: The Modern Day Devadasis* (London: Random House Group, 2014), 65.

2   In contrast to the previous song the *devadāsī* describes the compassion and protection that the goddess rewards her devotees. The goddess responds to believers "in the fecundity of fields, wombs, and all other forms of human thriving." When the goddess is angry the villagers will know as there may suffer a drought, sickness, or disease. See, Lucinda Ramberg, *Given to the Goddess: South Indian Devadasis and the Sexuality of Religion* (Durham: Duke University Press, 2014), 81–82.

© KONINKLIJKE BRILL NV, LEIDEN, 2021 | DOI: 10.1163/9789004450080_001

Here I met Mathamma Kanaganithian, a Dalit woman who had been dedicated to the goddess *Mathamma* as a child. Before we visited the village temple of the goddess, we sat in a church, positioned in the most affluent area of the community, where we were surrounded by members and ministers belonging to the Church of South India. It was here that Mathamma narrated the history of her dedication and her daily struggles as an ex-*devadāsī*. Mathamma had converted to Christianity, she was one of the many that the church reform programmes had focused on "saving". As a child she had been dedicated to the goddess in marriage because she was sick with small pox. She described how she was ashamed of her past that involved selling her body for sex, she had been a victim of violence, abuse and harassment from her community because of her role as a dedicated *Mathamma*. Yet these same villagers also came to her when their children were sick, when there was a village drought, when their crops were not growing or when they or a member of their family had a disease. They relied on her because she was a representative of the goddess. Mathamma now believed in Jesus Christ and was considered by the church members to be a "saved" member of the Dalit community. Yet despite her conversion, Mathamma still wore her *tali* around her neck, a symbol of her marriage to the village goddess. Following our conversation, we journeyed to the temple of *Mathamma* that was on the outskirts of the village, where the Dalit community lived, it was a very small, old hut. The goddess sat inside, ready to protect her devotees and all who pleased her and release her wrath on those who neglected her. It was here that my theological yātrā[3] began...

I delved into the world of the Dalit *devadāsīs* as an outsider, aware of my own "respective distinctiveness" as a white, British woman, yet having witnessed the multifaceted plight of Dalit women, I committed myself to the call to fight for Dalit justice. In doing so, I have sought to allow the voices and experiences of the Dalit women's pain-pathos to speak for themselves throughout this book, as it is the bodies of the Dalit women who shape it, who enable a profound theologising through their narratives of struggle and resistance. Noting that whilst the oppression of women is found in multiple contexts across the globe, the struggles experienced by the Dalit *devadāsīs* are distinct, and rooted in casteism, racism, sexism, and the collusion of Christian churches colonial missionary agenda, that has superimposed Western norms on to the bodies of the dedicated women. Therefore, this is a journeying into Dalit Theology that acknowledges that "other communities can participate in doing Dalit

---

3   The term yātrā means a religious and spiritual journey, pilgrimage or procession.

theology,"[4] as the non-Dalit, Dalit theologian, Sathianathan Clarke remarks, but in doing so there is a need to recognise one's own "respective distance and respectful relatedness to the distinctiveness of Dalit pain-pathos."[5] It is therefore essential to outline my own identity as an "outsider" looking in and therefore incapable of ever truly understanding the suffering narrated. As such, this is a book of contemplations on the role of God amidst such distinct suffering. My positions held have been fluid throughout this research as they have been shaped by the existential experiences of my fieldwork with *devadāsīs* in India, my time spent with the Dalit feminist movements and other influences, including working alongside the Church of South India and at Tamil Nadu Theological Seminary. I am aware therefore that I have no authority to speak for the Dalit women who have been dedicated to the goddesses, so I attempt not to speak for them but to allow their words to be spoken and to contemplate God based upon their existential bodily narratives.

This book will therefore explore the bodily experiences of Dalit women, specifically those who have been dedicated to village goddesses and labelled as sacred "prostitutes" or *devadāsīs*, in the context of the South Indian village. It centres on the narratives of these women because they are the ones who are too often overlooked and whose identity is embedded in casteism, sexism, classism and a history of socio-political and religious marginalisation. From childhood they have been dedicated to village goddesses, most commonly as a direct consequence of poverty, illness, caste, and hereditary obligation. They have become known as *"devadasi devachi, bayko saarya gavachi"*[6] (*devadāsī* servant of god, but wife of the whole town). This book therefore aims to theologise on the place of God in the midst of such narratives – as they have become the most marginalised of Dalit women. Their narratives are shaped by enforced sex work, sexually transmitted diseases, caste discrimination, rape, and paedophilia, whilst also being intertwined with village life, Dalit religiosity, reform

---

4   Clarke acknowledges the need for Dalit theology as a counter-theology to retain methodological exclusiveness to the Dalit pain-pathos however to be inclusive at allowing non-Dalit engagement, noting: "The intention of invoking theological inclusiveness of Dalit theology is to allow for Christian communitarian interrelatedness in the task of overcoming suffering for Dalits and all those who suffer the effects of oppression." See, Satianathan Clarke, "Dalit Theology: An Introductory and Interpretive Theological Exposition", in *Dalit Theology in the Twenty-first Century: Discordant Voices, Discerning Pathways* (New Delhi: Oxford University Press, 2010), 22.

5   Ibid, 22.

6   This is a common Marathi saying for dedicated girls and women. See, Pratibha Desai, "Exploitation of Scheduled Caste Women in the Name of Religion," in *Development of Scheduled Castes and Scheduled Tribes in India*, ed. Jagan Karade (Newcastle: Cambridge Scholars Publishing, 2008), 102–114.

and rehabilitation programmes and political and religious hegemonic battles over the identity politics of their bodies. Despite such identity specific oppression, Dalit Christian Theology has not yet offered a space for such narratives within Dalit theological discourse, as there remains a lacuna for the sexual narratives of the Dalit oppressed.

1   The Context for Theologising: Dalit Self, Gender and Identity

In order to theologise with the contemporary *devadāsīs* in India it is important to have an understanding of the caste system in order to situate the Dalits in a complex social system of stratification, noting as Ambedkar states:

> The caste problem is a vast one, both theoretically and practically. Practically, it is an institution that portends tremendous consequences. It is a local problem, but one capable of much wider mischief, for "as long as caste in India does exist, Hindus will hardly intermarry or have any social intercourse with outsiders; and if Hindus migrate to other regions on earth, Indian caste would become a world problem." Theoretically, it has defied a great many scholars who have taken upon themselves, as a labour of love, to dig into its origin.[7]

The term "caste" was designated by the Europeans to describe a complex social-structure that is shaped by the hereditary groupings of people who are ranked from birth. In the Indian context, caste has been used to denote the ideologies of *varṇa* and *jāti*. *Varṇa* translates from the Sanskrit as "colour", it is the belief that humanity's purpose within society is ordered within a four-fold system that is considered to be divinely authorised. The *varṇa* determines the function or occupation of a person within society. Each *varṇa* has its own *dharma*, or *varṇāśramadharma*, a life code of conduct that determines the hereditary vocation based upon the divine ordering of the cosmos, controlled by the *svadharma* (caste-duty, righteousness, obligations)[8]. The ideology of *dharma* is a central force in maintaining the order of the caste system. To quote Partha Chatterjee, "the conflicting relations between the differentiated parts of the system (namely *jātis*) are effectively united by the force of *dharma* so that

---

7   Bhimrao Ramji Ambedkar, "Castes in India: Their Mechanism, Gender and Development," in *Readings in Indian Government and Politics: Class, Caste, Gender, ed. Manoranjan Mohanty (New Delhi: Sage Publications, 2004), 132.

8   See, Rajendra Prasad, *A Conceptual-analytic Study of Classical Indian Philosophy of Morals* (New Delhi: Concept Publishing Company, 2008), 349.

the caste system as a whole can continue to reproduce itself."[9] Those at the top of the hierarchy are able to reproduce a hereditary homogenous system of power that they maintain is divinely justified through the *vedas*. The *jāti*, as Quigley remarks, refers to "named endogamous groups which are usually more or less localised or at least have a regional base."[10] The system of caste has been preserved through "the mechanism of differentiation, namely the ideology of 'purity' and 'pollution,'"[11] the *varṇas* are upheld through ritual purity and the fear of pollution. This has created a system of dominance, oppression and subordination that has legitimised the concept of 'untouchability'.

Caste has been outlined as being shaped by three main characteristics: mutual repulsion, hierarchical organisation and hereditary specialisation.[12] Untouchability for the sociologist, Tharailath Koshy Oommen should therefore be considered as "cumulative deprivation" that has systematically produced a separate group of people, outcastes, who are also amongst themselves, highly fragmented.[13] In Pocock's introduction to Célestin Bouglé's *Essays on the Caste System*, he writes, "the spirit of caste unites these three tendencies, repulsion, hierarchy and hereditary specialisation, and all three must be borne in mind if one wishes to give a complete definition of the caste system."[14] Caste is therefore a system of inequality, but an inequality that appears incomparable to the ordering of other nation states. As a result of its uniqueness, sociologists have attempted to expose its true history and nature for centuries.[15] Yet despite the significance of caste in comprehending and challenging the notion of 'untouchability', caste theories as Robert Deliége remarks "are largely based

---

9   Partha Chatterjee, *The Nation and its Fragments: Colonial and Postcolonial Histories* (Princeton: Princeton University Press, 1993), 180.

10   Declan Quigley, *The Interpretation of Caste* (New Delhi: Oxford University Press, 1999), 4–5.

11   Anshuman A Mondal, *Nationalism and Post-Colonial Identity: Culture and Ideology in India and Egypt* (London: Routledge Curzon, 2003), 97–98.

12   Alongside these social orderings, society under the caste system is divided into mutually exclusive groups, heirarchically ordered and intolerant to the mixing of blood through marriage and child birth, the change of profession and the acquisition of rank. See, Pokala Lakshmi Narasu, *A Study of Caste* (New Delhi: AES Publications, 1988), 2.

13   Tharailath Koshy Oommen, "Sources of Deprivation and Styles of Protest: The Case of the Dalits in India,"*Contributions to Indian Sociology* NS, 18 (1984): 46.

14   David Francis Pocock, *Essays on the Caste System by Célestin Bouglé* (London: Cambridge University Press, 1971), 9.

15   Triloki Nath Madan, "Louis Dumont and the Study of Society in India," in *Caste, Hierarchy, and Individualism: Indian Critiques of Louis Dumont's Contributions*, ed. Ravindra. S. Khare (New Delhi: Oxford University Press, 2006), 41.

on 'textual' sources, often in Sanskrit, that show little interest in the lowest levels of society."[16]

Until recent years the Dalits were historically excluded from socio-anthropological attempts at understanding the concept or origin of 'untouchability'. However, the social reformer *Babasaheb* Ambedkar, sought to transform the ways in which caste was comprehended, by noting that the caste system must be challenged in order to transform the poverty, stigmatization and oppression experienced by the Dalits, he wrote: "the outcaste is a by- product of the caste-system. There will be outcastes as long as there are castes." He called for the complete annihilation of the caste system, which he maintained has dogmatically produced an "odious" system of degradation, injustice and inequality.[17] As a result the origins of the caste system and the concept of 'untouchability' continue to be highly debated subject matters within historical, political, religious and sociological studies.

2   Hinduism, the Caste System and the 'Untouchables'

cātur-varṇyam mayā sṛṣṭam guṇa karma vibhāgaśaḥ
I have created a fourfold system in order to distinguish among one's qualities and functions
- *Bhagavad-Gītā*: Verse 13, Chapter XI

The *Bhagavad-Gītā* describes how Lord Krishna purposefully distinguished humanity into separate groupings, the *varṇas*, these are: *Brahmins*, *kṣatriyas*, *vaiśyas* and *śūdras*, and under the *varṇāśramadharma*, each held a predestined profession. The *Brahmins* are the spiritual leaders, the priests and law givers, the *kṣatriyas* are the warriors, the noble ones who are destined to be kings. The *Vaishyas* are bound to dutifully take care of the land through agriculture and business; and the *śūdras* are the labourers, the artisans, masons and farmers. The outcastes, the Dalits, are the ones who hold no place in society as their *dharma* has bound them to a life on the margins of society. The concept of 'untouchability' is articulated in the *Laws of the Manu*, where the *caṇāla* are described as communities of people who are expelled and rejected from villages. The *Manu* professes that "untouchability is the punishment for

---

16   Robert Deliége, *The Untouchables of India* (Oxford: Berg, 1999), 27–28.
17   See, Ambedkar in a letter dated 7, 1933 to Gandhijee, quoted in Shewta N. Mishra, *Socio-economic and Political Vision of Dr. B. R. Ambedkar* (New Delhi: Concept Publishing Company, 2010), 200.

miscegenation between a member of a high caste and that of a low caste or an outcaste. The children of such an unequal pair become Untouchables and the greater the social gap between the two parents, the lower the status of their children."[18] The *varṇa* system is made up of different *jātis* and ones *jāti* is determined from birth. The relationship between *varṇa* and *jāti* is in itself complex, according to the Indian sociologist Srinivas, the *varṇa* "provides an all-Indian framework into which the thousands of *jāti* may be fitted."[19] The *varṇa* is the "abstract and theoretical classification of Indian society" expressed in the four-fold classification of castes, each *jāti* is the actual social community into which an individual belongs.[20] *Jātis* themselves can be localised and exist only within certain regions of India,[21] they are therefore the endogamous sections of Hindu society. It is the rule of endogamy that confines members of the caste groups by marriage or kinship to the *jāti.*

Social regulations based upon the laws of purity and pollution influence the hierarchy of the divergent *jātis*, as Shankar remarks, "two *jātis* belonging to the same *varṇa* can mark the boundary of separation between themselves with as much vehemence as two *jātis* belonging to two different *varṇas*."[22] This adheres to Célestin Bouglé's study on caste, as he describes *jāti* as the prototype of castes as oppose to *varṇa*. He writes: "The chains which unite the members of the same caste were not forged from the scrap of those which united the representatives of the same class; they derive their links rather from those which united the descendants of the same lineage."[23] Food practices, endogamy, myths, occupations and languages differ between *jātis.* The 19th Century British writer Edward Blunt adheres to Bouglé's description, noting the complex social regulations of the distinct *jāti* castes as follows:

> One caste forbids the remarriage of widows, another permits it; one permits its members to accept food from certain outsiders, another forbids such acceptance from anybody but a caste fellow...certain castes are regarded as conveying pollution by touch: in other parts of India, the

---

18 S. M. Michael, *Untouchable: Dalits in Modern India* (London: Lynne Rienner Publishers, 1999), 31.

19 S. J. Tambiah, "From Varna to Caste through Mixed Unions," in *Character of Kinship*, ed. Jack Goody. (Cambridge: Cambridge University Press, 1973), 192.

20 Subramanian Shankar, *Flesh and Blood: Postcolonialism, Translation, and the Vernacular* (London: University of California Press, 2012), 32.

21 Mark Muesse, *The Hindu Traditions: A Concise Introduction* (Minneapolis: Fortress Press, 2011), 79.

22 Shankar, *Flesh and Blood*, 32.

23 Célestin Bouglé, *Essays on the Caste* System, trans. D. F. Pocock (Cambridge: Cambridge University Press, 1971), 42.

same or similar castes are regarded as conveying pollution...by mere proximity.[24]

Those who exist outside of the four segments of the *varṇa* system are the "outcaste" communities, who have also been referred to as '*avarṇas*,' '*atisudras*,' '*antyajas*' or '*panchams*,'[25] 'untouchable,' 'exterior caste,' 'depressed class,' and 'Dalit.' They are the people that according to the *Manusmriti* exist outside of the *Chaturvarṇa* (four castes) and are so polluting that their very touch is enough to defile the high-castes. For the German sociologist and economist, Max Weber, caste in India is a "closed status group"[26] determined by birth and controlled by religion. Hindu religiosity and Brahminical ideology, according to Weber, produced a more rigid societal structuring than was apparent in any other part of the world. This he maintained, was due to the doctrine of *karma,* a central ideological philosophy of Hinduism that constructed an "ethically determined cosmos" which he believed was responsible for creating the "most consistent theodicy ever produced by history."[27] Every aspect of life from "marrying the wrong kind of person, eating with the wrong kind of person, or even touching or glancing at the wrong kind of person could be ritually defiling" and would have significantly negative consequences.[28]

Throughout history those who exist outside of the caste system, have been confined to the margins of civic society, excluded from temples, and perceived as defiling to all others, they have been economically, politically, religiously and socially subjugated. The *Manu* describes the *candālas* as "dog-cookers"[29], their very sight is enough to pollute the Brahmins (3.239–42). Wasnik argues that the enforced marginalisation of the "outcastes" has been so extreme that

---

24   Edward Blunt, *The Caste System of Northern India* (Delhi: Isha Books, 1931), 1.
25   Krupakar Pralhad Wasnik, *Lost People: An Analysis of Indian Poverty* (Delhi: Isha Books, 2009), 68.
26   Richard Swedberg, *Max Weber and the Idea of Economic Sociology* (New Jersey: Princeton University Press, 1998), 139.
27   Max Weber, The Religion of India: The Sociology of Hinduism and Buddhism (New York: Free Press, 1962), 121; Weber's theory is influenced by the Hindu soteriological structure that as Gavin Flood describes, is "the idea that every action has an effect which must be accounted for in this or future lifetime, and that the experiences of the present lifetime are the consequences of past actions." The doctrine of karma is outlined in the Rig Veda, where good actions (punya) will lead to merit and evil actions will lead to further evil (pāpa). In the Upaniṣads the doctrine of karma is more clearly established, stating "the performed of action which bears fruit, wanders in the cycle of transmigration according to his actions (karma)." See, Gavin Flood, An Introduction to Hinduism (Cambridge: Cambridge University Press, 1996), 86.
28   Swedberg, *Max Weber,* 139.
29   Flood, *An Introduction to Hinduism,* 61.

the economic deprivation was only one aspect of their tribulations, as they "were forbidden to build houses of bricks, to use an umbrella or footwear. Their women were obliged not to cover their breasts. They were restricted in dress, speech, food and manner. Any violation of the customary norms of behaviour was dealt with very severe punishment – from severe ostracism to decapitation."[30] As Uma Chakravarti describes, "all the injunctions of dharma are predicated upon the labouring lower castes and their subordination and the reproduction of the labouring being as well as the reproduction of that person's subordination."[31] Today, the outcaste communities comprise of around 16.6 per cent of the Indian population, totalling at approximately 201.4 million people.[32] The Human Rights Watch have described the conditions experienced by these communities of people as follows:

> More than one-sixth of India's population live a precarious existence, shunned by much of society because of their rank as "untouchables" or Dalits - literally meaning "broken" people -- at the bottom of India's caste system. Dalits are discriminated against, denied access to land, forced to work in degrading conditions, and routinely abused at the hands of the police and of higher-caste groups that enjoy the State's protection... In what has been called "hidden apartheid" entire villages in many Indian states remain completely segregated by caste.[33]

3 The Touchable Untouchables: From Feminist to Dalit Womanist

In order to understand the complexity of Mathamma's, and that of other *devadāsīs* socio-political and religious narratives, it is vital to contemplate the role that caste plays in their lives and that of their communities. As a Dalit woman, Mathamma like that other dedicated women, is subjected to gender and caste-based persecution, as Dalit women are socially, economically and politically situated at an intersecting crossroad of caste and patriarchal subjugation. They are commonly described as being the "thrice marginalised", oppressed for their gender, caste and class. They are suppressed by the patriarchal hand

---

30   Wasnik, *Lost People*, 68.

31   Uma Chakravarti, *Gendering Caste Through a Feminist Lens* (Calcutta, STREE, 2003), 14.

32   "Official Dalit Population Exceeds 200 million," International Dalit Solidarity Network, accessed July 19, 2014, http://idsn.org/news-resources/idsn-news/read/article/india-official-dalit-population-exceeds-200-million/128/ .

33   Narula, Smita. Broken People: Caste Violence Against India's "Untouchables" (New York: Human Rights Watch, 1999)1–2.

of Brahminism that further stigmatises them for their 'untouchable' status, as well as by Dalit men who chastise the bodies of Dalit women through economic and sexual control. Violence against Dalit women is a direct consequence of gender, caste and class based discrimination that "acts as a crucial social mechanism to maintain Dalit women's caste and gender subordinate position to men and particularly dominant caste men."[34] Furthermore Dalit women are reportedly faced with significant limitations in their appeals for justice due to the impunity of patriarchal and caste influenced socio-political and legal structures.[35] Dalit women are also faced with further atrocities such as kidnapping, abduction and forced incarceration. In a Human Rights Watch interview with Asha Kowtal, a leading womanist figure for the Dalit women's resistance movement, she stated:

> Caste-based rape and violence against Dalit women and girls is escalating as we fight to claim justice. The amount of cases is growing and the brutality of the crimes becoming increasingly severe. Systems of justice meant to protect Dalit women at the national level are completely failing us. We are asking for immediate loud and clear global support in our struggle.[36]

For Dalit women like Mathamma and other contemporary *devadāsīs,* physical and sexual violence has been used as a means of reinforcing caste order and as an exercise of male privilege and power. Their placement at the bottom of the social hierarchy has determined that the bodies of Dalit women become touchable to both their own men and the high caste men in order to maintain the boundaries of social ordering, and the cries of such violence are met with the silence of a system that is rigid in its oppression, as outlined in by the Dalit poet, Chandramohan:

---

34 Aloysiuis Irudayam, S. J., Jayshree P. Mangubhai and Joel G. Lee. Dalit Women Speak Out: Caste, Class and Gender Violence in India (New Delhi: Zubaan, 2011), 3.

35 A cross-sectional survey by Suneeta Krishnan exploring the intersecting aspects of gender, caste and economic inequalities in martial violence in rural South India, revealed that low-caste and Dalit women belonging to poorer households, who held greater economic autonomy are more likely to report domestic violence. The survey displayed that the "poor, lower caste women linked their lack of social support to the accumulation of stress within the household and the incidence of conflicts. See, Suneeta Krishnan, "Gender, Caste, and Economic Inequalities and Marital Violence in Rural South India," Health Care for Women International, 26 (2005): 87–99.

36 "UN Rights Council: End Caste-Based Rape, Violence," Human Rights Watch, accessed June, 19 2014, https://www.hrw.org/news/2014/06/17/un-rights-council-end-caste-based-rape-violence.

No newspaper carried a headline or a photo feature,
No youth were roused to protests,
No city's life came to a standstill,
No furor in the parliament,

No nation's conscience was haunted,
No Prime Minister addressed the nation,
No TV channel discussions,
No police officials were transferred or suspended,
No candle light marches,
No billion women rising,
a tribal girl was raped and murdered![37]

It is for this reason that Gopal Guru maintains that the experiences of Dalit women require a "politics of difference" from mainstream Indian feminism. Based on the premise that such feminisms are limited in their capacity to represent the Dalit subaltern women who are communally, economically, socially, and religiously segregated. Indian feminists have therefore been forced to acknowledge that gender is only one aspect of the campaign for equal rights, noting that caste, class, urban and rural poverty are connected to the identity politics of the subaltern.[38] This rejection of the universalisation of women's experiences in feminist thought has led to an emphasis on the identity struggles of the body politics of Dalit women. Noting that the body of the Dalit woman is a site of agency, formed and situated in and by certain socio-political and religious conditions that have been historically formed. Whilst the subjective experiences of women in India are often shrouded by patriarchy and gender based violence, it is also true, as Anjali Bagwe states, that "women as subjects are deployers of alternative discourses who manipulate normative signs and create new spaces for themselves."[39] It is in such spaces of protest and courage that Dalit women have been speaking out against the cultures of

---

37   S. Chandramohan, "Rape and Murder of a Dalit Girl", quoted by Vidya Bhushan Rawat, in "The Poems of S. Chandramohan" accessed December, 17 2019, https://mayday.leftword. com/blog/post/the-poems-of-resistance-by-s-chandramohan/

38   Evangeline Anderson-Rajkumar describes Dalit womanism in the Indian context as "that double consciousness which emerges to renounce casteism and sexism as inherently evil to humanity, and stands in solidarity and spirit for justice and equality, regardless. Womanist spirituality is collective spirituality, one that is rooted in community." See, Anderson-Rajkumar, "Turning Bodies", 201.

39   Anjali Bagwe, *Of Woman Caste: The Experience of Gender in Rural India* (Calcutta: STREE, 1995), 19.

impunity that exist, and against the continued violence that women in India face.

This book therefore acknowledges that the political category of 'women' in contemporary India is complex. This has been brought to the forefront of international attention following the severity of the atrocities committed against the bodies of women inclusive of acts of brutal sexual violence.[40] Patriarchal structural violence is more ruinous under the hegemony of caste, as caste based atrocities including the rape of Dalit women often go unpunished.[41] As there exists dichotomous characterisations of upper caste and Dalit women,[42] that appear to have become so ingrained in the Indian patriarchal sub-conscience that the bodies of Dalit women are still thought of as being of lesser worth than that of the high-caste women. Noting that whilst it is apparent that the economic growth of India has positively impacted the Indian upper caste women, the disparities between the rich and poor have become even larger. The grave reality is that every day in India women face sexual, verbal, domestic, state, and other forms of gender-based violence. Dalit women experience the majority of such crimes. Irudayam, Mangubhai and Lee, suggest that this is fundamentally a result of socially-created dichotomies of honour and shame, as Dalit women find themselves having to "continually defend their right to bodily and sexual integrity, and basic human dignity."[43] Consequently, Dalit women have become suspicious of mainstream Indian feminism, noting that it is often dominated by high-caste and upper-class feminist concerns, and therefore fails to acknowledge the multiple and intersectional oppressions experienced by Dalit women.

Consequently, Dalit women in their struggles for transformation have not only began to re-define Indian feminism, but also dismantle the rigid patriarchal and caste hegemonic Indian society through various means of protest. Reading about the plight of Dalit women in a vast majority of literature creates an image of the downtrodden, silenced, weak and submissive social 'other', yet

---

40   On the 16 December 2012 a young woman was brutally gang-raped and murdered in New Delhi the gravity of the attack attracted international media attention, there has since been sporadic reporting on further sexual violence against women in India.

41   See, Praveen Kumar, *Communal Crimes and National Integration: A Socio-legal Study* (New Delhi: Readworthy Publications, 2011), 134.

42   The high-caste men and women depicted the low-caste and Dalit women as being immoral and dirty, and as T. Pillai-Vetschera remarks, "lazy, quarrelsome, not reliable, that the women enjoy much more freedom than rural high-caste women and above all that they (the women) have no morals and therefore deserve to be raped." See, Michael, *Dalits in Modern India*, 231.

43   Aloysiuis Irudayam, S. J., Jayshree P. Mangubhai and Joel G. Lee. *Dalit Women Speak Out: Caste, Class and Gender Violence in India* (New Delhi: Zubaan, 2011), 209–210.

such rhetoric risks undermining Dalit women's agency by instead reinforcing the notion of a silent victim. Autobiographical Dalit literature and my own encounters with Dalit women however exposed the inaccuracy of such characterisations. On the first day of my time in Andhra Pradesh my Telugu translator began by saying:

> *As a Dalit woman I feel sorry for high-caste women, we Dalit women are confident, we speak out, we work together, laugh together, cry together and fight together...the other women don't have that. They are reserved, scared and obedient, we are the rebels.*

The embodiment of Dalit women's struggles is very much interwoven within their self-definition of what it means to be a Dalit woman. Their bodies whilst being sites of struggle and contestation are also sites of protest and resistance, not just against caste discrimination but also against defined gender roles. According to Channa, the socio-political identities of high-caste and Dalit women are historically polarised through social stratification, "while the high-caste women suffered isolation and immobility, being confined to their homes, the low-caste women suffered from a stereotyping that made them into diametric opposites of the high-caste 'goddess,' a woman seen as the epitome of chastity and virtue."[44] It is through the fundamental principles of purity, honour and sexual control that the hegemonic structural systems of caste and patriarchy remain intact. The Dalit activist and academic Cynthia Stephen has therefore suggested that the term "Dalit womanism" is more suitable in order to address the Dalit women's protests and politics, stating, "I feel the best way to go for us is to call our struggle Dalit Womanism, and to acknowledge that the language that feminism speaks is, in our experience, also one of dominance which we have been struggling against." Stephen's critique resonates with that of the Black Womanist stance in the US, where the intersectional struggles of sexism, classism and racism act as a challenge not just to patriarchy but also to dominant white feminism. For Stephen, Dalit Womanism, demands understanding the located reality of the Dalit experience – politically and geographically, whilst being "sensitive enough to provide space for the expression of the diversity of the experiences of religious minorities, tribal and ethnic identities who are presently termed subaltern, and there can be no stopping the

---

44   Subhadra Mitra Channa, "Metaphors of Race and Caste-Based Discriminations against Dalits and Dalit Women in India," in *Resisting Racism and Xenophobia on Race, Gender, and Human Right,* ed. Faye Venetia Harrison (CA: AltaMira Press, 2005), 56.

process."[45] It is for this reason that the term Dalit Womanism will be used in this research, as oppose to Dalit feminism, as Dalit Womanist theology seeks to relocate Dalit women's experience from the margins of theological discourse to the centre, this includes the religious experiences as well as the embodied experiences of sexuality and violence, that are encountered within the narratives of Dalit women's lives.

4   Developing a Methodology for Theologising with Devadāsīs

When we gaze into the life and world of 'others' we do so with a lens that possesses particular cultural norms and understandings that have been imposed upon us through education, culture, and context and therefore are observations are never completely neutral. When I arrived in Nagalapurum, I stood before the goddess Mathamma in the temple, and I opened myself up to the goddess and her community, but such openness was limited by my own limited understandings. As a researcher I carried preconceived ideas learnt from textbooks and influenced by the narratives voiced for example, from the Christians of the Church of South India and others, such as the communities of women outreach workers, but it was only through ethnographic research that I was able to observe more thoroughly the complexity of the *devadāsīs* lives, their community, and their religiosity. However, it is also important to highlight the potential risks of ethnographic research in theology, as Gerardo Marti has commented, "insights generated by participant observation are constantly at risk of imposition of personal presumptions and asserted 'truths,' especially when researchers enter the field with strongly held convictions and compelling worldviews."[46] It is therefore vital that when encountering lived religiosity and experience as part of an ethnographic theological study, to expose oneself to world knowledges as freely as possible. This requires a certain amount of vulnerability as it involves divesting from preconceived understandings about identity, context, cultures, and beliefs. As a white feminist theologian, I must acknowledge that whilst immersing myself into the world of the *devadāsīs* I had the 'privilege' of knowing that any discomforts such as hunger or malaria were temporary for me. I could return to the safety of the college or back to the UK if necessary and therefore my understanding of life for the *devadāsī* will of

---

45   Cynthia Stephen, "Feminism and Dalit Women in India", *Countercurrents*, November 16, 2009, accessed March, 12, 2020. https://www.countercurrents.org/stephen161109.htm
46   See, Gerardo Marti, "Found Theologies versus Imposed Theologies: Remarks on Theology and Ethnography from a Sociological Perspective", *Ecclesial Practices 3, Brill, Leiden* (2016): 157–172, 157.

course be limited to that of an observer, an outsider, who though motivated to contemplate God in the temples and brothels of the *devadāsīs*, remained burdened with existing presuppositions that I may not have even been aware of. However, I sought not to be restrained by what Jeane Peracullo argued white feminist theologians have succumbed to, that being "centuries-old suspicion of the body, of eroticism, of play and wit, of slyness and seduction that Asian women in particular employ to negotiate for their space and their share of power."[47] In doing so, I allowed the sexual narratives of the women with whom I met, as well as the goddesses to whom they prayed, to challenge the imposed norms of white Christianity and white feminism, as their femininity did not comply with the established roles of women, and their religiosity was not constrained by the shackles of doctrine. Consequently, my theological journeying was full of surprises and the methodology of this research demanded an engagement with ethnography, anthropology, hermeneutics, and history in order to gain a deeper understanding of the status, lives and socio-religious identities of the dedicated women. This book therefore explores the lives and religiosity of the *devadāsīs* using ethnographic and anthropological approach, by relying on qualitative research, inclusive of participant observation, structured and unstructured interviews and conversations, and engaging with my own personal experiences as an outsider looking in.

Yet in order to situate the contemporary *devadāsīs* this theological endeavor also demanded an exploration of the socio-historical identities of Dalit women, as well as an understanding of the religio-cultural practices and beliefs of the Dalit people. As the complexity of Dalit identity cannot be overlooked when contemplating God in the brothels of the Dalit sacred sex worker. The history of casteism and the dominance of high-caste Hindu beliefs must therefore be grappled with in order to understand the means by which Dalit religious practices and belief systems have been marginalised and diminished as mere superstition and uncivilized false religion. Further, as this is a work of Christian theology, the role of the Christian Church and its collusion with Western colonialism and British imperialism cannot be overlooked, as the Church and dominant patriarchal models of Christian theology have been a contributing factor to the violence, shame, and marginalisation experienced by the women whose stories I shall share. This book therefore looks to the methodology of Dalit Theology which is fundamentally identity-specific and therefore demands an understanding of the socio-historical and religious beliefs,

---

47   Jeanne Peracullo, "Indecent Theology as Catachrestic Postcolonial Method: Gayatri Spivak and Asian Catholic Women" *The Criterion An International Journal in English, Vol. IV, II* (2013): 1.

traditions and understandings of the Dalit people. But then it seeks to disrupt the decency of Dalit Theological discourse by journeying with the narratives of the Dalit women who have remained on the margins because their stories include the indecency of rape, sex work, poverty, and paedophilia. It became necessary therefore to create a methodological framework that begins from the standpoint of Dalit women's bodies and therefore addresses what it means to be a woman in India, and more specifically a Dalit woman, as there is no universal female experience.

Whilst Dalit theologians have developed a research methodology which seeks to relocate the Dalit experience from the margins to the centre of theological discourse, a theologising with the Dalit *devadāsīs* requires a methodology that also challenges contemporary feminine norms. Because their lived experiences of womanhood that are embedded within the religious, sexual, political and economic realms, embody a feminism that must be explored through an intersectional lens in order to contemplate the hybridity of religious belonging alongside the distinctiveness of the suffering of the dedicated Dalit women. Embodiment is therefore a central theme of this book, as I seek to understand the experiences of the women who have been dedicated to the goddess and construct a theologising based upon the embodied experiences of the women as, in agreement with Lisa Isherwood and Elizabeth Stuart, "the body is both the site and recipient of revelation."[48] Approaching the Dalit body of the *devadāsīs* theologically therefore looks towards a womanist body theology, as it challenges dominant models of theological discourse that have privileged certain bodies over others. The womanist theologian, Eboni Marshall Turman, outlines the extent to which the body itself is the primary method of theology, as she talks of the marginalised and silenced body uncovering hidden experiences of history in order to create "positive space to begin the important work of constructing a moral vision" whilst recognising "the interconnected of all oppressions."[49] A Dalit body theology affirms such a vision, in that as Vinayaraj notes the "Dalit body has always been epistemological and theological,"[50] and thereby uncovers certain truths about God that are shaped by the Dalit experience, where the caste system that has enabled and reinforced such hierarchal systematic abuse to be perpetrated against those deemed as "outcastes", must

---

48   Lisa Isherwood and Elizabeth Stuart, *Introducing Body Theology* (Sheffield, Sheffield Academic Press, 1998), 11.

49   See, Eboni Marshall Turman, *Toward a Womanist Ethic of Incarnation: Black Bodies, the Black Church, and the Council of Chalcedon* (New York: Palgrave Macmillan, 2013), 7–11.

50   Y. T. Vinayaraj, "Dalit body without God: Challenges for epistemology and theology", in *Body, Emotion and Mind 'Embodying': The Experiences in Indi-European Encounters* (Berlin: LIT, 2013), 27–37.

be addressed from the bottom up, as the most significant underlying factor of subjugation. A Dalit body theology also acknowledges, that the historic identity of the Dalits that is embedded in narratives of suffering and oppression has also witnessed moments of resistance and protest through the subversion of dominant discourses expressed through the re-writing of myths of origin, the conversion into different religions and the denial to accept the Hindu ideology of purity and pollution. Such movements contradict claims made by the sociologist Max Weber, who maintained that Dalits never rebelled or protested against the system that binds them into their socio-religious and political state of servitude, instead maintaining that they "have internalised its values."[51] The psychological control that caste has had and continues to have on the Dalits has denied the Dalits of an identity and history and attempted to continue to dictate the social, political and religious positioning of individuals based upon caste hegemony. The chapters contained in this book therefore seek to expose the suffering committed against the bodies of Dalit women, they also uncover narratives of resistance and liberation, whilst contemplating God in the midst of pain and trauma and therefore it is important to recognise that the reader may encounter narratives that are emotionally, intellectually and theologically challenging to engage with.

5   The Book

In Chapter One of this book, we journey to the rural villages of Tamil Nadu to meet Mathamma, and other dedicated women, in order to situate the *devadāsīs* in contemporary Indian society using ethnographic, sociological and anthropological research. Outlining how the contemporary *devadāsīs* exist today as outcaste, marginalised, sacred 'prostitutes', who have become objectified as "harlots" in need of reform as their profession and institution has been criminalised. The identity of these women has been transformed significantly from 'ritual specialists' rooted in auspiciousness[52] dedicated to temple deities in marriage, to village sex workers, often trafficked to the city and

---

51   Deliége, *The Untouchables,* 51.
52   Kersenboom-Story details the historically auspicious nature of the chosen *devadāsī* stating: "The *devadāsī* was neither a vestal virgin nor an ascetic nun, nor they are opposite, a public woman or sacred harlot. Her function and identity has a third possibility...she was primarily a ritual specialist whose professional qualification was rooted in auspiciousness: her powers were believed to bring good luck and ward off evil." See, Saskia Kersenboom-Story, *Nityasumangali: Devadasi Tradition in South India* (Delhi: Motilal Banardsidass Publishers, 1997), 131–147.

consumed by sexually transmitted diseases. The *devadāsī* system has become an increasing phenomenon amongst rural Dalit communities within South India, where young girls are dedicated to village deities and ordained by the goddess in marriage (*maduve*), they then become the property of the village and are frequently sexually exploited.[53] The contemporary sacred sex workers find themselves in the middle of hegemonic battles for power – inclusive of caste, colonialism, political agendas, religious dogmas, reform programmes, racial and gender discrimination – each fighting to determine their control over the bodies of women. This chapter will explore the historic, religious and contemporary identities of the dedicated women, based upon socio-historical research alongside ethnographic fieldwork that details the existential experiences of the devotees of the goddess, which become the starting point for theologising. Alongside this it looks to the role of the goddess in the life of the dedicated women and the village, in order to gain a greater understanding of Dalit religiosity.

Chapter Two considers the theological methodology for contemplating God with the narratives of the sacred 'sex workers'. By firstly addressing the need for such a theology to be both contextual and practical, it outlines the way in which Indian Christian Theology has transformed Christ into a Brahmin, through a systematic Christian theology that is Sanskritic, in order to produce a discourse that satisfies the 'purity' of the high castes. This comes at the expense of the Dalits who despite making up the majority of Christians in India – are essentially irrelevant within such theological discourse. It therefore uncovers the hegemonic evils of caste violence and discrimination in order to explicate the category of Dalits within the socio-political and religious context of caste-ordered India. Centuries of socio-economic, religious and political

---

53   In Karnataka, 1588 female sex workers were interviewed, of these 414 entered sex work through the *Devadāsī* tradition, these *Devadāsī* female sex workers were more likely to be illiterate, live in rural areas, and be initiated at a much younger age. See, James F. Blanchard, "Understanding the Social and Cultural Contexts of Female Sex Workers in Karnataka, India: Implications for Prevention of HIV Infection," *The Journal of Infectious Diseases*, Vol. 191, Supplement 1. (2005): S139-S146; A report from the Integrated Child Development Services (ICDS) found that the rate of mother and infant mortality in the Chittoor district of Andhra Pradesh, where the majority of my field work was conducted, is alarming. The research attributed the cause of the deaths to the dedication of child girls to the goddess *Mathamma* – where upon attaining puberty the girls were forced into marriage. The majority of the dedicated girls die young as a result of childbirth, sexually transmitted diseases and malnutrition – only 1 percent are said to live above the age of 45. For the full report and for further information on the health implications of the dedicated girls who belong to the Madiga caste see, "MICDA Mathamma Eradication Project, Chittoor District, Andhra Pradesh," Ashanet, accessed July 25, 2014, https://www.ashanet.org/projects/project-view.php?p=409.

subjugation have determined that the Dalits have been deprived of their personhood, as the discriminatory system of caste has denied people of their humanity, religion, history, identity and agency. Yet as this chapter will discuss, throughout history there have been significant moments and movements of resistance where Dalits have fought against caste violence and discrimination. It therefore looks to Dalit Liberation Theology as a countercultural theology of resistance that is fundamentally shaped by the identity specific pain-pathos of the Dalit people. It considers the ways in which Dalit theologians have reflected on the Dalit identity of Jesus – who is Himself considered a Dalit as a "broken" and "outcaste" God. It also looks at the ways in which Dalit theologians have reflected upon the religiosity, worship, art, song and dance of the Dalit people in their discourse, in order to make such theologising relevant and liberative to the lives of the Dalit people. However, it suggests that to date such theologising has remained predominantly androcentric as the narratives and experiences of Dalit women and the Dalit divine feminine are missing.

In response, the following Chapter explores Dalit Womanist theological discourse that is shaped by the bodies of Dalit women and Dalit feminist hermeneutics that applies the existential experiences of Dalit women to Biblical narratives, in order to produce models of liberation and resistance. It gives significant attention to the plight of Dalit women who are faced with multiple layers of discrimination as a result of the hegemonic forces of patriarchy, casteism, capitalism and colonialism. It does so noting that the voices and experiences of these women must not be lost amid what Gopal Guru refers to as the "whitewashing" of Dalit women's experiences in the "call for women's solidarity."[54] As it aims to pragmatically demonstrate that the body politics of women in India are always in a flux and are influenced by a variety of factors inclusive of colonialism, gender, caste, and poverty. Noting the existing lacuna in Indian Christian Theology and Dalit Liberation Theology for the voices and experiences of the most marginalised of Dalit women, in particular those whose narratives would be deemed "indecent". In response, inspired by the Indecent Theology of Marcella Althaus- Reid, it suggests that in order to be truly identity-specific and liberating to the most marginalised of Dalit women, Dalit Liberation Theology must be born out of the sexual narratives of the oppressed.

Chapter four therefore uses a Dalit feminist hermeneutical lens in order to apply the lived experiences of the *devadāsīs* to the Biblical texts which describe the violence committed against the "harlots", "concubines", and "prostitutes"

---

54   Gopal Guru, "Dalit Women Talk Differently," *Economic and Political Weekly, Vol. 30. No. 41/42* (1995): 2549.

of Scripture. It re-reads the text of Ezekiel 23, where violent, misogynistic, androcentric language describes the destruction of the two sisters Oholah and Oholibah, the personified nations Samaria and Jerusalem. Followed by a re-reading of the tortured "concubine" of Judges 19. In doing so, the lived experiences of the contemporary sacred 'sex workers' expose the dangers of such passages that have been used to justify and permit violence and atrocities committed against the bodies of women. Using an Indecent Dalit hermeneutical lens, this chapter then re-reads the narrative of "the 'Prostitute' at Christ's Feet with her Matted Hair", in Luke 7: 36–50, in order to present a model of resistance – where the 'prostitute' becomes prophetic, revealing Christ's promise in a kin-dom to come. Throughout history women have been persecuted by the hegemonic powers of patriarchy, purity and pollution and imposed moral orders that have sought to control and subjugate their sexuality and body politics. This chapter highlights how by failing to criticise the Biblical narratives where God is the dominant male other, liberation theologies do little to challenge the hegemonies of power that destroy, rape, murder and vilify the most marginalised of women.

Chapter five journeys further in this theological yātrā by focusing on the silenced goddess in Dalit theological discourse, in order to highlight both the need to be identity specific and move towards a more liberative and indecent model of Dalit Theology, for the sake of the most marginalised of Dalit women. As theologising with the contemporary sacred sex workers further requires engaging with the lived religiosity of the Dalit villagers where the goddess plays a central role and where Jesus has become a local village deity. This chapter therefore explores the lived religious identity of Dalit villagers in order to encounter the Jesus who walks with sex workers, answers their everyday needs and sits alongside them in the temple of *Mathamma*. It will therefore explore notions of multiple religious belonging and religious hybridity apparent in the narratives of the contemporary *devadāsī*s and consider the possibilities of a Dalit the(a)ology that reconsiders the role of the goddess in Dalit theologising. This final chapter seeks to provide a model of Dalit Liberation Theology that supports the need to be affirmative to the Dalit identity yet challenges existing Dalit theological discourses to see beyond the hetero-patriarchal gaze. The worship patterns, beliefs, mythology and the suffering of the Dalit communities bring about a the(a)ologising with the divine that is rooted in a relationship with a God/dess that acts in the here and now, transgresses purity laws, and responds to the most indecent of needs. This chapter therefore challenges Dalit theological discourse to continue to journey towards an Indecent Dalit theologising that crosses religious boundaries in order to be truly indigenous and liberating to the most marginalised within the Dalit communities.

Meeting Mathamma: Sacred 'Prostitute' and Mother Goddess

My name is Mathamma Kanagarathinam and this is my story adi andrha (from the beginning).

When I was a young girl, about three years old, I became sick and so my parents and grandmother dedicated me to the temple. After puberty I served the temple by dancing. The higher caste men would abuse me, they would threaten me if I did not do what they wanted and they said that I was their property. I became a temple prostitute.

When I gave birth to a child these people would say that this is the child of god, and they would also be used by the village and the higher caste men.

There are seventy families in my village; out of these families, three families have dedicated one of their children to Mathamma. It is the tradition that when the female child becomes sick they are dedicated in order to save the life of that child and ward off evil, because Mathamma has saved the life of the child, the child is believed to be divine and an incarnation of the goddess, so the child must spend their life serving the goddess and the village. I wear my Mangalyam (marriage necklace) as a symbol of this promise because I belong to the goddess. This was made known to me at the ceremony.

During the marriage ceremony when I was given to Mathamma, a buffalo was offered as a sacrifice, and I had to walk on fire during the festival. I then had to dance for a week.

There are many superstitious beliefs surrounding those who are dedicated. For example, if I want to live with one person, then I can, or if I want to live with many, then this is also ok, but if I want to get married to one person then it is believed that, that man will die and so mostly we never get married. It is not allowed in my village. My first role as a dedicated Mathamma is as a prostitute; my second is as a temple dancer.

The men that I live with or stay with have other wives and families, so I have to provide for myself and for my children, my children are not recognised, they are treated badly by the whole village, so my problems are passed on to them.

For me, the goddess has taken me into the street, she has made everyone scold me, and tease me and they always say bad words to me. But if I go, and if I do not do the things that I have to do to please the goddess, then the goddess will punish me, so I have no choice. I am a child of god, the property

© KONINKLIJKE BRILL NV, LEIDEN, 2021 | DOI: 10.1163/9789004450080_002

of the goddess and can be used by everyone. My future and my childrens
belong to Mathamma, Mathamma controls how I live.[1]

∴

This is the story of Mathamma Kanagarathinam, who is from the rural village
of Nagalapurum in the Chittoor district of Andhra Pradesh, a predominantly
Mādiga community, that is embedded in extreme poverty, illiteracy, sickness
and deprivation. The practice of *Mathamma* dedication has existed in this
region for centuries, where child girls are offered in marriage to the goddess
Mathamma, usually when the girl is sick or in extreme poverty, in order to
spend the rest of their lives as *Mathamma devadāsīs*. Through personal ethnographic fieldwork this chapter exposes the narratives of the women who have
been dedicated to the goddess *Mathamma* and in their own words describes
how they have been raped, abused from childhood, trafficked, vilified, marginalised and oppressed. It does so in order to situate the place for theologising by
exploring the identities of the contemporary *devadāsīs*. Alongside describing
the existential pain-pathos of the dedicated Dalit women, this chapter aims to
reveal the influence of the goddess in the lives of the women and their community in order to deconstruct liberal and orthodox thinking and bring to
the forefront questions over purity, sexuality, marriage, power and the divine
authority of the goddess. Research of the *Mathamma devadāsīs* in this chapter is based upon exploring the socio-demographic characteristics of various
communities of dedicated female sacred sex workers. Personal interviews
were conducted based upon a standardized questionnaire, whilst daily conversations and mealtimes enabled more profound insights into the complexities of the *Mathammas* lives. Identifiable *Mathammas* were found with the
help of the Church of South India, Madras Diocese, who have worked on various reform and rehabilitation programmes within different rural communities
in the states of Andhra Pradesh and Tamil Nadu.[2] Interviews only took place

---

1   Mathamma Kanagarathinam, interview, Nagalapuram, Andhra Pradesh, December 12, 2014.
2   Christian church organisations in the area have been working on the rehabilitation of the
    Mathammas, yet based upon practical analysis of over a one month period of living along-
    side *Mathamma's* community, the women are further marginalised in the process of reha-
    bilitation as despite many accepting the missionary agenda to accept Christ as liberator and
    saviour, they still live in social exclusion, marginalisation, and extreme poverty, instead of
    three meals a day, they receive one meal from the church, and due to their prior social 'posi-
    tioning' they do not attend worship in the church and have not been allowed to be baptised.

following informed consent. I stayed in the villages with the women in their homes along with a Telugu speaking translator, where I was able to observe their daily lives amidst their community, in order to witness the daily existential experiences of the dedicated women.

1   Situating the *Devadāsīs*

The contemporary *devadāsīs* have been condemned outside of the discriminatory space of Indian history, existing today as outcaste, marginalised, sacred 'prostitutes'. They have become objectified as 'harlots' in need of reform and their profession and institution has been criminalised. The term *devadāsī* translates from Sanskrit as *deva,* god and *dasi,* female slave; it has been designated to a vast number of communities of women who have come to be regarded as sacred prostitutes. Sociological and anthropological studies have portrayed the *devadāsīs* as 'ritual specialists' rooted in auspiciousness[3] dedicated to temple deities in marriage, whose functions have been transformed and fragmented throughout history. Literary and epigraphic sources have used the term to describe women who have been dedicated to religious deities within the Indian Hindu context and embody a spiritual union with the divine that is transmitted in divergent worship expressions, inclusive of temple dancing and sacred prostitution. Their present-day social cataloguing situates their identities as illegal,[4] marginalised sacred 'prostitutes'. Society has rebuked these women to an indecent, immoral and impure social status. As a result, the majority of contemporary *devadāsīs* face persistent violence, emitted in varying forms, by oppressive structures of hegemonic control, and divergent systems of subjugation, including: poverty, sexual exploitation, stigmatisation and caste based marginalisation. The term *devadāsī* has come to be used as a collective categorical noun that incorporates different groupings of women who have been dedicated to deities; inclusive of those who take on the names *jogini, jogin,* or *mathamma* and will therefore be employed throughout this

---

3   Kersenboom-Story highlights the auspicious nature of the chosen *devadāsī*, stating: "The *devadāsī* was neither a vestal virgin nor an ascetic nun, nor they are opposite, a public woman or sacred harlot. Her function and identity has a third possibility...she was primarily a ritual specialist whose professional qualification was rooted in auspiciousness: her powers were believed to bring good luck and ward off evil." See, Kersenboom-Story, *Nityasumangali*, 131–147.

4   See, "Andhra Pradesh Prohibition of Dedication Act 1988", Department for Women, Children, Disabled & Senior Citizens, Government of Andhra Pradesh, accessed December, 12, 2013. http://wcdsc.ap.nic.in/entitlement_women.php.

book as a bracketed term to denote such groupings of contemporary sacred 'prostitutes', who continue in their thousands to be dedicated to temple goddesses in South Indian villages every year.

It is extremely difficult to obtain official statistics on the number of *devadāsīs* within South India, based upon the ostracized nature of the contemporary *devadāsī* institution, coinciding with the outlawing of the practice, and the fact that the majority of dedications occur within rural communities, that are isolated and embedded in immense poverty. The NGO, Aashray, claims that there are approximately 100,000 Joginis in the state of Andhra Pradesh, yet this figure has been disputed by other NGOs working within the states of Andhra Pradesh and Tamil Nadu, who claim it is much higher. Extreme poverty within rural villages has, according to the Dalit Solidarity Network, led to the dedications of minor Dalit girls occurring on a daily basis in certain areas.[5] Amongst the rural *Mādiga* communities within south India, the *devadāsī* system has become an increasing phenomenon, where young girls are dedicated to village deities and ordained by the goddess in marriage (*maduve*), they then become the property of the village and are frequently sexually exploited.[6] According to Torri, the system has become emblematic of "the social control and hegemonic masculinity of upper caste men" being "asserted and maintained through defilement and appropriation of lower caste and dalit women's sexuality."[7] Such claims are justified based on the fact that the vast majority of contemporary *devadāsīs* belong to pseudo-castes[8] or Dalit sub-castes and as a result of which face continuous marginalisation and exclusion from all social and political spheres.

The 'untouchable' status and explicit caste discrimination continues to be rampant amongst many villages within South India. Mathamma Kanagarathinam belongs to the *Mādiga* caste, a Dalit sub-caste. Nagalapurum, where Mathamma Kanagarathinam is from, is home to seventy families, the villagers as a whole face extreme poverty, malnutrition, disease and illiteracy. Different caste groups within the village occupy different hamlets. The *Mādigas* are one of the

---

5 This refers to an analysis of the districts of Mahaboobnagar and Andhra Pradesh. See, "Devadasi Increases", Dalit Freedom Network UK, accessed December 12, 2013, http://www.dfn.org.uk/news/archive/191-devadasi-increases.

6 According to a study by Blanchard et al, in Karnataka, 1588 female sex workers were interviewed, of these 414 entered sex work through the *Devadāsī* tradition, these *Devadāsī* female sex workers were more likely to be illiterate, live in rural areas, and be initiated at a much younger age. See Blanchard, "Understanding the Social": S139-S146.

7 Maria-Constanza Torri, "Abuse of the Lower Castes in South India: The Institution of the Devadasi," in *Journal of International Women's Studies* Vol. 11 (2009): 31.

8 See Erika Belkin, "Creating Groups Outside the Caste System: The Devadasis and Hijras of India" (PhD diss., Wesleyan University: 2008).

largest Dalit sub-caste groups in India, predominantly based in South India, in the states of Andhra Pradesh, Tamil Nadu and Karnataka. Their traditional specialisation is in leather work, which is the rationale behind their 'untouchable' scheduled caste status; they are an economically depressed community, commonly pushed to the margins of rural villages.[9] The ritual practice of dedicating *Mādiga* women to the goddess *Mathamma* in South India is intertwined with the interconnectedness of caste and gender based oppressions. As a Dalit woman, like many Dalit women, those dedicated are economically deprived and socially marginalised, as a consequence of their imposed 'impure' status. It is important to therefore understand the role that caste plays in situating the lived experiences of the contemporary *devadāsīs* inclusive of Mathamma. The Dalits are considered by the high caste people to be ritually impure, "deriving from their association with death and organic pollution. They are employed in occupations which are essential for removing impurity from social life, and work as sweepers, scavengers, grave-diggers and tanners."[10] The extent of their 'impure' status has determined that they exist on the outskirts of civic society, often forbidden from drinking water from wells, walking on certain paths, wearing fine clothes and jewellery and forbidden from touching certain objects, people and places due to their very touch, shadow or presence being considered defiling. Further, "they are despised and are expected to adopt a servile and obsequious attitude when addressing high caste people. They can be beaten by their superiors and formerly could be sold like cattle."[11] A Dalit devotional song describes their conditions as follows:

> *I search for God, whom should I hear?*
> *I made stone temples, carved God out of stone*
> *But priests are like stone,*
> *They imprison God.*
> *Whom shall I hear?*
> *We were born Untouchables*
> *Because of our deeds.*[12]

---

9   For further information on the socio-economic marginalization of *Mādiga* communities see, K. Rajesekhara Reddy, "Fertility and Mortality Amongst the Scheduled Caste Mādigas of Andhra Pradesh, India," *Current Science* Vol. 88. No. 10 (2005): 1664–1668.

10   Robert Deliége, "The Myths of Origin of Indian Untouchables," *Man, Royal Anthropological Institute of Great Britain and Ireland* Vol. 28, No. 3 (1993): 535.

11   Deliége, "The Myths of Origin of Indian Untouchables", 535.

12   "Dalit Devotional Song", quoted in Sagarika Ghose, "The Dalit in India," *Social Research,* Vol. 70, No. 1 (2003), 83.

The 'polluted' nature of the Dalits is said to be justified according to the *Manusmriti*, "in the same way as a menstruating woman, a widow, or a person who has recently been bereaved is polluted."[13] The ritual concept of pollution and purity serves as a 'sacred' weapon, that is used to legitimise the social and religious inferiority of Dalit and women through menstrual taboos.[14] However in reality caste pollution rules do not apply when it comes to the sexual abuse and harassment of the bodies of Dalit women, as Mencher remarks, "the most insidious dimension of the practice of untouchability leaves a woman's body open to violation while forbidding her touch in any other form."[15] Dalit women's bodies are sites of patriarchal and caste contestation, and the contemporary *devadāsī* system has become rooted in a Dalit womanhood that is shaped by the pain of caste and gender based oppression. However, the bodies of the *devadāsīs* are also sites of protest as shall be discussed, their lived religiosity, daily experiences, sexuality, and femininity disrupts imposed norms. As such the *devadāsī* system remains highly disputed in anthropological, religious and feminist studies, as to some their narrative is one of gender and caste-based oppression – where religious superstition has enabled sexual exploitation and caste subjugation. To others it is a display of female religious empowerment and counter-cultural religiosity that challenges the high-caste status-quo. [16] Historically the identity of the *devadāsīs* has been transformed, once

13 Women are condemned as polluting during menstruation and as the laws of purity determine the ownership of power, women are further marginalised during such periods based upon their uncontrollable natural bodily functions. Harper for example describes how "*Muttuchettu* (pollution) derived from a menstruating woman is more defiling than that from an Untouchable." The 'pollutive' potency of a menstruating woman within Brahminical orthopraxis is considered so defiling that the woman is forced to leave her home throughout her monthly cycle. See, Ghose, "The Dalit in India", 84.

14 The Havik mutu women are forced to exist in a state of polluted exile for five days, where a woman must "change her clothes, comb her hair or wear kumkuma (a red spot considered a mark of beauty) on her forehead, and for two to three days she does not bathe. During this time, she may not enter the house or a temple, draw water from a well, nor come near any supernatural power..." See, Edward B. Harper, *Religion in South Asia* (Seattle: University of Washington Press, 1964), 159–161.

15 Joan P. Mencher, "Conclusions", in *Life as a Dalit: Views from the Bottom of Caste India*, eds. Subhadra Mitra Channa and Joan P. Mencher (New Delhi: Sage Publications, 2013), 402–428, 418.

16 This view is held most prominently by the Dalit reformers who consider the institution to be a form of sexual exploitation and caste based marginalisation, see Torri, "Abuse of Lower Castes in South India"; Other scholars have however highlighted that that the identity of the *devadāsī* is far more complex and note that issues of reform should be considered alongside the socio-historic and religious identities of the institution. See, Amrit Srinivasan, "Reform or Conformity? Temple 'Prostitution' and the Community in the Madras Presidency," in *Structures of Patriarchy: State, Community and Household in*

considered artists and auspiciously empowered temple dancers, their sexuality became the subject matter of reform, their bodies through no fault of their own have become a battle ground of conflicting ideologies, and the inescapable structures of purity and patriarchy have dictated that their contemporary status be one of indecency and immorality.

2 The *Devadāsī* and the Politics of Her Body

My Fame was that I
Was recognised as a whore
Even as a new born babe.
My story should bring
The head of this civilisation
Low into the depths of hell.
In which chapter of the volumes
Of the famous history of your country
Do you intend to write it?[7]

The body of the *devadāsī* is a sight of debate, contestation, passion, judgment, violence, motherhood, marriage, sacredness and profanity, as such it has become a place of both practical and textual discourse. The origin of the *devadāsī* phenomenon has been debated amongst anthropologists and historians, with some suggesting it can be traced back as far as Indus Valley civilisation and others maintaining that the origins of the tradition can be found in the Vedic literature.[18] Throughout history the socio-political and religious identity of the dedicated women has been transformed dramatically, as it has been shaped and distorted by the ideologies of the many powers that have ruled and colonialised India. The women that were once considered auspicious sacred dancers have become "religious prostitutes" practicing an "evil and backward custom."[19] It is for this reason that this book focuses on the *devadāsīs*, as their

---

Modernising Asia, ed. Bina Agarwal (London: Zed Press, 1988); Kirsti Evans, "Contemporary *Devadāsīs* Empowered Auspicious Women or Exploited Prostitutes?" *Bulletin of the John Rylands Library* Vol. 71–80 (1998); S. Anandhi, "Representing Devadasis: 'Dasigal Mosavalai' as Radical Text" *Economic and Political Weekly*, Vol. 26. No. 11/12 (1991).

17   *Challapalli Swaroopa Rani,* "Dalit Women's Writing in Telugu," *Economic and Political Weekly,* Vol. 33, No. 17 (1998): WS22.

18   Kersenboom, *Nityasamangali,* 2.

19   Anagha Tambe highlights how the contemporary *devadāsī* practice involves the dedication of low caste and Dalit women in southern Maharashtra, where they are considered to

FIGURE 1   Family of the *devadāsī Mathamma*, Nagalapurum, Andhra Pradesh
PHOTOGRAPH BY THE AUTHOR

bodily experiences are of great social, theological and political significance. As it is by locating the various facets of patriarchal subjugation in its various manifestations throughout different socio-cultural contexts that we can reflect on the politics of the body of the *devadāsī*. In doing so we witness, as Vijaisri remarks, that "the institution of sacred prostitution is intricately linked to the cultural construction of sexuality and caste identity and the mode of production."[20] The contemporary *devadāsīs* also make visible the violence

---

be temple prostitutes and remain a subject matter of reform and rehabilitation. See, Anagha Tambe, "Reading Devadasi Practice Through Popular Marathi Literature" *Economic and Political Weekly* Vol. XLIV, No. 17 (2009): 85–92.

20   Priyadarshini Vijaisri, *Recasting the Devadasi: Patterns of Sacred Prostitution in Colonial South India* (New Delhi: Kanishka Publishers, 2004), 14.

of patriarchy apparent within the praxis of the church – that has further marginalised the dedicated women.

The historic auspiciousness of the *devadāsī* practice is outlined in great depth by Kersenboom-Story, as she explores the identity of the *devadāsīs* from within the folds of the Hindu tradition. She presents the phenomenon as a sacred art, stating: "this auspiciousness is implored by the society in the case of wedding ceremonies, in processions of the gods, and while carrying the sacred water to the temple."[21] The power of the *devadāsī* is considered effective "through her female sexuality that is identified with that of the goddess", as well as through ritual values such as the pot or lamp, and through her art.[22] In agreement, Anandhi focuses on the prestige and honour gifted to the *devadāsīs* during the medieval period.[23] Nair however remarks that "we must not exaggerate the power enjoyed by *devadāsīs*, who despite their relative autonomy nevertheless remained dependent on that triad of men within the political economy of the temple, the priest, the guru and patron."[24] Whilst Kersenboom-Story grants significant attention to the sacred femininity and auspiciousness of the *devadāsīs*, she fails as Vijaisri notes, to address how the "ideal of sacred femininity itself got transformed and underwent a decisive change on its incorporation into the greater tradition."[25] Historically the *devadāsīs* were married to the goddess and held prestigious temple positions, performing daily rituals, singing, dancing and leading festival processions.[26] Yet the *devadāsī* functions and status have shifted dramatically, as although they remain married to the goddess, they are no longer considered *Veśya darśanam punyam papa nāśanam* (auspicious and the destructors of sin).[27]

Anthropologists have attributed their change in status in part due to British imperialism of the 16th century onwards that forced a socio-political and religious shift on to the *devadāsī* identity-politics.[28] The Christian missionary model of morality had a detrimental effect on the way in which society came

---

21   Kersenboom-Story, Nityasamangali, 47.

22   Ibid, 67.

23   Anandhi, "Representing Devadasi", 739.

24   See, Janaki Nair, "The Devadasi, Dharma and the State," *Economic and Political Weekly* Vol. 29, No. 50. (1994): 3157–3167.

25   Vijaisri, *Recasting the Devadasi*, 8.

26   See, K. C. Tarachand, *Devadasi Custom: Rural Social Structure and Flesh Markets* (New Delhi: Reliance Publishing House, 1992); C. J. Fuller, *Servants of the Goddess, the Priests of a South Indian Temple* (Cambridge: Cambridge University Press, 1984).

27   The 18th century French missionary Abbé Dubois, uses the proverb to describe his encounter with the religious praxis of the dancing girls and remarks on the sacredness. Quoted in Kersenboom, Nityasamangali, 2.

28   Evans, "Contemporary *Devadāsīs*", 27.

to regard *devadāsīs*. Srinivas notes that "the devadasis—deputed as slaves of Gods for service in temples—were deprived of their singularly privileged social and economic position in the name of community reform by mostly male, upper case Hindu professionals who were strongly influenced by Victorian Christian missionary morality and religion."[29] This was especially apparent during the "anti-nautch" movement, as the sacred sex workers of the temple proved to be a contentious subject matter for the colonialists who sought to impose their universalising Christian morality upon the colonialized. Take for example the words of the Christian missionary Dubois in his description of the temple dancers:

> As soon as their public business is over, they open their cells of infamy, and frequently convert the temple into a stew...in order to stimulate more briskly the passion which their lewd employment is intended to gratify...perfumes, elegant and attractive attire, particularly their beautiful hair, multitudes of ornamental trinkets with infinite taste to the different parts of the body...the charms which these enchanting sirens display to accomplish their seductive designs.[30]

The subject of gender and sexual control was a major factor in the independence debates of the 19th century. *Sati* for example, which involves the burning alive of widows on the husband's funeral pyre, was abolished by the British in 1829. Child marriage, female education and the stigmatisation of widows, were also brought to the forefront of reform movements. Widow remarriage was legalised in 1856, the age of consent to sexual intercourse went from 10 years in 1860 to 12 years in 1891. Female infanticide was prohibited and child marriage was forbidden in 1929.[31] Yet despite seemingly empowering social reforms for women in India, Vina Mazumdar notes that they had little effect on the majority of Indian women, as widow remarriage, dowry, polygamy and property rights mostly concerned the middle classes and the higher castes. The campaign against British imperialism became interwoven with women's reform movements[32] to the extent that the British used the so-called 'modernisation' of the place and role of women within Indian society as a means of

---

29   Bagwe, *Of Woman Caste*, 19.
30   Abbe J. A. Dubois, *Hindu Manners, Customs and Ceremonies* (London: Oxford at the Clarendon Press, 1928) 387–389.
31   Joanna Liddle and Rama Joshi, "Gender and Imperialism in British India," *Economic and Political Weekly* Vol. 20, No. 43 (1985): WS73.
32   Joanna Liddle and Rama Joshi, *Daughters of Independence: Gender. Caste and Class in India* (New Delhi: Zed Books, 1986), 22–23.

demonstrating their own universal moral agenda and legitimising their rule. James Mill for example, noted in his influential *History of British India*, that the place of women in a society determines the advancement of that given society. Stating how "among rude people, the women are generally degraded; among civilised people they are exalted." Mill concentrated in particular on the degrading manner in which the Hindus treated their women.[33] Suggesting therefore that the British were comparatively rational and moral and therefore offered a more enlightened and civilised society to that of the colonialized peoples.

Yet retracted from such socio-historical analyses are the narratives of the most downtrodden women within that given society. For example, in India the British army increased demand for prostitution as a means of fulfilling the sexual needs of the military and facilitated the Contagious Diseases Act in 1868 that in effect protected the men and justified the exploitation of the women. The Indian women who were prostitutes were treated as commodities by the British, they became by-products of the commercial aims of imperial rule.[34] In agreement with Liddle and Joshi, British attempts to impose a moral agenda on the treatment of women in India, "failed to understand the particular form of male supremacy in their own culture, or to analyse how they created and reinforced aspects of male oppression within Indian culture, seeing no parallels between the different cultural forms of male dominance in the two countries."[35] During the British colonial rule of India, women were used as subjects in the debates over reform and independence, yet the complexities of their personal narratives were removed. As Lata Mani remarks, "tradition was thus not the ground on which the status of woman was being contested. Rather the reverse was true: women in fact became the site on which tradition was debated and reformulated."[36] The image of Indian womanhood was transformed through various enlightenment and reform programmes that used education, social action and legislation to progress with the modernisation agenda. Yet the low caste and Dalit women who were deemed as being unchaste and unvirtuous in comparison to high caste women were often made irrelevant in the changing face of Mother India, where the bodies of the low

---

33   See, James Mill, *The History of British India, 2 Vols.* (New York: Chelsea House, 1968), 309–310.

34   Liddle and Joshi, "Gender and Imperialism in British India", WS74.

35   Ibid, WS72.

36   Lata Mani, "Contentious Traditions: The Debate on Sati in Colonial India," *Recasting Women: Essays in Colonial History* ed. Kumkum Sangari et al. (Delhi: Kali for Women, 1989), 117–118.

caste women were considered to be of lesser value. Take for example colonial legislations on rape:

> On the one hand, take the case of a high caste female, who would sacrifice her life to her honour, contaminated by the embrace of a man of low caste, say a Chandala or a Pariah. On the other...a woman without character, or any pretentions of purity, who is of easy access. In the latter, a woman from any motive refuses to comply with the solicitations of a man, and is forced by him, the offender ought to be punished, but surely the injury is infinitely less than...in the former.[37]

It is for this reason that scholars such as Dirks maintains that under the British, the caste system became more pervasive, uniform and totalising, as they promoted laws that enabled caste and class persecution to become justified under religious social order.[38] Dalit and low caste women were conveyed as being binary opposites to their high caste 'virtuous' counterparts, in order to naturalise and strengthen Brahmincal patriarchal representations of womanhood. Gupta notes that the ideal virtuous Indian woman was portrayed by the Indian nationalists and reformers as being one who should cover up, not speak loudly, not fight or gossip and not converse too much with other women, noting that these were often characteristics identified with Dalit women.[39] In stark contrast, as Gupta remarks:

> Dalit women were said to live in temporary marriages, have questionable sexual morals and experience frequent divorces and desertions. They were seen as sex objects by the high-caste men...the Dalit female body, while represented as 'unfeminine', was also perceived as lustful. She was unattractive but alluring. Her body was both at the same time-repulsive and desirable, untouchable and available, reproductive and productive, ugly and beautiful. Sexual exploitation of Dalit women was an everyday fact, which was often expressed in terms of the alleged 'loose' character of the Dalit women themselves.[40]

---

37   Vasudha Dhagamwar, *Law, Power and Justice* (Delhi: Sage, 1992), 115.
38   See, Nicholas B. Dirks, *Castes of Mind: Colonialism and the Making of Modern India* (New Jersey: Princeton University Press, 2001).
39   According to sociologists Kenneth Nielson and Anne Valdrop, the visible pace of socio-economic transformation in India has been astounding and this in turn has had a positive effect on the socio-political and economic positioning of women in the country. See, Gupta, "Representing the Dalit Woman, 114–12.
40

During colonial rule the British both improved and worsened the conditions of women in India. The hegemonic forces of caste and patriarchy were not structurally attacked and whilst the reformers made concentrated efforts to challenge what they referred to as 'immoral' religious rituals such as *sati*, and advocated for widow re-marriage, the majority of Indian women, particularly those belonging to low castes or Dalits, were unaffected by the 'positive' changes brought about by the modernisation agenda of colonial India. The dedicated women became the subject of hegemonic ideological control, as Vijaisri remarks, "the sacred prostitute, the ultimate model of feminity in the pre-colonial period, was now to strive and transform herself to emulate the virtues of this new woman."[41] Thus the multifaceted aspects of her socio-religious identity were vehemently disregarded as the acts of a debauched 'harlot' according to the patriarchal hegemony of British colonialism and Indian modernity.[42]

3   Dalit Reform, the *Devadāsī* and Her Devi

In 1947 a law was passed that criminalised the *devadāsī* system, this was part of the "modernising process" of Mother India, a period that "signalled shifts in the definition of domestic and non-domestic sexuality."[43] According to Nair "what was put in its place, both in the nationalist imagination and in bureaucratic practice, in the name of a new abstract legality was a more thoroughly patriarchal family order which maintained the illusion of mutual respect and companionship."[44] This process was shaped by a politics of morality where women in particular were shamed and stigmatised if they did not conform to the regulated gender norms. This led to transformed perceptions of the *devadāsī* system, where it was deemed an immoral, impure and improper subaltern religious profanity, consequently reform initiatives were imposed that campaigned to separate the divine from the erotic. This form of postcolonial patriarchy that was itself impacted by the British colonialists defined a 'new woman' of Mother India. This 'new woman' was portrayed as the opposite to the indecent low-caste or Dalit woman, the latter was considered "coarse, vulgar...sexually promiscuous... maidservants, washer-women, barbers, peddlers

---

41   Vijaisri, *Recasting the Devadasi*, 137.
42   Reformist scholars also tarnished the Tantric arts with the same brush of immorality, referring to the Tantric practices as "gross impurities", "bestiality" and "obscenity." See, Vijaisri, *Recasting the Devadasi*, 2.
43   Nair, "The Devadasi, Dharma and the State", 315–317.
44   Ibid, 365.

... prostitutes."[45] The *devadāsīs* were systematically shamed and castigated in the process of modernisation, they became victims of nationalist patriarchal, caste and class warfare as the Indian elites began to see it as their duty to rescue the dedicated women, attitudes that echoed the colonial agenda of "civilising the natives".[46] The Christian missionary and Indian Church projects also set their sights on reforming and 'saving' the women who were deemed indecent Dalit 'prostitutes'. As a subaltern group the *devadāsīs* were then pushed further into the margins of society, as a result, it was mainly Dalit women that were then dedicated to the goddess, where they could be further degraded as impure, immodest and sexually promiscuous women.[47]

The Dalit activist, Ambedkar, appeared to accept such concepts of purity and chastity as a means of modernity and liberation for the Dalit women, focusing in particular on the Dalit women who had been dedicated to village goddesses. In his attempts to convert the Dalit people to Buddhism in order to escape the folds of Hinduism, he maintained that the purity of the body of women was a precondition for the 'new' way of life. He stated: "women are jewels of society. Every society endows immense credit for the chastity of women... the status of the family depends on the wives behaviour."[48] He therefore campaigned strongly against the practice of the *devadāsīs* that went against such normative family models and for him opposed the self-respecting identity he desperately sought to endorse within the consciousness of the Dalit people. Under the influence of Ambedkar, the Dalit social reformer Deveraya Ingle undertook a pragmatic campaign to eradicate the dedication of Dalit girls to the goddess. Using drama, song and protest, he reached out to the villages where the practice was taking place in order to challenge what he believed to be "outcaste superstitions" imposed by the high castes.[49] Women became a means by which all castes sought to gain respect and "what is crucial in this context is primarily the singular or dominant model of femininity emerging and articulated during this period, cutting across caste lines...the sacred prostitute was a deviant female whose very survival was lethal for the pride and

---

45   Partha Chaterjee, *Nation and Its Fragments: Colonial and Postcolonial Histories* (NJ, Princeton: Princeton University Press, 1993), 127.

46   See, Rajalakshmi Nadadur Kannan, "Gendered violence and displacement of devadasis in the early twentieth-century south India", Sikh Formations, Vol. 12, Nos. 2–3 (2006): 243–265.

47   Vijaisri, *Recasting the Devadasi*, 16.

48   Ambedkar appears to consider the practice of the Dalit *devadāsīs* as an embarrassment to Dalit progress and the Dalit liberation movement. See, Vijaisri, *Recasting the Devadasi*, 178.

49   See, Vijaisri, *Recasting the Devadasi*, 176–177.

vitality of the community."[50] Visible in this argument is the need to observe a sexual behaviour and moral order that is fundamentally patriarchal alongside this is the fear of Dalit identity being rooted in 'Sanskritic Hinduism',[51] which for many Dalit reformists would prevent an affirmative Dalit identity that was free from the shackles of caste.

Ambedkar therefore opposed the religious, structural, and sexual practice of the *devadāsī* system, deeming it indecent and immoral, and maintaining that it was embedded within the folds of oppressive Hindu worship. The religiosity of the *devadāsīs* and their wider community is therefore extremely complex, according to the sociologist Michael Moffatt, Dalit religiosity repeats the practices of high caste Hinduism, as it partakes in the hierarchy of caste and recognises that they must play their part in the ordering of the social reality in which they must exist. Moffatt suggests that repetition occurs due to the 'Untouchable' communities being socially excluded, resulting in the psychological actualisation of the model of social ranking, "thus they ismorphically transform or map hierarchy into a caste system among themselves."[52] He goes on to suggest that there is further evidence of implicit religious repetition and consensus in the worshipping of the same gods and goddesses as the upper castes; as Lynch remarks: "Untouchables are excluded from the worship of *Mariammam*, territorial goddess of the high caste hamlet (*uur*), and predictably replicate her worship among themselves."[53] Ambedkar and Christian Dalit reform movements in particular, oppose such practices under the premise that it would force Dalits to remain under the folds of Hinduism and therefore the caste system. This is a notion that will be grappled without throughout this book when exploring the liberative potential of the Dalit deities within Dalit theological discourse. Proposing that what Moffatt's analysis concludes as unarticulated repetition in high caste goddess worship, could in fact be a tool of Dalit emancipation, used to refute the system by using goddess worship as a means of rebellion. As taking into account the significant transformations

---

50   Ibid, 178.

51   M. N. Srinivas developed on the notion of 'Sanskritic Hinduism', he suggests that "every caste and tribe across the subcontinent was, as he saw, engaged in a long term process of conforming its practices and ideas to those of 'Sanskritic Hinduism'" a way of life exemplified by Brahmins. M. N. Srinivas, *The Cohesive Role of Sanskritization and Other Essays* (New Delhi: Oxford University Press, 1977), 48. See also, Simon R. Charsley, "Caste, Cultural Resources and Social Mobility," in *Challenging Untouchability: Dalit Initiative and Experience from Karnataka*, ed. Simon R. Charsley et al. (New Delhi: Sage Publications, 1998), 52.

52   Owen M. Lynch, "A Review of an Untouchable Community in South India: Structure and Consensus by Michael Moffatt," *Journal of South Asian Studies*, Vol. 39, No. 3 (1980): 644.

53   Ibid, 643.

of the caste system that have occurred over-time – where rebellions, protests and movements of Dalit resistance against the caste order have happened and continue to occur, present a model that is not timeless but open to debate. In agreement with Gorringe, a "history of conversion to Buddhism, Sikkhism, Islam and Christianity, migration and flight both within and out of India and the attempt to Sanskritise caste practices all testify to the numerous 'weapons of the weak' which have been used against the dominant values of society."[54] The praxis of repetition by certain Dalit and low caste communities is arguably due to centuries of repressive doctrine being employed against them in order to sustain the order of society, reducing many Dalits into a psychological state of acceptance that leads to cases of repetition. However, Dalit religiosity also present a counter-cultural model of resistance against dominant religious forces, where lived religiosity of the Dalit people, goes beyond repetition and is instead shaped by the day to day needs of the community. The complexity of the lived religious experiences of the Dalit communities can be witnessed in the narratives of the *devadāsīs*.

When I met Mathamma Kanaganithian, I was with Dalit activists and members of the Church of South India, they maintained that the *devadāsī* system is a mode of exploitation, and labelled the dedicated women, who sat before us, as "enforced prostitutes". At this the women looked ashamed of themselves. As one activist, named Preci stated: *"they are prostitutes in the village, they worship false goddesses, because the Brahmins have tricked them. Their children are now illegitimate because they have led such immoral lives."*[55] Shortly after making this statement, the minister of the local church offered everyone tea, excluding the *devadāsī Mathamma*. The dedicated women went outside and drank on their own. Purity, pollution, and untouchability therefore appeared ingrained even with the praxis of the church. Later that day a man in the village had come to Mathamma Kanaganithian and offered her a bowl of rice – she described how he was calling on her to pray to the goddess for the healing of his son, on leaving he touched her feet. Mathamma described how even Christians come to her to ask her to call on the goddess for help, but the Church has told her that her beliefs are dangerous. She described how despite this, she still fears the goddess and prays to her but does not tell the people in the church that she is doing this.[56] Mathamma's narrative reveals the extent to which her religious and social positioning and belonging within her community has been

---

54   Hugo Gorringe, *Untouchable Citizens: Dalit Movements and Democratization in Tamil Nadu* (New Delhi: Sage Publications, 2005), 117.

55   Dalit Women's Self-Respect, interview, Madurai, December, 10, 2013.

56   Priyadarshini Vijaisri remarks that, "the debates are largely influenced by the western scholarships that looks for parallels to sisterhood/womanhood in other cultures." See,

impacted by the dominant religious forces, in this case the Church. Her body has been pushed to the margins both physically and symbolically, as a result of sexual and sacred acts. Yet despite being condemned as an immoral practice, the fear, adoration and centrality of the goddess was also apparent, as was the rebellious sacred bond she shares with the goddess to whom she secretly prays.

4   Dedicated to the Goddess

Devdasi devachi bayako, sarya gavachi- Servant of God but wife of the whole town[57]

Mathamma Kanagarathinam was dedicated by her parents at the age of four to the goddess because she was sick. Following a promise of dedication to the goddess, Mathamma was healed, this was determined to be a sign that she was a divine intermediary, who would enable the village to communicate with the goddess. A ceremony of dedication took place[58] in the style of a traditional marriage, where she was symbolically offered to the goddess, who then granted her to the whole community. It is in this moment, as Torri describes, that Mathamma became the "property of a divinity that benevolently concedes her to the whole community."[59] During the ceremony of dedication a necklace was tied around her neck, this is referred to as the *pottu, mangalyam* or *tali* and used to mark the identity of dedicated women, who are forbidden from ever removing it, the consequences of doing so would be severe from the goddess. Traditionally the dedicated women are then considered to be divine and auspicious, yet this identity has become fragmented.[60] At the age of twelve a "deflowering ceremony" took place for Mathamma Kanagarathinam, where a high-caste man paid Mathamma's parents for her virginity, following this, other men of the village would pay Mathamma for sex, these men belonged to different caste groups. If Mathamma resists the requests for sex it is deemed as an insult to the goddess. Following the dedication and "deflowering ceremony"

Priyadarshini Vijaisri, "In Pursuit of the Virgin Whore: Writing Caste/Outcaste Histories," *Economic and Political Weekly* Vol. XLV, No. 44 (2010): 64.

57   This is a common Marthi saying to describe the role of the *devadāsīs*.

58   The practice of dedicating young girls and women to deities is known in anthropological terms as 'theogamy.' See, Kamal K. Misra and K. Koteswara Rao, "Theogamy in Rural India: Socio-cultural Dimensions of the Jogini System in Andhra Pradesh," *Indian Anthropologists* Vol. 32 (2002): 1–24.

59   Torri, "Abuse of Lower Castes in South India: The Institution of Devadasi": 33.

60   Vijaisri, *Recasting the Devadasi*, 618.

Mathamma became the property of both the goddess and the village. Her body became a divine representation that was used for sexual exploitation.

Dedicated women are not permitted to get married therefore Mathamma and the other women that have been dedicated to *Mathamma* from different villages have never been married. Many of the women who I spoke to had been dedicated in childhood by their parents due to sickness; the other women were dedicated by family members as a result of extreme poverty. The children of those dedicated faced further stigmatisation from their community, as a result of their dedicated mother's unmarried status. It is interesting to take into account a description of the children of sacred prostitutes during the time of British colonial rule that continues to apply to their current social positioning, as described by Yatharardhavasini:

> We need not expect morality from the children of the dancing girl caste; who after they go home from school are the usual spectators of dancing performances the dancing master being in attendance with his musical instruments. The prostitutes take upon themselves to train up their children from infancy and teach them nothing but how to lure the other sex. How then can we allow are children to read with them?[61]

The children of the *Mathammas* often continue to be refused an education; they are also refused access to legal Scheduled Caste state provisions,[62] and as a result are further marginalised by the community and state.[63]

Visible in Mathamma's narrative is the violence that is committed against her, not only physical violence, but also social, cultural, psychological, and symbolic violence. Her historically sacred role has been transformed and her body has become a site of patriarchal oppression, where the goddess has been used against her in order to control her. Mathamma has been systematically shamed to the margins of her social and religious community, as have her children who carry with them the burden of their mother's oppression. Her indigenous religiosity has been manipulated through what Bourdieu refers to as a

---

61   Yatharardhavasini, 7th August, 1878, quoted in Vijaisri, "Recasting the Devadasi": 151–152.
62   See, Maggie Black, *Women in Ritual Slavery: Devadasi, Jogini, and Mathamma in Karnataka and Andhra Pradesh, Southern India* (London: Anti-Slavery International, 2007), 21.
63   The *devadāsī* practice was criminalised in 1934 under the Bombay Devadasi Protection Act by the British Government, the law made it illegal to dedicate girls to the goddess, later the Karnataka Devadasis Act was instilled and was adopted by the State Legislature in 1982. Despite the criminalisation of the practice, thousands of girls are dedicated to the goddess every year, the criminalisation of the practice often mean it is hidden from the public eye and the exploitation of Dalit minor girls goes unreported as result.

'symbolic violence' that has led to her sexual exploitation. Her everyday experiences of social stigmatisation and physical sexual abuse have been determined and imposed by multiple contexts of power that have enabled "various
forms of normative violence to continue with impuity."[64] Mathamma is consequently exploited not just by the men of the village, but also those around her
who have imprisoned her within the imposed boundaries of sexual morality,
shaming her and her children to a lifetime of subordination. Meanwhile the
Dalit reform programmes and the Christian church initiatives that aim to offer
a pathway to 'salvation' risk making Mathamma invisible in the process, as her
body becomes categorised as an indecent sex worker shackled to caste Hindu
religiosity and her subaltern religiosity and sexuality is silenced by the dominant forces in the name of reform and 'salvation'.

The peripheral and subaltern discourses of the *devadāsīs* are not monolithic,
and therefore to silence or ignore them is to reproduce systems of domination
and oppression, and to therefore ignore opportunities for liberation. This was
visible in the religious experiences of the women I met, as the majority of *Mathammas* interviewed were committed to their worship of the goddess, as one
woman stated: *"my identity is with the goddess, people may wish to remove me
and my family entirely but I was called by the goddess, and I still have hope in
her."*[65] In contrast, when asked of the role that the goddess *Mathamma* plays
in the life of Mathamma Kanagarathinam, she stated: *"I am the property of the
goddess, Mathamma controls how I live."*[66] Yet, Mathamma Kanagarathinam
knew nothing of the oral myths surrounding the goddess, all that Mathamma
knew was to live in fear of the goddess and obey the high caste men. Her status
as a dedicated sacred prostitute had been communicated to her as the dominant forces of the village saw fit, this is a dramatic shift from the narratives of
the early Christian missionaries, where the women were Priestesses holding
respected and feared identities.

5   The Mother Goddess *Mathamma*

In the villages of South India, the mother goddess plays a central role and yet
there appears to be a lacuna in the studies of village religiosity. As Wilber T.

---

64   See, Suruchi Thapar-Bjorkert, Lotta Samelius and Gurchathen S. Sanghera, "Exploring
       symbolic violence in the everyday: misrecognition, condescension, consent and complic-
       ity", *Feminist Review,* 112 (2016): 145–162, 145.
65   Prasu, interview, Chittoor District, Andhra Pradesh, December, 16, 2014.
66   Mathamma Kanagarathinam, interview, Nagalapuram, Andhra Pradesh, December, 12,
       2014.

Elmore remarked back in 1925, "it is estimated, and probably conservatively, that eighty per cent of the people of South India address their worship almost exclusively to minor, i.e. local and village deities, and yet these deities receive little attention in the studies of Hindusim."[67] The "great gods" include *Vishnu* and *Siva* and there are also the local village deities, known as *Gramadevata*. The *Gramadevata* play a central role in the lives and worship of the people of the towns and villages, as they are worshipped for being protectors from evil, illness, disease and hunger. Jaganathan describes how "people consider the deity of the concerned place as their own guardian deity or the one who protects the village from illness and helps them in their prosperity and goodness of place."[68] In South India, the goddesses who are protectors of the villages will mostly carry a name that ends with *'Amma'* or *'Amman'*, translating as mother. The motherhood of the goddess takes on various forms, as the femininity of the divine goddess is as Kersenboom-Story notes, "credited with a highly eruptive, dynamic power that is hard to control. This force can be applied for the welfare, fertility, health and justice of human society but it may also break loose and result in epidemic diseases and other calamities."[69] Kamala Ganesh remarks:

> The mother goddess can be interpreted as expressing ideas of power, autonomy and primacy in the widest sense of the terms. She conveys not so much the idea of physical motherhood but a world view in which the creative power of femininity is central: the goddess mediates between life and death and contains in herself the possibility of regeneration…[70]

Devadāsī history is rooted in the worship of the goddess *Yellamma*, otherwise referred to as *Renuka* or *Mariamma*. [71] The stories surrounding how *Yellamma* became a mother goddess vary amongst different regions and communities within India. Arun Jaganathan maintains that a vital aspect of understanding

---

67   Wilber T. Elmore, *Dravidian Gods in Modern Hinduism a Study of the Local and Village Deities of Southern India* (Madras Christian Literature Society, 1925), ix.

68   Arun Jaganathan, "Yellamma Cult and Divine Prostitution: Its Historical and Cultural Background," *International Journal of Scientific and Research Publications,* Volume 3. Issue 4. (2013): 1.

69   Kersenboom-Story, *Nityasamangali,* 59.

70   See, Kamala Ganesh, "Mother Who is Not a Mother: In Search of the Great Indian Goddess," *Economic and Political Weekly* Vol. 25, No. 42/43 (1990): WS-58.

71   There are striking similarities in the myths surrounding the goddesses of South Indian villages, as Jaganathan remarks: "all these seem to have a common base for their origin based on the *Renuka* myth described in *Puranas* or any other stories mostly having connection with this myth." See, Jaganathan, "Yellamma Cult and Divine Prostitution":1.

the development of the myths, narratives and worship patterns of the goddess *Yellamma*, is embedded in the caste structure of India, witnessed by the fact that *Renuka*, otherwise referred to in South Indian regions, inclusive of Karnataka and Andhra Pradesh as *Yellamma,* is most popular with the lower castes as oppose to the Brahminical caste groups.[72] Jaganathan describes how "*Renuka*, as mentioned in *Purana* is the mother of *Parasurama* who according to Indian mythology is considered to be the incarnation of *Visnu* and his cult."[73]

The myth of Renuka is narrated as follows: one day upon taking a bath outside, the wife of *Jamadagni* witnessed *Gandharvas* "sporting" in the reflection of the ball of water that she held in her hand.[74] Because of the desire she felt upon accidently witnessing this, she lost her chasity and thus the power that came along with it. Her husband witnessed that her powers had vanished and upon doing so, he ordered his son *Parasurama* to cut off his mother's head. *Parasurama* agreed, yet an 'Untouchable' woman came to Renuka's protection, unable to separate the two women, *Parasurama* cut off both of their heads. For his obedience *Parasurama* was rewarded by his father and received the granting of a wish in return. He desired that his mother be bought back to life. This wish was granted, and *Parasurama* who was ordered to sprinkle water upon the head with the body to bring his mother back to life, however he accidently attached the wrong heads to the two bodies. He placed his mother's head on to the body of the 'Untouchable' woman, and the other woman's head was rejuvenated on to the body of his mother. Both were brought back to life with the wrong heads. Witnessing the miracle that had taken place the local villagers began to worship both women as goddesses. The body with the head of *Renuka* became known as *Mariamma* and the body with the head of the untouchable woman came to be known as the goddess *Yellamma*[75]. Throughout time and

---

72   The worship of *Renuka* or *Yellamma* can be seen in many parts of India, however Jaganathan notes that it is in the regions of Vindhya Mountains that worship of the goddess is predominant, as it is here that the mythical stories of a mother goddess have shaped an identity and historical cultural background for the lives of thousands of women whose lives have been dedicated to her worship. See, Jaganathan "Yellamma Cult and Divine Prostitution": 1.

73   *Renuka,* is known to be wife of *Jamadagni* and the mother of *Parasurama.* The earliest reference to the goddess is in *Mahabharata*, in *Vanaparva*; it is here that her death and rebirth are explained. Jaganathan translates the narrative according to *Vanaparva* of *Yellamma* and her husband *Jamadagni* who are described as having five sons, *Rumanvan, Susena, Vasu, Visvavasu* and *Parasurama*. See, Jaganathan "Yellamma Cult and Divine Prostitution": 1.

74   Her ability to carry water in a ball on her hand was a sign of her auspiciousness.

75   The word '*Yella*' means all and '*Amma*' means mother, together the name of the goddess translates as 'mother of all'. However, in the context of Tamil, '*Yella*' also can be translated as the border of a village. As a result of which the location of the temples at which she is

dependent upon differing contexts, the myth has developed amongst different communities and villages and by different caste groups. The socio-anthropological development of the myth of *Yellamma* reveals both the patriarchal and caste-based influences on cultural mythology and religious practices.

Yellamma was considered a perfect religious wife who was devoted and obedient to her husband, for her purity of mind she was blessed with a prosperous home and healthy family. It was in the moment that she dared to be tempted with "impure thoughts" that she was punished with death. For Ramberg the story exposes how "the regulation of women's sexual capacity is fundamental to patriarchal social organisation…so too is the terrific power of feminine sexual desire here capable of destroying the calm of a great sage and inspiring matricide."[76] She was brought back to life because her son wished it, and her husband authorised it, and she was rejuvenated to once again be a holy and devoted, pure, wife. It is for this reason that Robert Bohn refers to the story of *Yellamma* as being "a patriarchal or male-created myth" because of the clear portrayal of male dominance. Yet as Bohn further remarks, it is "in this same myth, as well as in the contemporary rituals surrounding *Yellamma's* worship, we can find glimpses of an earlier non-patriarchal myth."[77] Bohn maintains that the story of *Yellamma* is rooted in the matriarchal history of India's early religious traditions and practices. He argues that this can be witnessed during the celebrations of *Yellamma* which occur most prominently during the full moon. Full moon festivals are associated with the harvest and linked to fertility; it is in *Yellamma's* sudden sexual consciousness that also surrounds the story and worship of *Yellamma* that Bohn believes can be traced back to the early fertility cults. He therefore suggests that such matriarchal roots have been distorted and rewritten as a result of partriarchal and caste hegemonies. He argues that the beheading is a later addition to the myth added my men who seek to also destroy the memory of *Yellamma*, as "female sexuality cannot be allowed to exist independent of women's designated role as mother. She must be passive, subordinate, non-self-activating."[78] The mythical narrative of the goddess is, in agreement with Ramberg, one that challenges normative family values in the same way that the lives of those dedicated to her do.[79]

Though there is a significant lack of religious and historical sources relating to the identity of the goddess *Mathamma* and of those dedicated to her, early

---

worshipped are located on the borders of the village, in order that she will be the protecting mother. See, Jaganathan "Yellamma Cult and Divine Prostitution": 2.

76   Ramberg, *Given to the Goddess*, 11.
77   Robert Bohn. *Notes on India* (Boston: South End Press, 1982), 123.
78   Bohn. *Notes on India*, 124.
79   Ramberg, *Given to the Goddess*, 9.

reference is made by the colonial ethnologist, Edgar Thurston, in his research on southern India, he states: "Mātanga or Mātangi is a synonym of Mādiga. The Mādigas sometimes call themselves Mātangi Makkalu, or children of Mātangi, who is their favourite goddess. Mātangi is further the name of certain dedicated prostitutes, who are respected by the Mādiga community."[80] *Mathamma* is the goddess of certain *Mādiga* communities, *Mātangi* is the name given to the Mādiga woman when she becomes possessed by the goddess *Mathamma*. According to Kersenboom, the goddess *Ellamma* is regarded as the original form of *Mathamma*.[81] *Mathamma* is also referred to as *Māthangi*. The traditional beliefs surrounding the goddess have been orally passed down through the generations of *Mādiga* communities. [82] The narrative coincides with the myths surrounding the goddesses *Yellamma* or *Mariyamman*.[83]

The mythology clearly echoes that of the goddess *Yellamma* and *Mathamma* communities believe that the goddess *Mathamma* like *Mariyamman* has the powers to ward of enemies and cure illnesses.[84] The goddess is deemed as being beautiful, holding the looks of a young bride and being gifted with the ability to heal, bring fertility to people and the land, fight for the oppressed,

---

80   Thurston, *Castes and Tribes*, 49.

81   Ibid, 56.

82   See for example the myth for *Mariyamman* as described by Younder, "Paraśu Rāma's mother was believed to be exceptionally virtuous, which could be witnessed by her ability to carry water in a ball on her hand everywhere she went. One day she glanced at handsome angel-like beings, as a result her ball of water fell apart and her sari, that would fly over her head, fell down and became wet. When she returned home, her husband was enraged to see she was no longer an honourable woman, so he demanded that their son cut off her head. Reluctantly, Paraśu Rāma obeyed his father; his mother clung to her Harijan (untouchable) maid, and her son accidently cut off both their heads. He repented of his act and his father allowed him to put his mother's head back on and bring her back to life, however Paraśu Rāma accidently attached the wrong heads to the wrong bodies. His mother and the maid were brought back to life and the untouchable body came to be called *Mariyamman*, which translates as 'switched mother'. It is as a 'mother goddess' that she is worshiped as a virtuous deity who opposes injustice." See, Younger, "A Temple Festival of Mariyamman": 508.

83   According to Paul Younger the legend of the goddess has been developed from the brahminic and Sanskritic texts that tell the story of Paraśu Rāma, the son who beheaded his mother. See, Paul Younger, "A Temple Festival of Mariyamman," *The Journal of the American Academy of Religion*, Vol. XLVIII, No. 4. (1980): 493–516.

84   Stories relating to *Mathamma, Yellamma, Ellaiyamman* and *Mariyamman* are all very similar, stemming from the same source and goddess, beginning with the human form Renuka, each village appears to have slightly adapted the story with divergent added or emitted features. See, Sathianathan Clarke, "Paraiyars Ellaiyamman as an Iconic Symbol of Collective Resistance and Emancipatory Mythography," in *Religions of the Marginalised: Towards a Phenomenology and the Methodology of Study*, eds. Gnana Robinson (Delhi: ISPCK, 1998), 35–53.

and defeat enemies of her worshippers.[85] Anandhi Shanmugasundara, high-lights how communities "also look at *Mathamma* as containing uncontrollable sexuality and as a formidable feminine force that needs to be pacified through the dedication of women."[86] The goddess who is both dangerous and miraculous is central to the religious life of the villagers. The goddesses of the rural Dalit communities[87] hold a distinct identity to that of the Caste-Hindu deities, as they represent an "autonomous cultural system," that continues to exist within rural communities today.[88]

Dalit religions have existed on the margins of Indian society throughout history, yet in contrast to Hindu deities there are no written narratives for the Dalit goddess religions. Instead myths and traditions are orally transmitted, and over time it appears that high caste beliefs have become intertwined with the outcaste beliefs, thus transforming worship styles and practices, and removing the autonomy of outcaste religiosity. Reference is made to outcaste religious practices by the 19th Century Christian missionary Henry Whitehead, he notes that the Mādiga communities of rural India worshipped female deities within temple institutions watched over by Priestesses. The temples had "male attendants, who are supposed to guard the shrine and carry out commands of the goddess, but their place is distinctly subordinate and servile."[89] During this period the *Mathammas* were not deemed as village sex workers but instead held prestigious religious positioning within their societies. The caste implications are also historically noted by Kersenboom, who highlights that all castes had fear of the goddess *Mathamma* and contributed to her worship, yet "caste distinctions prevent any but Mādigas from taking an active part in the ceremonies."[90] It is for this reason that scholars such as Vijaisri have maintained that the feminine autonomy and caste distinctions of the dedicated women to the seemingly liberative goddess "perceive a different religious principal at work, which recognises the mysterious powers of the outcaste woman, the dangerous and benign power she recreates for the village community."[91] Revealing a subaltern religious praxis of liberation for the Dalits.

---

85   Younger, "A Temple Festival of Mariyamman": 504.
86   Anandhi Shanmugasundara, Gender, Caste and the Politics of Intersectionality in Rural Tamil Nadu," *Economic and Political Weekly* Vol. XLVIII No. 18 (2013): 66.
87   There are reportedly 3000–5000 Mathammas within these regions of Tamil Nadu and Andhra Pradesh. See, UN report by the Institute of Social Sciences, *Trafficking in Women and Children in India* (New Delhi: Orient Longman, 2005), 618.
88   Vijaisri, *Recasting the Devadasi,* 34.
89   Henry Whitehead, *Indian Problems in Religion Education Politics* (Bombay: Bombay Press, 1921), 17–18.
90   Kersenboom, *Nityasumangali,* 55.
91   Vijaisri "In Pursuit of the Virgin Whore": 64.

FIGURE 2   Ex- *devadāsī*, Chittoor District, Andhra Pradesh
PHOTOGRAPH BY THE AUTHOR

However, the narrative of the contemporary *devadāsī*, Mathamma Kanaga-rathinam, appears to oppose the notion of a self-governed divine identity, as her fear and bitterness towards the goddess is held alongside her hatred of the high-caste men and Dalit men who have sexually exploited her. The traditional narratives themselves therefore need to be explored with a hermeneutic of suspicion, based upon the existential realities of the contemporary *devadāsīs*. Yet in agreement with Vijaisri, "the very existence of the custom diversifies the scope of analysis on crucial issues relating to sexuality, outcaste culture and religion...while the influence of the matangi on the cultural identity of the outcaste sacred prostitute provides a link to establish their distinct iden-tity within the institution of sacred prostitution."[92] Fundamentally the world

---

92   Vijaisri, *Recasting the Devadasi*, 304.

FIGURE 3   Inside the temple of *Mathamma*, Nagalapuram, Andhra Pradesh
            PHOTOGRAPH BY AUTHOR

of the contemporary *devadāsīs* is complex, it exposes us to narratives of violence committed against the bodies of the most marginalised of Dalit women
and omitted through various hegemonic forces. Whilst the historical identity,
mythology and religious praxis reveals a Dalit goddess who is on the side of
the oppressed, and a religious world that is fundamentally counter-culture and
shaped a divine feminine who challenges normative social constructions.

6   A Goddess of Pain, Blood and Discharge

The Dalit feminist poet Meena Kandasamy describes how in the strength of
the goddess, Dalit women find hope in the midst of their daily oppression, she
writes:

> *My Maariamma bays for blood. My Kali kills. My Draupadi strips. My Sita
> climbs on to a stranger's lap. All my women militate. They brave bombs, they
> belittle kings.... Call me names if it comforts you. I no longer care.*[93]

---

93   Meena Kandasamy, *Ms Militancy* (New Delhi: Navayana Publishing. 2010), 6.

This was visible in Mathamma's village where women would come to Mathamma when they needed to call upon the goddess to aid them in their pain related to childbirth or menstruation, when a member of their family was sick, or even when they needed liberation from their abusive partners. In the rural villages of South India, the divine is the Mother Goddess, as Brubaker describes: "Whatever her name, her story, her physical representation, or the details of her worship, the goddess in question is the tutelary deity of a South Indian village. The village topocosm is her domain, its destiny is in her hands, and its inhabitants are her people."[94] The first encounter with the divine for the Dalit people throughout history is rooted in the mythology of the mother goddess, it is the goddess, who is considered the divine protector from small pox, the one who will bring the rain for harvest, and bless the women with fertility. It is the goddess who understands the cries of lament, the prayers for change and gives the Dalit women of the village the courage to go on.

The *devi* of the Dalits is central to communal life, as she is a matriarchal force of justice and protection who takes on the needs of the community, no matter how mundane, and exists alongside the Dalit people in their village. As a Dalit woman in Ramangulam village, Madurai, stated: *"What else are we going to ask God except for good rain, good growth of trees, plants and healthy life without disease for all."*[95] The Dalit *devi* is a practical goddess that takes on the needs of an oppressed people, as such Dalits do not consider their deities as divine others, glorified and removed in the realms of paradise, but they are practical village goddesses, existing in the here and now, enabling and liberating the oppressed. Take for example the worship of the Dalit goddess *Mansani*, who is considered a protector of women, as she knows their pain and removes their suffering. As Muthu describes, during menstruation "women may have severe pain and excess blood discharge. They take for this herbal medicine 'uthiramalai' thinking of *Mansani*, and after taking it thrice, their pain ceases. The women who get cured by this, offer 'uthiramalai' to the Goddess...also at the time of delivery related pain *Masani* is considered the remover of all disease..."[96] Dalit religiosity instantly challenges notions of purity – through the worship of the goddess who understands and removes the blood flow of suffering women. According to Kumari, "worship of these Deities (i.e., *Maremma, Pochamma, Yellemma, and Mathamma*) symbolises that the world originated from female *sakthi* (power); and all these goddesses, though they differ in

---

94   Richard L. Brubaker, "Barbers, Washermen, and their Priests: Servants of the South Indian Village and Its Goddess," *History of Religions*, Vol. 19. No. 2 (1979): 129.

95   K. S. Muthu. *Dalit Deities* (Madurai: The Dalit Resource Centre, 2005), XIV.

96   Ibid, 71.

names in different villages, are the offspring of the ultimate female *shakthi* (power).[97] The strength and power associated with this female power of the Dalit *devi* is described by Rao:

> Numerous writings of foreign travellers and works of anthropologists show that before the advent of Christianity in India, Dalits had a religious system of their own. Dalits are concerned with their local village goddesses. The female goddesses appear predominant. Unlike in Hinduism they emerge independent, unblushing erotic female figures. Be it the Mariamma, Poleramma, Peddamma, or local deity, they have nothing in common with the goddess of the Hindu pantheon...[98]

The deities of the Dalits stand outside of the realm of dominant Hindu religiosity, as Kumar remarks, "all these mother goddesses are not part of the dominant religion (i.e. Hinduism) in India. All these Dalit goddesses are treated as demons (*Asuras*) in Hindu Scriptures and named as *Kśūdra Devatas* (Deities of the lowest people)."[99] Y.B. Satyanarayana's biographical novel, *My Father Baliah,* supports this description, stating:

> "The deities they pray to are not the same as the Hindu ones...unlike in Brahminism, where the priest is Brahmin, male and hierarchical, and the Varnashrama Dharma is institutionalised, there are no priests for these deities, and every untouchable is a priest unto himself or herself."[100]

The goddesses of the Dalits like the Dalit people themselves exist outside of the realms of Hinduism both physically and metaphorically, as their temples are mostly on the margins of the villages. They take on the form of an impure deity, as they are associated with blood, death, and left-over food, all of which opposes the Brahminical laws of purity. As a vital aspect of the orthopraxis of Brahminism and the history of the Hindu religion as a whole is the socially operative division of purity (*śauca, śuddhi*) and pollution (*aśauca, aśuddi*)

---

97   B. M. Leela Kumari "The Untouchable "Dalits" of India and their Spiritual Destiny," in *Another World is Possible: Spiritualities and Religions of Global Darker Peoples,* eds. Dwight N Hopkins and Marjorie Lewis (London: Routledge, 2014), 9.
98   Y. Chinna Rao, "Dalits and Tribals Are Not Hindu," *Frontier*, Vol. 32, No. 37 (2000): 156.
99   Kumari, "The Untouchable "Dalits", 17.
100   The biography describes the life of the authors father who belonged to the Dalit *Mādiga* community in Telangana in Andhra Pradesh. It portrays the existential lives of those belonging to Dalit communities over a period of time. See, Y. B. Satyanarayana, *My Father Baliah* (New Delhi: Harper Collins Publishers, 2011).

attributed to the sacred laws of Hinduism. The polarity of purity and pollution operates on a hierarchy, where the Brahmins are at the top and the "outcastes", the Dalits, are at the bottom. Célestin Bouglé's study on the caste system illustrates how the place of purity in occupational caste-based hierarchies is the defining factor in the social ranking of *jātis*, noting that the supremacy of the Brahmins is directly attributed to their role as sacrificial priests. Unlike the degrading occupations of the "outcastes", the place of the Brahmin is in the priesthood, "partaking in the world of the gods".[101] The purpose and role of the Brahmins is to create a pure environment. The social stratification of varṇa, that is interrelated with the concepts of purity and pollution, reinforces existing inequalities through occupational and social grading that determines inequitable access to land, politics, education, religion and basic human rights.

Purity and pollution therefore play a significant role in Dalit religiosity, as C. S. Fuller argues, the spiritual distinction between Brahmins and 'Untouchables', also remains a vital aspect of the hierarchal separation between both. Fuller writes: "Purity and pollution embody more than high and low status, and have ethical and spiritual aspects, expressing the proper relationship between men and gods."[102] It is because purity and pollution "define an idiom by which respect to the gods is shown,"[103] that the role the 'Untouchables' play in ritual worship, by controlling the 'impure' spiritual forces, that they become viewed as permanently 'impure'. The idiom of purity therefore controls the religious and societal interactions, as Mary Douglas writes "purity and impurity are principles of evaluation and separation. The purer must be kept uncontaminated by the less pure."[104] It is for this reason that those at the bottom of the caste system are ideologically imprisoned by caste restrictions,[105] regulations and rituals, as Ghurye reminds us, "ideas of purity, whether occupational or

101   Deliége, *The Untouchables of India*, 32.
102   C. J. Fuller, "Gods, Priests and Purity: On the Relation Between Hinduism and the Caste System," *Man, New Series*. Vol. 14, No. 3 (1979): 459.
103   Ibid, 470.
104   Mary Douglas, "Introduction", in *Homo Hierarchicus: The Caste System and Its Implications*, ed. Louis Dumont (London: Paladdin, 1972), 16.
105   The Jesuit missionary Gerard Baader described the plight of Dalits and the impact of the socially ingrained purity laws in the early 20th century, stating: "It is reported from Jattarodid, suburb of Nagpur, that a Caste Hindu woman accidentally fell into a well while drawing water. Hearing the cries for help, two Harijan (Mahar) youths rushed to the spot and attempted to dive into the well to save her life. They were, however, prevented by Caste Hindu women from doing so, on the ground that the water of the well would be polluted by contact with the would-be rescuers. The girl in the meantime was drowned." see, Gerard Baader SJ, "The Depressed Classes of India: Their Struggle for Emancipation," *Studies: An Irish Quarterly Review*, Vol. 26. No. 103 (1937): 399.

ceremonial, which are found to be a factor in the genesis of caste, are the very soul of the idea and practice of untouchability."[106] The deities of the Dalits are themselves considered impure by the high caste people, consequently they enable a subversive lived theology for the Dalit people, as Dalit village worship appears to undermine the purity laws through subversive worship.

Despite the role of the goddess in the lives of the Dalit people, for the Dalit revolutionists Ambedkar and Jyoti Phule, and many contemporary Dalit Christian activists, village religiosity is embedded within the folds of Brahminical Hinduism and therefore considered "holistically digressive". As Vijaisri remarks, "the past was seen as lacking any reason for celebration or even invocation and providing critique of religion that was perceived as a basis for an oppressive structural order. This further led to disassociation from religious traditions that in modernistic parlance were superstitious and irrational."[107] Dalit religiosity has therefore been removed from Dalit political discourse and degraded in the process of "modernisation," this is also the case in the vast majority of Dalit Christian theology as shall be discussed in the following chapter. The Dalit religious experiences that are intricately related to the mythology of the village goddesses have also become stigmatised as ignorant and irrelevant. However, despite attempts by the British colonialists and reformists to eradicate Dalit goddess worship "India's population remains about 75 per cent village-based and local goddesses are regarded as protectors of these villages."[108] Worship of Dalit village deities therefore remains a vital aspect of kinship and community.

7   Sacred Sexuality and the Demand for Decency

The *devadāsis* present a politics of the body that is impacted by intersectional forces of oppression alongside a subversive religiosity and profound history. This can be witnessed in the transformation of the role of the *devadāsis* and their place in society, as they display a timeline of womanhood and sexuality that has challenged the norms of Indian femininity and crossed the boundaries

---

106   G. S. Ghurye, *Caste, Class and Occupation* (Bombay: Popular Book Depot, 1961), 214.
107   "Only religious traditions that had the potential for liberating outcastes like Buddhism, with its strong egalitarian and humanitarian ethos were deployed in the struggles for identity...Thus, the corpus of studies that seek to reconstruct the outcaste traditions are singularly flawed by the absolute denial of all cultural posts." See, Vijaisri "In Pursuit of the Virgin Whore": 67.
108   Sree Padma, *Inventing and Reinventing the Goddess: Contemporary Iterations of Hindu Deities on the Move* (London: Lexington Publishers, 2014), 2.

of enforced notions of decency. This can be witnessed in the poetry of the *devadāsis*, as written by Kṣetrayya:

> *When lustily I jump on top*
> *And pound his chest*
> *With my pointed nipples, he says,*
> *"That girl Kanakāngi is very good at this."*
> *I slap him hard with all five fingers.*[109]

Ramanujan outlines how the 17th century poetry of the *devadāsis*, indicates a "mode of experiencing the divine that is characterised by emotional freedom, concrete physical satisfaction, and active control."[110] The erotic language of the poetry and seemingly liberated sexuality of the *devadāsis* suggests a femininity that challenges the boundaries of decency before succumbing to patriarchal and colonial forces of respectability. According to Lynn Gatwood's *Devi and the Spouse Goddess*, this is also as a result of the Indian feminine that has been transformed throughout history due to the destructive power of patriarchy and caste. Gatwood suggests that Indian womanhood can be placed into two distinct categories, on the one-hand, "the control-free, non-Sanskritic type she calls Devi" and on the other, "the control-defined, Sanskritic type she calls the Spouse Goddess."[111] Gatwood suggests that Dalit women's sexuality is juxtaposed with the decent and pure caste Hindu women through patriarchal cultural norms. She does so based upon the premise that the two are separated by the process of "spousification", "by which the unifying, communally-oriented, egalitarian, martially independent, and sexually autonomous Devi type can become remade through the controlling institution of marriage into the dualistic, household-orientated, hierarchal, martially subject, and sexually inhibited Spouse Goddess."[112] Such processes of patriarchal respectability have also been used by the reformist movements that have imposed upon the *devadāsis* a path of "spousification" as a means of promoting patriarchal norms and so-called self-respect. As conventional marriage has been used as a means of rehabilitation for the dedicated women, so that they can be initiated back into the domestic sphere and gain a level of decency.[113]

---

109   Kṣetrayya, "Woman to her friend", in *When God is a Customer: Telegu Courtesan Songs by Kṣetrayya and Others.* (Berkley, CA: University of California Press, 1994), 91.

110   Ibid, 91.

111   Ellison Banks Findly, "Reviewed Work: Devi and the Spouse Goddess by Lynn E. Gatwood" *Journal of the American Oriental Society* Vol. 107, No. 4 (1987): 781.

112   Ibid, 781.

113   Vijaisri, *Recasting the Devadasi*, 825–827.

Dalit reform movements have therefore accepted the dominant models of decency that marginalised the *devadāsīs,* and did so in order to also challenge aspects of Dalithood that they maintain to have been 'sancritised'; where religious practices that appeared to take on a Hindu worship style were considered to be fundamentally detrimental to the conscientization of the Dalit movement. This is visible in Lucinda Ramberg's anthropological explorations of the *devadāsī* system, where she describes how there has been a Dalit reformist focus on the abolition of the *jogati* religious practice of *bettale seve,* a naked procession practiced and performed by the devotees of the goddess *Yellamma.* Many Dalit women activists have strongly protested the naked rites of procession, suggesting that it is indecent and a casteist form of humiliation applied to dedicated Dalit women. As a means of challenging the practice Dalit movements have attempted to force clothes on to the women and involved the police in order to prevent the procession from taking part. Krishnappa, a leader of the Dalit Sangha Samiti, described his disdain for the practice, as follows:

> *Taking the women in the nude is really uncultured and barbarous. This type of procession going on in Karnataka is shameful on the part of the people's representatives to the government...So we have attacked the government [saying, 'You] must stop this or we will fight against the government.' In this way we converted a social issue into a political issue.*[114]

For Ramberg what becomes apparent here is the westernisation of the Dalit reformist movements that are imposing their own moral ideology on to the body politics of the Dalit subaltern *joginis.* She notes that just as the Christian missionaries of South India believed that they had saved the souls of the uneducated savages by clothing the converts and making them decent, the same such standards of "comportment signifying sexual restraint have been reformulated in the context of the anti-caste politics, and Dalit women have long exhorted to conform to them."[115] She further notes that whilst the reform movements maintain that such religious practices are intended to castigate the bodies of Dalit women, that her own research and that of Epp's, found that the *bettale seve* was not only practised by Dalit women, but by those belonging to various castes including "Brahmans, Lingayats and Marathas..."[116] The *joginis* also questioned the manner in which the Dalit reform movement attempted

114   Krishnappa is quoted in an interview with Linda Epp, "Violating the sacred?": 332.
115   Lucinda Ramberg, *Given to the Goddess: South Indian Devadasis and the Sexuality of Religion* (London: Duke University Press, 2014), 123–125.
116   Ibid, 125.

to force change on them as devotees of the goddess, questioning why they were taking action against the *joginis* but not against semi clothed *jain monks* or cabaret dancers.[117]

Such examples within feminist movements force the question of representation to be addressed, as it appears that the bodies of the Dalit *devadāsīs* and *joginis* have become political sites of reform that are being used to serve the agendas of others and the existential religious and social discourses of the Dalit women themselves have been silenced in the process. Such processes of reformation and interaction of and with the so-called 'subaltern' groups adheres to Spivak's argument that the subaltern cannot speak or appear without the thought or influence of those who hold power, as the *joginis* have automatically been categorised as the ignorant and the oppressed.[118] Yet in agreement with Maggio, "all actions to a certain extent offer a communicative role"[119] and whilst the Dalit reform movements who in this case hold the discursive power appear to be speaking on behalf of the *joginis* by suggesting that based upon their nudity they are the oppressed, the subaltern voice appears to be retrieved in the continued acts of rebellious worship performed by the *joginis* that can be considered as being counter-cultural as they challenge notions of decency.

For Gramsci such control over the subaltern involves the dominating elite weaving and convincing an all-embracing worldview that gives meaning to repression.[120] In the case of the British they brought with them their Bibles – their universal moral agenda. The Hindus imposed their Brahminical ideology and caste rigidity and both groups continued to legitimise the domination of women through religiously justified patriarchal hegemony. Further, images of ideal womanhood based on the faithful and devoted wife became enshrined within reformist endeavours, this in turn meant sexual disciplining and stricter controls over the movements of high caste women in order to maintain social boundaries and caste hegemony.[121] Such processes of control over the bodies of the *devadāsīs* adheres to the feminist Donna Haraway's epistemological reasoning regarding sexuality and power, where the politicization of the bodies of

117   Ibid, 125.

118   See, G.C. Spivak, "Can the Subaltern Speak?", in *Marxism and the Interpretation of Culture*, eds. C. Nlson et al. (Chicago, IL: University of Illinois Press, 1988), 271–313.

119   See, J. Maggio, "Can the Subaltern Be Heard? Political Theory, Translation, Representation, and Gayatri Chakravorty Spivak" *Alternatives 32* (2007), 419–443, 421.

120   See, Cosimo Zene, *The Political Philosophies of Antonio Gramsci and B. R. Ambedkar: Itineraries of Dalits and Subalterns* (New York: Routledge, 2013)

121   Charu Gupta, "Representing the Dalit Woman: Reification of Caste and Gender Stereotypes in the Hindi Didactic Literature of Colonial India" *Indian Historical Review* 35 (2008): 110.

the contemporary *devadāsis* have become a "field of inscription of socio-symbolic codes."[122] Furthermore, Dalit reform programmes have instilled within the dedicated women a sense of self-ignorance and betrayal of the Dalit cause that further marginalises the contemporary *devadāsis*.

8   From Goddess to 'Slut': Locating a Devadāsī Theology

The religiosity of the Dalits has been deemed a superstitious obstacle to social progress performed by the ignorant masses, yet visible in such interpretations are the dynamics of power in determining what does and does not count as religion. In agreement with Ramberg, "to ask what counts as religion is to pose a question about forms of knowledge as they intersect with relations of power. Whose ways of talking to gods and spirits are designated as religion, and whose are stigmatised as superstition?"[123] 'Outcaste' village goddess worship has become rooted in the complexities of antagonistic battles between the modern-day reformists and the Brahminical Hindu ideologies that have resulted in a transformation in the role of the *Mathammas*. They have become the exploited by-products of a clash of ideologies that has resulted in the agency of the dedicated women being removed. The body of the *Mādiga Mathamma* has become the manipulated subject of male desire, their enforced roles as sex workers from childhood has left many with Aids/HIV, and Sexually transmitted diseases and reproductive tract infections.[124] From a young age the social order has determined that they are available for sexual exploitation, as their sexuality is considered an impure corruption that requires controlling. As one *Mathamma*, from a rural community in Andhra Pradesh, said, "*I am not considered relevant enough to be treated by the doctor despite being sick, but my body becomes relevant when the landlord needs to release his anger or fulfil his sexual desires.*"[125]

The contemporary *devadāsis* are predominantly Dalit, they exist in extreme poverty, are usually dedicated to the temple at the request of the high caste men from as young as two years old. They are then raped in the name of religion,

---

122   Haraway "draws our attention to the construction and manipulation of docile, knowable bodies" and how they are being constructed through the disembodied gaze. See, *Nomadic Subjects: Embodiment and Sexual Difference in Contemporary Feminist Theory*, ed. Rosi Braidotti (New York: Columbia University Press, 1983), 207.

123   Ramberg, *Given to the Goddess*, 5.

124   See, Maggie Black, *Women in Ritual Slavery: Devadasi, Jogini, and Mathamma in Karnataka and Andhra Pradesh, Southern India* (London: Anti-Slavery International, 2007).

125   Prasu, interview, Chittoor District, Andhra Pradesh, December, 16, 2014.

many go on to become village sex workers, thousands are trafficked into the brothels of the cities. Aids and HIV is prevalent amongst these communities of women[126], and due to the lack of education with regards to sexual health, the diseases spread quickly amongst the villagers. Contraceptive precautions are taboo, therefore alongside suffering from sexually transmitted diseases many women will have unwanted pregnancies, dangerously performed abortions and stillbirths are therefore common amongst the dedicated women.[127] Daughters of the *devadāsīs* often face the same predicament as their mothers, as they are considered as *devadāsīs* from birth, as one young woman from Tamil Nadu said: *"I was born in the brothel, I have served in the brothel and I will die in the brothel, this is the life God has given me."*[128] The *devadāsī* practice exists today as a criminal practice of sex slavery and human trafficking, committed against the bodies of Dalit women. Apparent in the fact that 93 per cent of contemporary *devadāsīs* belong to Scheduled Castes and 7 per cent are from Scheduled Tribes. Sexual access to the *devadāsī* is considered to be a right by all men in the village, especially the high caste men.[129] As despite being so-called 'untouchables', such purity laws are consciously ignored by the upper caste men in relation to the sexual exploitation of the low caste, casteless women. Sacred prostitution has therefore become a means of reinforcing control over the body politics of the lower castes and Dalits within the caste complex. The social ramifications of caste persecution play a vital part in the continuation of the practice of dedication in its current form, as poverty, malnutrition, family insecurity, and high-caste patron or landlord privilege over outcaste agency all act as a means by which the sexual exploitation of Dalit women is able to occur.[130]

Mathamma's narrative also reveals the ways in which the Christian Church in South India has become embroiled in the war on the bodies of the dedicated sacred sex workers, as they have sought to 'liberate' the women from sex work by offering them 'salvation' in Christ, whilst also dismissing their subaltern religiosity as dangerous superstition. Yet the relief offered through the Church has proved vital for many contemporary *devadāsīs* who receive food, health care, and for some an education, and for many, hope in Jesus Christ who offers ultimate liberation. In exchange many *devadāsīs* have professed faith in Christ,

126   Matilda Battersby, "Prostitutes of God," *The Independent*, September, 19 2010, accessed February 19, 2014 http://www.independent.co.uk/news/world/asia/prostitutes-of-god-2082290.html.

127   See, Maria-Constanza Torri, "Abuse of Lower Castes in South India": 43.

128   Bama, interview, Madurai, Tamilnadu, November, 11, 2014.

129   See, Tambe, "Reading Devadasi Practice through Popular Marathi Literature": 88.

130   See, Misra and Rao, "Theogamy in Rural India": 1–24.

but with that must come a rejection of the goddess as many Dalit Christians
and activists have fiercely rejected the religious past that they maintained is
rooted in the evils of Hinduism, which they argued is the fundamental basis
for their oppressed status.[131] As a result, they have "uncritically pursued the
reformist programmes and failed to grapple with the complexity of cultural
identity"[132], that hold direct links to their indigenously rooted past of the
devadāsīs. In doing so they have also ignored the specific socio-economic factors intertwined with the agency of those who become sex-workers, where
many rely on the payments from the patrons to feed their children and pay
their landlord. Furthermore, they have excluded women as 'sacred prostitutes'
based upon patriarchal constructions of ideal womanhood that have marginalised the dedicated women and chastised them for their roles as village sex
workers. The *Mathamma* has to contend not only with the homogenised ideologies of caste and gender based persecution, but in her search for liberation
she is constrained by alienating moral agendas of the church, and the reformist and rehabilitation programmes, that fear the sexuality of women outside of
marriage and attempt to deny the cultural space in which she exists.

My fieldwork in South India exposed me to the complex lives of the contemporary *devadāsīs*. As Dalit women they live in the fringes of society and as
sacred sex workers they are vilified by all, even their fellow Dalits. Many of the
women suffer from sexually transmitted diseases, many are forced to have sex
to feed their children, or satisfy their landlords, others are trafficked to the cities
as they are no longer of use in the village. Multiple powers have enforced the
devadāsī practice to the margins of society where they have been subjected to a
multitude of oppressions, and their religious identities have been condemned
as backwards and superstitious. Efforts have therefore been made to allow their
voices to be heard, and their religious identities to be contemplated within a
framework of analysis that works towards an identity-specific liberation theologising. As this book aims to explore if there is an opportunity to establish a
self-proclaimed, empowering identity for the outcaste sacred 'prostitutes' that
is indigenously rooted, counter-cultural and liberative based upon a re-reading
and reclamation of their historic socio-religious identities. It does so because
the contemporary *devadāsīs* have been marginalised and vilified by all. Their
narratives of suffering have been brought about through no fault of their own
and such pathos requires the attention of Dalit movements of liberation.

---

131   Ambedkar was the great reformer of the Dalits, he focused his mission on activism of the
        Dalits as oppose to exploring their mythic and religious anthropological identities, he
        "rejected anthropology in favour of activism" See, Epp, "'Violating the Sacred': 18.
132   Vijaisri, "In Pursuit of the Virgin Whore": 67.

FIGURE 4   Mathamma goddess in Nagalapurum
PHOTOGRAPH BY AUTHOR

Symbolically, physically, and emotionally the *devadāsī*s have been violated, yet amidst such abuse there are moments of indecent rebellion, a language of subversive religiosity, sacred protest through prayer to 'impure' goddesses, and a love of Christ who promises ultimate liberation. Whilst Mathamma sits alongside church leaders praying secretly to the goddess whilst also worshipping Christ she presents a lived religiosity that is shaped by her daily needs. As such, the brothels of the sacred sex worker, her temple and her bed, remain hybrid spaces where money is exchanged for sex, where prayers are recited for rain, where goddesses are called on for period pains, and where the Dalit Christ lives with the people who search for liberation from their daily oppression. It is in such spaces, where Dalit women are 'slut-shamed' and condemned to the margins of the Dalit community, for feeding their children, pleasing their patron, and worshiping the goddesses they fear, that we must come to contemplate Christ. Because it is in such moments that the we may gain a greater understanding of a broken Christ through the lens of a broken body. The chapters that follow will therefore look to the ways in which Indian Christian theology, and Dalit Christian theology, have found space for voices of the *devadāsī*s in contemplating God.

What Theology Hides under the Sari of a Sacred Sex Worker?

> Practical theology starts with description...the action of describing that opening movement, as it were, in the symphony of practical theological inquiry is not merely to excavate theological assumptions but is an act that is itself theological...because it attends to the one describing; a person (or persons) made in the image of God.[1]

∴

How do we theologise on and with the multifaceted identity of contemporary sacred sex workers? How do we talk about God in the brothels, or on the deathbed of the dying sex worker who is losing her battle with AIDs; or in the back alley of Chennai where a teenage girl greets her patron; how do we talk about God with the woman who has had her sari ripped off, her naked body paraded around the village and her flesh beaten and stoned; or with the *devadāsī* who cries out to her goddess for rain as her village faces starvation. Should we start by asking where God is, or who God is? Asking these questions in the midst of such suffering is a theological imperative that requires a theological *yātrā* with narratives of rape, murder, trafficking, caste-persecution, and multiple layers of religious belonging. It therefore cannot be a decent, ordered or systematic theology if it is be truthful to the lives of the oppressed, because as Mario Aguilar writes: "any human being who is being tortured today is a son or daughter of God created in her image, thus synchronic questions about the presence or absence of God must be asked regardless of the indecency of the moment of torture."[2] Such theologising is practical because it requires relocating and contemplating God in the most indecent of spaces, but it must also be liberative because it requires God knowing the suffering of the oppressed and acting in the here and now for transformation from their brokenness.

---

1   Eric Stoddart, *Advancing Practical Theology: Critical Discipleship for Disturbing Times* (London: SCM Press, 2004), 17.
2   Mario I. Aguilar, *Religion, Torture and the Liberation of God* (New York: Routledge, 2015), 2–3.

This chapter continues a theological *yātrā* with *Mathamma devadāsīs* in order to explore the theological methodologies that may enable identity-specific and liberative contemplations on God in the context of the sacred 'prostitutes' of South India. The journeying begins with the multifaceted religious hybridity of Christianity in India that is encapsulated in Indian Christian Theology where Christ is deliberated on through a Vedic lens. Before moving to a Bhakti religious protest where the voices of the Dalits are heard in poetic religious resistance. The challenge however is finding a place for the struggles of the Dalit women in a theologising that appears committed to a Brahminical Christ or Hindu religiosity. As the life and experiences of Mathamma reveal that such an understanding of Christ is of little relevance in the lives of the most oppressed of Dalit women. It is here that the *yātrā* takes us to the liberative discourses of Dalit theology, where Mathamma may find a voice, as it is a theology shaped by the brokenness of the Dalit experience, apparent in what Nirmal refers to as the 'dalitness of Christ'[3], and centres on the need to be indigenously rooted and identity specific and fundamentally a praxis focused theology of liberation for the Dalit people.

1   Towards Theologising with Mathamma

There is a brief tale that has been shared with me at least three times now by three different friends in India, that is relevant in working towards a practical theologising with the contemporary sacred 'prostitutes':

> Once upon a time a parachutist found himself caught up in a storm and he was swept off several kilometres away from where he was scheduled to land. Instead he somehow landed up on top of a tree. Confused but grateful to be alive, he looked down and was very happy to see someone passing by. He called down, *"Excuse me Sir, can you tell me where I am?"* The man on the ground responded, *"You are on top of a tree."* At this, *the parachutist asked, "Are you a theologian?"* The man on the ground appeared shocked, *"why yes I am"* he said, *"but how did you know that?"* the Parachutist responded *"Oh, that it is easy, because what you said is correct, but is useless to me."*

---

3 Arvind Nirmal, "Towards a Christian Dalit Theology," in *A Reader in Dalit Theology* ed. Arvind P. Nirmal (Madras: Gurukal Lutheran Theological College and Research Institute, 1991), 54.

The truth is there are many useless theologies that offer little hope to those stuck in the most difficult moments of life, when people are in need of real help and direction in the midst of their suffering. For Felix Wilfred, "what enhances theology is not its claim to offer a total and satisfactory explanation of the entire reality, but the help it can give people to relate harmoniously the various dimensions of reality."[4] Much like the man passing by offering no real help to the man stuck on a tree, a theology that is exempt from the realities of life, of poverty, grief, racism, casteism, sexism, and other such forms of oppression is useless to those 'stuck on a tree', whether or not it is deemed systematically correct, such theologising without an understanding of place and context especially for the oppressed and most downtrodden offers little hope to those suffering or experiencing *dukkha* (when life is denied). A theology that is "integral and integrating" is one that "centres round the experiences of the poor and the suffering"[5] and in their midst of their suffering finds moments of hope and liberation.

Therefore, in order to theologise with the contemporary *devadāsīs* the theological discourse must emerge from the narratives of their lives and delve into the contextual experiences of what it means to be a Dalit female sacred sex worker in the South Indian village. Apparent within such theologising is the need to address the pluralistic religious experiences and identities of subaltern communities that within the Indian context take on diverse worship expressions. Such religious praxis acts as a direct challenge to homogenous doctrines of faith and praxis. Emphasis must therefore be placed upon the multitude of local village deities, religious practices, myths and beliefs that belong to the Dalit people and enable Christian theological dialogue with subaltern religiosity that centres on the Goddess who responds to the needs of the people at a given time and place. In doing so Christian theologising in India takes on a hyphenated religious belonging as it is fundamentally dialogical with other faith traditions.[6] For Panikkar such theologising is life giving as it "is not like water that flows in a river, it is rather like water that falls on the fertile soil and goes back up to the clouds having produced green pastures and frondose forests."[7] It is based on the existential experiences of a context that is rich with culture, history, diversity and life. To theologise on and with the multifaceted

4   Wilfred, *On the Banks of the Ganges,* 24.
5   Ibid, 24–25.
6   When theologising in India it is important to remember that Christians make up only a very small minority of a vast population of over a billion people, and are surrounded by a multiplicity of other faith traditions.
7   R. Panikkar, "Indian Theology. A Theological Mutuation," in *Theologising in India*, eds. M. Amaladoss et al. (Bangalore: Theological Publications in India, 1981), 24.

identity of contemporary sacred sex workers involves journeying through the layers of Christian theology in India, in order to gain a greater understanding of the hybridity of the contemporary *devadāsīs'* lived religiosity as well as the barriers to belonging that they have experienced amongst religious communities. As persistent poverty, sexual labour, goddess dedication, Christian salvation, and social stigmatisation, demand a theology shaped by the struggles of the Dalit women who have been dedicated. Consequently, this book focuses on working towards a Dalit Theology of the sacred sex workers, because, as will be discussed, Dalit theology professes a need to be 'identity-specific' and fundamentally focused on the liberation of the Dalit people in their struggle to overcome systems of oppression, injustice and suffering.

Theologising with the contemporary sacred sex workers must therefore be identity-specific in order to understand the complexities of the religiosity and daily struggles of the women. It requires situating the *devadāsīs* in the context of caste discrimination, gender violence, poverty, and subaltern oppression, in order to challenge dominant theologies for failing to address the everyday needs of persecuted people. This is visible in mission efforts of the Church, noting as George Ooommen states, the Indian Church has not sufficiently engaged in the struggles of the Dalit people for liberation, focusing instead on "defending the right to convert and looking after Christian communal minority rights."[8] This was visible in Mathamma's narrative and that of other dedicated *devadāsīs*, where the "psychological dependency, political passivity and communal exclusiveness among Dalit Christians" was visible within the Christian missions and reform projects that at times led to the further marginalisation of the dedicated Dalit women. In speaking to a dedicated Mathamma named Agga, she stated:

> *Every day I am hungry, I am desperate, my children starve, my youngest is sick. The Church people come, and they give me food, and I am grateful, but one day they may stop coming to the village and then we will all starve. So, I keep the men satisfied just in case. But can I still be a Christian?*

The needs of the *devadāsīs* are often invisible to the missional agenda of the Church, like that of many abused women struggling to exist, the idea that sex work may offer more security in response to the daily needs of the dedicated

---

8   George Oommen, "Majoritarian Nationalism and the Identity Politics of Dalits in Post-Independent India", in Joseph George (ed.), *The God of All Grace: Essays in Honour of Origen Vasantha Jathanna* (Bangalore: Asian Trading Corporation and the United Theological College, 2005): 338–350, 339–340.

women than that of the Church, is unthinkable. This is because our theologies are too often constructed in ways that offer no space for the voices of the women's bodies that are deemed 'indecent' or 'immoral'. A theology that assumes the supremacy of male voices, androcentric dogmatics and gendered socio-political and sexual norms, is irrelevant to the bodies of the contemporary *devadāsīs*. As such theologies throughout history have only ever served to disempower women and justify violence against the bodies of those women who do not accept imposed gendered norms. Such violence is commonly expressed in the form of honour killings, forced marriages, domestic violence, rape, and infanticide. So what use is religion to the *devadāsīs*? According to Ambedkar in his work on *Conversion as Emancipation* he stated:

> *I tell you specifically that man is not for religion, religion is for man. To become human, convert yourselves. To achieve strength, convert yourselves. To secure equality, convert yourselves. To get liberty, convert yourselves. To make your domestic life happy, convert yourselves....*[9]

What might such a conversion look like for the Dalit *devadāsīs*? What religion is for woman and not solely constructed for the liberty of man? Can strength and equality be realised in a religion that has enabled the marginalisation of women who find strength in a Dalit goddess as well as the Dalit Christ?

2   Indian Theology and the Brahmin Christ

Indian Christian theologians have traditionally followed a "pursuit to harmonise Hindu philosophical thought and Christian theology in their quest for an authentically indigenous theological expression."[10] The fusion of religious identities can be witnessed in 17th century Tamil Nadu, where the Italian Jesuit, Robert De Nobili, composed music and liturgy in Tamil and Sanskrit to entice Brahmin converts. Claiming he "was by birth a raja, by profession a Brahman Sannyasi"[11] he preached on the lack of requirement for converts to give up their caste identities, he gave up wine, meat, fish and eggs, and sought to lead the life of a pure and holy Guru. His indigenization process of Christianity was very

9   Bhim Rao Amedkar, *Conversion as Emancipation* (New Delhi: Critical Quest, 2004), 38.
10   Rajkumar, *Dalit Theology and Dalit Liberation*, 34.
11   Joseph Thekkedath, *From the Middle of the Sixteenth Century to the End of the Seventeenth Century 1542–1700* (Bangalore: The Church History Association of India, 1982), 216.

much aimed at the high castes.[12] Furthermore, De Nobili introduced Christianity to the orthodox Hindus as '*Satyavedum*', meaning the 'true religion', and attempted to prove its orthodoxy in the *Vedas*. De Nobili broke the boundaries of missiology through acculturation of Christianity, yet he focused solely on converting the Brahmins, in doing so he failed to acknowledge the indigenous worship styles, beliefs and resources of the low castes and Dalits. Furthermore, he was guilty of failing to "see the evil in the Indian caste system," as *Sarveswara* (God) was conveyed solely as the God of the Brahmins, and he believed that caste was simply a justified means by which to order society.[13]

Indian Christian theology continued to follow a Brahminical style of apologetics that was described by Menon as being, "Hindu in culture, Christian in religion, and oriental in worship."[14] A theological praxis that theologians such as the Indian prelate, Joseph Parecattil, continued into the 20th century, and considered a necessity in order for Christianity to be accepted within the pluralistic context of India. Parecattil belonged to the Syro-Malabar Catholic Church and justified the need for indigenization and acculturation through the praxis of the Eucharist, by maintaining that indigenization first began when the Word of God was made incarnate, he notes that "if Christ were to become incarnate in our country today, he would have chosen the local dress, would have whispered the local dialect; he would have been an Indian in its full sense."[15] He therefore maintained that the local church should be shaped by the culture and context into which it is embedded and allow the indigenous identity of the Indian people to shape the liturgy and worship.[16]

Earlier Indian Christian theologians had followed a similar path but went beyond acculturation of worship and created a systematic Hindu-Christology. A. J. Appasamy for example, outlined a Christian doctrine of *Avatāra*, beginning with a verse from the *Bhagavad-gītā* that reads: "*Whenever there is a decline in law, O Arjuna, and an outbreak of lawlessness, I incarnate myself. For the protection of the good, for the destruction of the wicked and for the establishment of law...*"[17] Appasamy's missiology spoke of Christ to Hindus "from the inside,

---

12   Zoe Sherinian, *Tamil Folk Music as Dalit Liberation Theology* (Indiana: Indiana University Press, 2014), 74–75.

13   M. Stephen, *A Christian Theology in the Indian Context* (Delhi: ISPCK, 2001), 8.

14   K. P. Kesava Menon, foreward to *Christianity in India*, ed. A. C. Perumalil and E. R. Hambye (Alleppey: Prakam, 1972), 7.

15   Joseph Parecattil, foreward to *The Missionary Consciousness of the St. Thomas Christians* (Cochin: Viani Publications, 1982), xv-xvi.

16   See, Jacob Nangelimalil, *The Relationship between the Eucharistic Liturgy, the Interior Life and the Social Witness of the Church according to Joseph Cardinal Parecattil* (Rome: Editrice Pontifica Universita Gregoriana, 1996).

17   *Bhagavad-gītā*, IV. 7.8.

feeling with their intense feelings, longing with them their deepest longings, thinking with them through their most baffling problems, following with them their highest ideals, doing all these in that measure and to that degree which our loyalty to Christ permits."[18] His Christian doctrine therefore outlined that Jesus is the ultimate *Avatāra,* and that amongst all other religious figures on earth, Jesus is the only true incarnation of God.[19] Christ was therefore considered to be the purna *Avatāra,* yet unlike in Hindu philosophy where the *Avatāra* comes to punish the deserving and save the righteous before returning to God, Christ is God who came to save the sinners.[20] His *Christianity as Bhakti Marga* comprehends Christianity as ultimate *Bhakti*-devotion to Christ that resulted in mystical union with the Divine (mokṣa).[21] Appasamy's theologising emerged from the philosophy of the caste Hindus, as he appealed to them to explore the *Vedas* and witness the relevance of Christ within their Holy texts. Like others before him, Appasamy's appeal to the mysticism of Hinduism apparent within Christianity excluded those who existed outside the folds of Hinduism, the Dalits, and therefore re-created Braminical Hinduism within the Church.

The 19th century Indian Christian theologian, Brahmabandhab Upadhyaya, was also "of the conviction that the Christian doctrines are there already in Hinduism among its admitted errors." He professed that the revelation of God in Jesus Christ is "further clarification and affirmation of the main Vedanta doctrines."[22] Upadhyaya used *Advaita* (the philosophy of non-Dualism) to articulate a Vedantic Trinitarian Christology, where Christ is considered to be the fulfilment of the Hindu longings, *Sat* (reality), *Cit* (consciousness) and *Ananda* (bliss).[23] His *Hymn of the Incarnation* captures his Hindu-Christian theology as follows:

> *The transcendent image of Brahman,*
> *Blossomed and mirrored in the full-to-overflowing*
> *Eternal intelligence – Victory to the God, the God-Man.*
> *Child of pure virgin,*

---

18   A. J. Appasamy, *What is Moksha?* (Madras: CLS, 1931), 9.
19   A. J. Appasamy, *The Gospel and India's Heritage* (London: SPCK, 1942), 259.
20   Stephen, *A Christian Theology,* 53.
21   See, A. J. Appasamy, *Christianity as Bhakti Marga: A Study in the Mysticism of the Johannine Writings* (London: Macmillan and Co. ltd, 1927).
22   K. P. Aleaz, "The Theological Writings of Brahmabandhav Upadhyaya Re-Examined," *IJT* 28, no. 2 (1979): 56.
23   Brahmabandhab Upahyaya, "The Hymn of Incarnation," in *An Introduction to Indian Christian Theology,* ed. Robin Boyd. (Madras: CLS, 1994), 77–78.

Guide of the Universe, infinite in Being
Yet beauteous with relations,
Victory to God, the God-Man.24

The hymn, originally written in Sanskrit, deliberately uses Hindu symbolism and doctrine in order to make Christ relevant to the Hindu faith.[25] Christ takes on the identity of the highest Brahmin, who is victorious over all others, and infinite ruler of the universe. His eternal purity is acknowledged in the virtuousness of the virgin birth, where he was born free of pollution. Upadhyaya was a Christian *Samnyasi* who believed in following the *samaj dharma* (moral obligations of Hinduism) and Christianity as his *sadhana dharma* (way of salvation and religious life).[26] Upadhyaya further advocated a need to adhere to the caste system which he maintained was vital for social cohesion and self-respect, stating:

> The caste-system is a natural evolution of the Hindu social instinct. Far-sighted, learned men formulated it in consonance with the genius of the people. The greatness of the Hindu race was achieved largely through the regulating influence of caste. It was caste that preserved the Hindus from being transformed into hybrids of the Semitic stock.[27]

Upadhaya like those before him developed an indigenous Indian Christology that enables us to encounter a religious deity who is 'pure' and 'infinite', and free from the shackles of human violence and exempt from the pain of the everyday lives of the Dalit people. Such a Christology does little to ideologically dismantle the oppressive caste system in which the sacred sex workers have found themselves victim too. Whilst Indian Christian Theology has created radical and divergent theological discourses based upon the hybrid identities and multiple religious belonging of the Indian theologians and Christian converts, it has been guilty of perpetuating Brahminism within Christianity. Despite being spiritually indigenous it has shielded the Hindu-Christ from the Dalits and the poor. For the Dalit theologian Kothapalli Wilson, Indian

---

24   Ibid, 77.

25   Upahyaya approached the Trinity through the Hindu concept of *sacchidananda*, and his theologising combined Hindu philosophy of the natural order with Christianity's cosmic supernatural order.

26   Bob Robinson, *Christians Meeting Hindus: An Analysis and Theological Critique of Hindu-Christian Encounter in India* (Milton Keynes: Regnum Books, 2004), 19.

27   William Allan Furley-Smith, *Brahmandhab Upadhyay: An Enigmatic Catholic Freedom Fighter 1861–1907* (Melbourne: Melbourne College of Divinity, 2011), 29.

Christian Theology that was shaped by colonial Christianity, and created a "salvation theology" that brings about "political passivity and communal exclusiveness among Dalit Christians"[28] as a result of this "salvation theology", he called for a shift of theological discourse in order to concentrate on communal narratives of oppression in the here and now as oppose to being distracted by the Kingdom to come. Ambedkar, like Wilson, maintained that religion should bring about liberation in the present if it is to be the religion that offers hope, freedom and transformation for the Dalits, he stated:

> A religion which preaches what will or will not happen to soul after death, may be useful for the rich. They may entertain themselves by thinking over such religion at their own leisure. It is quite natural that those who have enjoyed all sorts of pleasures in their lifetime, may consider such religion as a real religion, which mainly tells them of the pleasures they are to get after death. But what of those who by remaining in a particular religion have been reduced to the state of dust...who have not been treated even as human beings, are these people instead of thinking of religion from a material point of view, expected to look at the sky by merely closing eyes? What is the use of this rich and idle people's Vedanta to the poor?[29]

Though Ambedkar speaks of the failures of Hinduism in relation to Dalits, his words also speak true to the theology of high-caste Indian Christianity. Christian theologising in India has transformed throughout the various stages of history and dependent upon the different contexts and locations in order to make the Christian faith relevant. In doing so, Indian Christian theologians and missionaries have attempted to use indigenous religious and cultural practices to interpret the Gospel and create worship styles that have been acculturated to the Indian context. Yet Indian Christian Theology failed to recognise that the vast majority of Christians in India were in fact Dalits, despite concentrated efforts to evangelise the high-caste Hindus. Perhaps by acknowledging this fact, Indian theology would have provided a liberation *motif* within its discourses, as "it became clear that Depressed class converts continued to complain of indifference and neglect."[30] As such, the lack of a model of liberation

---

28   Kothapalli Wilson, *The Twice-Alienated: Culture of Dalit Christians* (Hyderabad: Booklinks Cooperation, 1982), 59.

29   Bhim Rao Amedkar, *Conversion as Emancipation* (New Delhi: Critical Quest, 2004), 38.

30   Arvind P. Nirmal, "Towards a Christian Theology," in *An Eerdmans Reader in Contemporary Political Theology*, ed. William T. Cavanaugh (Grand Rapids, Michigan: William B. Eerdmans Publishing Company, 2012), 539.

within such theologising was criticised strongly by the likes of the Dalit theologian A. P. Nirmal, who noted that the theologians before him had "trodden the *jnana marga*, the *bhakti marga*, and the *karma marga*..." yet they had failed to reflect on the Dalit struggles.[31] As a consequence Indian Christian Theology and the Indian Church itself[32] remained exempt from the narratives of the oppressed. As Indian Christian religious models of inculturation that focused on the evangelisation of the Hindus created a deeply spiritual theological discourse, and a Brahiminised Christology, where Christ was conveyed as being the ultimate reality and the eternally pure logos. Yet such a theology remained inaccessible to the majority of the Dalit Christian demographic and furthermore would offer little to the Dalit female sex worker, who is deemed polluted and indecent, as it emerges solely from the lives of the elite. However, the mystical and aesthetic contemplations of Indian Christian theology enable a theological *yatrā* that moves beyond colonial concepts of Christ, thereby enabling indigenous contemplation on Christ through the symbols and myths of India, though such theology is further enriched when it comes from the bodies of the marginalised as is visible in the *bhakti* theology, which may speak greater to the experiences of the *devadāsīs*.

3   The Bhakti Movement: A Subaltern Voice of Resistance

O god, my caste is low; how can I serve you?
Everyone tells me to go away: how can I see you?
When I touch anyone, they take offence.

---

31   For Nirmal, Christian missiological efforts concentrated too much on the notion of the 'problem' of other faiths in so called third world contexts, and were therefore distracted by syncretising with other faith traditions and became 'Brahminised' in the process of interreligious theological discourse, and were therefore distracted from the conditions of the oppressed. See, Nirmal, "Towards a Christian Theology", 537 – 539.

32   The Brahminical ideology within the South Indian Church remains a dominant feature despite conversion to Christianity, during my time working for the Council for World Mission with the Church of South India (CSI) and Church of North India (CNI) and at the Tamil Nadu Theological Seminary, the caste identity of the Christians continued to play a vital role in church pastorate decisions, lectureship roles, student scholarship and admissions, Church jobs and Bishop appointments. Mosse's research within Tamil Nadu engaged with the same issue of caste-discrimination within the church context, he notes how Dalits were "poorly represented on church leadership and governance structures such as parish or pastoral councils, finance committees or social service societies." See, David Mosse, "Dallit Cristians, Catholic Priests and Dalit Activism in Contemporary Tamil Nadu" Unpublished Conference Paper. Quoted in Zoe Sherinian *Tamil Folk Music as Dalit Liberation Theology* (Bloomington: Indiana University Press, 2014), 21.

Chokhamela wants your mercy.[33]

Chokhamela was a 14th century poet-saint belonging to the *Mahar* caste[34] in Maharashtra, India and a vital figure of the early *Bhakti* movement. His poetry expresses a spiritual and devotional questioning of the repressive orthodoxy of Brahminical hegemony apparent within Hinduism. Challenging cries of protest have surfaced through the Dalit arts, in literature, song, dance and poetry since as early as the 11th century,[35] articulating the injustices of caste persecution and challenging dominant and oppressive theologies. Whilst questioning the inadequacies of the religiously justified caste system that has forced millions of people into a state of socio-political servitude from birth. The *Bhakti* movement was a socio-religious expression of protest conveyed through the aesthetics, articulating the aspirations of the oppressed, including the Dalits and women. It based its theology on the premise that *Bhakti* (devotion) was a way to salvation. As Rajkumar describes: "it was a counter-movement, which questioned the 'upper caste' Hindu belief that *Gnana* (knowledge), *Karma* (good deeds) and *Dhyana* (reflection) were the only ways to salvation."[36]Leela Mullatti further highlights how "the *Bhakti* movement totally rejected the needs of Brahmins in religious performance", as a result of the fact that "Brahmins were exploiting the ignorant masses; making them undergo various sin cleansing rituals to propitiate God and obtain His grace."[37] In response the theology of *Bhakti* centres on the partaking in a devotional relationship with a personal God. The *Bhakti* poets expressed themselves in their own vernacular, articulating their observations of the world around them and incorporating images, experiences and emotions of everyday life, whilst appealing to the divine. Karen Pechillis Prentiss notes that "female *bhakti* poets in regional languages often use images of their own bodies to comment on the world around them." [38] This can be witnessed in the poetry of Janabai, a low caste 13th century *Bhakti* poet:

---

33   Abhanga 76 quoted by Amar Nath Prasad, *Dalit Literature: A Critical Exploration* (New Delhi: Sarup & Sons, 2007), 11.
34   Mahar is a Dalit/untouchable caste group.
35   I refer here to the works of Madara Chennaiah, a cobbler-saint, one of the earliest known writers of Dalit literature who wrote in the twelfth-century Vachana Movement. See, Hemant Rawat, *Dalit and Backward Women* (New Delhi: Lakshay Publications, 2011).
36   Rajkumar, *Dalit Theology and Dalit Liberation*, 33.
37   Leela Mullatti, *The Bhakti Movement and the Status of Women: A Case Study of Virasaivism* (New Delhi: Abhinav Publications: 1989), 4.
38   Karen Pechillis Prentiss, *The Embodiment of Bhakti* (Oxford: Oxford University Press, 1999), 27.

Cast off all shame,
and sell yourself
in the marketplace;
then alone
can you hope
to reach the Lord.

Cymbals in hand,
a veena upon my shoulder,
I go about;
who dares to stop me?

The pallav of my sari
falls away (A scandal!);
yet will I enter
the crowded marketplace
without a thought.

Jani says, My Lord
I have become a slut
to reach your home.

The female *bhakti* poet saint Janabai (1298–1350) uses powerfully rebellious language that narrates contempt for the socio-political and Brahminical religious order. She protests against societal rules and regulations, such as keeping her breasts covered in an open market place, and uses her own body as a weapon of resistance. She also laments about her low caste status as a *dasi* (servant), and her pathos as a woman. Yet throughout she remains devoted to the god who journeys with her in her suffering:

Jani sweeps the floor,
The Lord collects the dirt,
Carries it upon His head,
And casts it away.

Won over by devotion,
The Lord does lowly chores!
Says Jani to Vithoba,

How shall I pay your debt? [39]

Janabai presents a God that takes on an impure status, a Lord that collects the dirt and with her suffers the oppression of a low-caste status. Kosambi remarks on how "bringing God down from celestial heights to the sinful earth is the familiar problem of correlation between the secular and the divine in *bhakti*."[40] Janabai and other *bhakti* saint poets have been criticised for "submitting to the norms of their epoch and society" yet their devotional worship style and theology of radical love and equality contradicts the status quo of caste hierarchies and socio-economic divisions. The religiosity is one of devotion and hope for liberation. It rests on the belief that God will be able to destroy the social evils of caste and gender divisions.[41]

Bhakti poets have however been criticised by contemporary Dalit protest and literary movements for not being radical enough as they maintain that they do not challenge the system of caste. According to Amandeep, the "*bhakti* poets remained very much within the domain of the sacred, as they failed to carve out literature outside the literature of Hinduism."[42] Despite protesting against social inequality and economic injustices, many contemporary Dalit scholars argue that the *Bhakti* poets still operated within a religious framework that prevented absolute social transformation. Paswan and Jaideva for example note the movements "radical stance and its inclusiveness", however maintain that the poets "were largely confined to the religious plane, and action for social equality from it was trivial."[43] They use the example of the *Bhakti* poet-saint Chokhamela, who despite his radical protests against the ideology of pollution, still attributed his low status and deprivation to the sins of his past life, thus accepting the imprisoning ideology of casteism.[44] Oomen agrees to such a position, emphasising that the poets of the *Bhakti* movement shared certain characteristics, namely that they were reformists – as they aimed to eradicate untouchability but failed to attack the caste system. Secondly, "the participants developed a dual identity; a religious ideological identity with fellow

---

39   Janabai, "Jani Sweeps the Floor," in *Women Writing in India: 600 B.C. to the Early Twentieth Century*, ed. Vilas Sarang et al. (New York: The Feminist Press, 1991), 83–84.

40   Irina Glushkova, "Norms and Values in the Varkari Tradition," in *Intersections: Socio-cultural Trends in Maharashtra*, ed. Meera Kosambi (New Delhi: Orient Longman Limited, 2000), 51.

41   Ibid, 50–51.

42   Amandeep, "Dalit Aesthetics: A Study of the Bhakti Period," *Journal of Literature, Culture and Media Studies* Vol. II (2010): 2.

43   Sanjay Paswan, *Encyclopaedia of Dalits in India Literature: Education, Literature, Political Science, Sociology, Women Studies* (Delhi: Kalpaz Publications, 2002), 16.

44   Ibid, 16.

participants of the movements." They further did not challenge the socio-economic status of Dalits as "the equality professed by them remained a mirage."[45] Jayant Lele however believes that there is in fact revolutionary potential within the *Bhakti* poetry when explored through a hermeneutics of liberation, as Lele suggests, there are hegemonic and liberating moments apparent within *Bhakti* traditions that are hidden behind the hegemonic ideologies, stating:

> Valued symbols, myths, beliefs and rituals of a tradition bear in them, as meanings, the actuality of everyday experience and the imaginative or creative potentiality of its transition. Symbols have dual meanings which allow an understanding of particular experience, as well as its re-interpretation within the universality of a living tradition. This universality is, at another level, a paradox of liberation and hegemonic appropriation, of the legitimacy of a social order and its legitimation, of the moments of necessary and unnecessary oppression.

The symbols of liberation within the *Bhakti* movement become apparent when exploring the poetry with a hermeneutic of suspicion that looks beyond the inherited colonial and neo-colonial perspectives that focus solely on the hegemony of traditions. The symbols of liberation can be witnessed in the revolutionary language that opposes the dominant social order.[46] *Bhakti* according to Lele is therefore a "modernizing force by virtue of its negation of tradition and liberation through criticism," as it embodies both the realities of the world, encourages social action and calls on the spiritual. Many Dalit writers have however rejected the liberating aspects of the *Bhakti* movement, maintaining that it is irrelevant to their struggle due to the belief that it is so intertwined with Brahminical ideology that it has lost any radical and transformative potential. Instead of witnessing liberating symbolism for the Dalit cause within the *Bhakti* movement, they consider Chokhamela and his contemporary followers as having been manipulated by the hegemonic classes.[47]

However, such criticism does not appear to take into consideration the direct opposition that the *Bhakti* movement professed in its condemnation of the hegemony of Brahminism and elite exclusivity supported through *vedic* education. The *Bhakti* poets were contextually radical in their direct resistance of *Sanskrit*, and as Ram Puniyani remarks they instead adopted the languages

---

45   Rawat, *Dalit and Backward Women*, 65.
46   Jayant Lele, "The Bhakti Movement in India: A Critical Introduction," *Journal of Asian and African Studies* XV, 1–2 (1980): 6.
47   Ibid, 7.

that were more popular with the masses.[48] The *Bhakti* movement of the poet saints created a spirit of resistance that journeyed through the centuries challenging Brahminical power, caste based oppressions, and social divisions based on economics, religion and gender. Yet it was the voices that came much later that would shape the Dalit liberation movement as we know it today and inspire a counter-cultural discourse of united resistance of the 'broken-people' of India, who promoted a society that was free from the caste system, endogamy, poverty, and socio-political inequalities.

4   The Dalit Revolutionists Impact on Indian Christian Theology

One of the greatest revolutionists of the Dalits was 'Mahatma' Jyotirao Phule, a leading figure in the history of the Dalit liberation movements, who during the 19th century was outspoken in his criticism of the plight of the *śūdra-atiśūdra* (low-castes and the Dalits). He campaigned against the Brahminical hegemonic powers and violent caste discrimination that existed throughout India and appealed for ideological, social and political revolution that prioritised the needs of the poor, the low castes, the Dalits, and the women. For Gail Omvedt, his political ideology represented "the fulfilment of the renaissance desire for social transformation along revolutionary lines."[49]Phule was born into a *śūdra* caste (the Mali caste)[50] in Pune in 1827 and was greatly influenced by the western Christian education he was exposed to in his formative years whilst attending a Scottish Christian missionary school.[51]

Phule's subaltern discourse on the need for revolutionary transformation against caste discrimination was expressed in his book *Slavery*, which he dedicated to the African-American slaves and freedom fighters, whom he hoped would act as an inspiration to the *śūdras* of India. As Naregal remarks, "Phule cleverly attempted to insert lower-caste subordination into a global discourse

48   Ram Puniyani, "Religion: Opium of the Masses or..." in *Religion, Power and Violence: Expression of Politics in Contemporary Times*, ed. Ram Puniyani. (New Delhi: Sage Publications, 2005), 38.
49   Gail Omvedt, "Jotirao Phule and the Ideology of Social Revolution in India," *Economic and Political Weekly* Vol. 6. No. 37. (1971): 1969.
50   The Mali caste were mostly gardeners responsible for taking care of fruits, vegetables and flowers, they were considered as backward caste.
51   The Christian missionary evangelical discourse professed that "the Hindu religion had deprived them, as *śūdras*, of their real rights in matters of education and religion." See, Rosalind O'Hanlon, *Caste, Conflict and Ideology: Mahatma Jotirao Phule and Low-Caste Protest in Nineteenth-Century Western India* (Cambridge: Cambridge University Press, 1985), 6.

of marginality by asserting equivalence between the subjugation of non-literate, labouring communities—across space and time—at the hands of groups who controlled inscription."[52] In doing so, Phule created a narrative of shared global oppression, or rather universal Dalitness that gave a new depth to the narrative of *śūdra-atisśūdra* suffering. He criticised the *Bhakti* movements, for being too confined to the religious sphere and therefore void of rationalism and lacking in an absolute social critique that would bring about transformation for those at the bottom of the hierarchy.[53] For Chakravati "it was because Phule attempted to make the lower castes conscious of the injustices and inequality of the caste system as a whole that he rejected the Sanskritization moves of the local *kunbis*, a peasant caste, who were trying to take on the rituals of the upper castes."[54] Phule and his fellow reformers sought to establish an ideological basis for social and religious transformation that would set in motion a revolution of new values in India. They did so by encouraging a new identity for those who were downtrodden by caste, economic inequality and socio-religious depravity, which as O'Hanlon describes "lay obscured by the fictions in Hindu representations of the proper ordering of society."[55] A newly shaped identity of the *śūdra-atiśūdra* was central to the campaign of Phule and his fellow reformers.

Together they saw a need to contextually reverse an imposed downtrodden identity by using existing symbols, religious rituals, and popular myths that they gave new meaning to.[56] Phule's mission for the future of India revolved around a notion of universal brotherhood and shared equality that carried theological implications of non-acceptance towards a transcendental God who was too far isolated from the social sufferings of the masses. The mystification of Brahmanism, in his opinion, destroyed the fabrics of society by keeping the poor ignorant and entrapping them through the fictitious philosophy of *daiva* (fate) and *prarabdha* (predestination). In contrast, Phule believed in a Divine creator, whom he referred to as *Nirmik*, and considered as the divine originator of all things yet separate from the human world.[57] He therefore maintained that the mythic world of Hinduism lacked reason and consciously disregarded the oppression of the *śūdras*. He argued that the superstitions of Brahmanism could be overcome through education, which he regarded as the essential

---

52   Veena Naregal, *Language, Politics, Elites and the Public Sphere: Western India Under Colonialism* (London: Wimbledon Publishing Company, 2002), 52.

53   Ibid, 52- 53.

54   Chakravarti, *Gendering Caste*, 121.

55   O'Hanlon, *Caste, Conflict and Ideology*, 8.

56   Ibid, 8.

57   Michael, *Untouchable Dalits*, 47–48.

apparatus for *śūdra-atiśūdra* social transformation. Education was deemed as the "*traittya ratna*, or the third eye, which enabled those who possessed it to see beyond what the normal eye could not see, that is, it would provide the lower castes with a new mode of social perception."[58] A means by which power relations could be altered, and the rigidity of caste hierarchy could be destroyed.

Phule and his fellow reformers further highlighted the dangers of believing in religious texts such as the Rigveda that despite underpinning the order of Indian society, only a few could read. As a result of which the biblical teachings of the missionaries resonated much greater with the Dalits and low-castes. A letter written to the periodical *Dnyanodaya* by a 14 year-old Dalit girl reflects on the impact such views had on the Dalit communities:

> "*The Brahmans, who are very fond of their creature comforts, say that the Vedas belong exclusively to them. So it is clear that we ourselves have no religious book. If the Vedas are for the Brahmans, then they should conduct their behaviour according to them. If we are not free to look at any religious book at all, then it is clear that we are deprived of religion.*"[59]

Phule was further influenced by the missionary polemic with regards to the place of women in Indian society and made concentrated efforts to highlight the failures of Hindu society in educating women, the injustices in relation to the prohibition of widow remarriage, and the sinful practices of enforced child marriages.[60] Quack remarks that unlike others before him, Phule was no "arm-chair reformer."[61] He actively took part in the national debates for political and religious reform and vehemently opposed the power of the Brahmins as well as strongly critiquing Hindu religious texts, myths and deities that he maintained were a tool of dominion that enabled caste hegemony. Phule's socio-political and religious critique of Indian society maintained that the Hindu religion was built on fabricated mythology that 'divinely' justified the shackles of the *shudras*.[62] However for Omvedt, Phule failed to provide sufficient economic analysis for the struggle of the Dalits, yet was clear in his vision of the need for liberation that was witnessed in the major impact he had in the 19th

---

58   Chakravarti, *Gendering Caste*, 122.
59   *Dnyanodaya*, quoted in O'Hanlon, *Caste, Conflict and Ideology*, 120.
60   O'Hanlon, *Caste, Conflict and* Ideology, 73.
61   See, Johannes Quack, *Disenchanting India: Organised Rationalism and Criticism of Religion in India* (New York: Oxford University Press, 2012), 65.
62   Aparna Devare, *History and the Making of a Modern Hindu Self* (New Delhi: Routledge, 2011), 35.

century in shaping Dalit consciousness and promoting the need for a united *śūdra-atiśūdra* identity that paved the way for later revolutionists and reformers inclusive of Ambedkar who continues to have an impact on Christian Dalit theology and the reform movements of the *devadāsīs*.[63]

B. R. Ambedkar (1891–1956) is arguably the most influential revolutionist in the contemporary Dalit liberation movement. As a Dalit, he campaigned vigorously throughout his lifetime for the political and constitutional reform and the annihilation of caste. In S. R. Bakshi's description of Ambedkar, he writes: "he came before his countrymen and before the world as a professor, a barrister, an erudite person, a legislator, a constitutionalist, a social reformer, a political leader, a cabinet minister, a 'Modern Manu' (constitution-maker)and above all a community leader."[64] Ambedkar's socio-political philosophy was rooted in the amelioration of the lives of the Dalits through political and religious enlightenment, the enhancement of education, and uniting the Dalits whilst promoting economic transformation for those who have existed in dire states of poverty.[65] He regarded the caste system as a malevolent social organism that did not promote morality but instead endorsed exploitation based on an ideology of division and degradation induced by the high-castes. Imperative to his politics were the equal rights of men and women, and the dignity of all human beings. He therefore campaigned vigourously against the practice of untouchability and the evils of caste. Like Phule, Ambedkar considered the awakening of Dalit consciousness to be vital in order to build an empowered Dalit identity.[66] His impact on the Dalit cause can be witnessed in the writings of the Dalit poet, Mool Vansh Katha:

---

63   Omvedt, "Jotirao Phule": 1969.

64   S. R. Bakshi, *B. R. Ambedkar: His Political and Social Ideology* (New Delhi: Deep & Deep Publications, 2000), 2.
        Ambedkar was himself a Dalit, he was educated at an English school in Satara, it was here that he experienced discrimination through segregation from his class mates due to his "untouchable" status. Ambedkar later attended Bombay University, where he was further persecuted by other students who refused to be "polluted" by his presence; he overcame such obstacles to gain a place at Columbia University in New York where he studied economics. In 1919 as a Dalit university graduate, he became a voice for the Dalits in the formation of the new Bombay provincial government. See, Deliége, *The Untouchables of India*, 176 – 179.

65   Bakshi, *B. R. Ambedkar*, 3.

66   The Mahar Conference of Untouchables and Non-Brahmins that was convened in 1927 aimed to help shape a Dalit identity by highlighting the psychological dimensions of a history shaped by pollution and untouchability. In an address to his fellow Dalits at the Mahar Conference at Bombay in 1936, Ambedkar described the inhumane atrocities committed against his Dalit sisters and brothers in order to raise awareness to the shared plight of the oppressed:*"Beating has also been occasioned by your wearing better clothes*

Even the gods failed to act in favour of the Dalits and the deprived
Greater than all these gods, was Bheem Rao Ambedkar;
For it was he who gave rights and dignity to those
Deprived through the ages.
Liberator and hope of these feeble and weak,
Ambedkar, your name shall remain immortal
Till the existence of the universe continues to exist.[67]

Ambedkar did not stop with political provisions for the Dalits he journeyed
further in the search for a counter-cultural Dalit identity, having made a vow
not to die a Hindu. He grappled with the place of religion in society throughout
his speeches and writings, including *Annihilation of Caste* (1936), *The Buddha
and the Future of His Religion* (1950), and *The Buddha and His Dharma* (1957).[68]
Like Phule, Ambedkar longed for a theology that identified with his politics
of equality and fraternity; he eventually found this in his politicised Buddhist
theology that rested on rational human values and social equality. According
to Fitzgerald, it was the values of religion that were imperative as they held
society together, in contrast the "concepts of the supernatural were not essential for Ambedkar. Indeed, he came to see supernaturalism as irrational and
irrelevant to true religion."[69] It was in Buddhism that Ambedkar developed
his political theological praxis and it was the Buddha that exemplified hopeful
resistance for the Dalit movement. He wrote:

> *"Knowing that there was so much unhappiness in the world the Buddha
> realized that it was wrong for him to sit as a sanyasi [ascetic] with folded
> arms and allow things to remain as they were. Asceticism he found to be*

---

and ornaments, and by the use of copper vessels for fetching water (instead of earthenware
jars). There have been, and there still are, instances of beating by Caste Hindus because of
the purchase and use of land, because of the failure to remove carcasses of bullocks and cows,
and because of declining to eat them; similarly, because some Untouchables have taken to
shoes and sandals, are seen in open streets, and have failed to salute Caste Hindus...There
are hypocrites who give sugar to ants and refuse water to the dying. Dr Ambedkar, in his
address to the Mahar Conference at Bombay, 31 May 1936 as quoted in Gerard Baader SJ,
"The Depressed Classes of India": 400.

67   Mool Vansh Katha, "Bohistattva Bharat Ratna Baba Saheb Dr Bheem Raoji Ambedkar,"
       in *Multiple Marginalities: An Anthropology of Identified Dalit Writings*, eds. Badri Narayan
       and A. R. Misra. (New Delhi: Monohar Publishers & Distributors, 2004), 92.
68   See, Timothy Fitzgerald, "Ambedkar, Buddhism, and the Concept of Religion," in *Untouch-
       able Dalits in Modern India*, ed. S. M. Michael. (London: Lynee Rienner Publishers,1999),
       59–60.
69   Ibid, 61.

useless. It was vain to attempt to escape from the world...What is necessary is to change the world and to make it better."[70]

Ambedkar's intention was to develop a historically rooted indigenous identity for the Dalits, as he "was giving the liberation movement of untouchables an organisation, definite direction and also ideological platform necessary for a revolution."[71] Uniting the Dalits towards a shared conversion to Buddhism, was for Ambedkar, a representation of radical transformation; the need to convert he stated, was "for becoming strong...for securing equality...for getting liberty... so that your domestic life may be happy...so that you may be liberated."[72] As Hebden remarks, "Ambedkar was not proposing conversion as a means of concealing caste identity but rather making that identity a thing of pride."[73] Emancipation for the Dalits, according to Ambedkar, could therefore be achieved through the education of the masses that would bring about consciousness that would lead to the psychological awakening of the inadequacies of Hinduism and therefore to a conversion to the Buddhist religion. Ambedkar was a radical reformer that promoted a theological praxis of faithful resistance to socio-political and economic oppressions, through political initiatives, and the demand for an end to degrading social and religious practices inclusive of 'untouchability', a direct product of the caste system, which he maintained must be annihilated. Ambedkar attempted to transform the national identity of India through philosophical, sociological and theological reforms, he envisioned a new ideal of Mother India, the *devadāsīs*, as outlined in previous chapters became a by-product of such socio-religious transformations.[74] Ambedkar became the leading reformist for the Dalit movement, as his radical political and social agenda has without doubt shaped the vision of a just society for the contemporary Dalit activists and paved the way for a Dalit theology of Liberation.

---

70   B. R. Ambedkar, *The Buddha and His Dharma* (Delhi: Siddarth Books, 2006), 112.

71   Shastree, *Religious Converts in India,* 12.

72   See, Madan Gopal Chitkara, *Dr. Ambedkar and Social Justice* (New Delhi: A P H Publishing Corporation, 2002), 229.

73   Keith Hebden, *Dalit Theology and Christian Anarchism* (Surrey: Ashgate Publishing, 2011), 85.

74   Hebden, *Dalit Theology,* 83.

5   Dalit Liberation Theology

Dalit Christian theologians have followed the path of Phule and Ambedkar, who maintained that there was no hope or freedom for the Dalits within the folds of Hinduism.[75] Dalit Christian theology also sought to disassociate itself from Indian Christian Theology, as when contemplating Christ in the Asian context, the non-Dalit Dalit theologian Sathianathan Clarke notes that "the significations of the Bible cannot be understood in isolation from the pre-existing world of religious texts that is part of the social memory and practice of Asian communities."[76] Whilst the Indian theologians took such texts and practices seriously, they failed to acknowledge those within the communities who were marginalised from Brahminical Hinduism, existing outside of the caste system. Thereby remaining helpless to the needs of the many as it "left the *bahujana*, the majority, out of its purview."[77] The lacuna of the existential experiences of the persecuted Christians, meant that however indigenous Indian Christian Theology was or is, if it is not borne out of the experiences of those excluded from Hindu philosophical praxis, the Dalits, or offering liberation from their daily oppressions, then it is considered irrelevant in their plight. Instead Indian Christian Theology attempted to continue the "master-narrative" of Hindu ancestors and the Christian story was deemed as being a fulfilment of Hindu truths.[78] As a result of which, Clarke describes Indian Christian Theology as being embedded within the ideology of caste Hinduism and as such has "tended to serve hegemonic purposes." [79] In contrast Dalit theology was born out of the experiences of the Dalit people and therefore politically motivated in the campaign for Dalit liberation. It emerged during the uprising of Third World theology and was therefore influenced by the liberation theologising of

---

75   Whilst Ambedkar advocated Dalit conversion to Buddhism, exhorting his followers to stop worshipping Hindu gods and observing Hindu beliefs and practices, others within the Dalit panther movements pushed Dalits to follow a secular path, maintaining that "all religions are instruments of social control and political manipulation in the hands of the powerful and well-to-do sections in every religion." See, A. M. Abraham Ayrookuzhiel, "The Dalits, Religions and Interfaith Dialogue," *Journal of Hindu-Christian Studies:* Vol. 7, Article 6 (1994): 17.

76   Sathianathan Clarke, "The Task, Method and Content of Asian Theologies," in *Asian Theology on the Way: Christianity, Culture and Context*, ed. Peniel Rajkumar et al (London: SPCK, 2012).

77   Nirmal Minz, "Meaning of Tribal Consciousness," *Religion & Society* 6 (1989)

78   Rajkumar, *Dalit Theology and Dalit Liberation*, 37.

79   Satianathan Clarke, *Dalits and Christianity: Subaltern Religion and Liberation Theology in India* (Oxford: Oxford University Press, 1998), 43.

Latin America[80] that initially enthused Nirmal's *Shudra Theology.* [81] As such, Dalit theological discourse irrupted as a means of protest, against the caste hegemony that continued to manipulate and control the Church, noticeable in the continued caste persecution of Dalit Christians. As Dalit Christians were often forced to pray in segregated churches, bury their family members in segregated ceremonies, and take communion from separate chalices.[82] Additionally, despite Dalit Christians making up around 65 per cent of the 10 million Christians in South India, only 4 per cent of the parishes were delegated to Dalit priests.[83] For Chatterji, the hegemony of caste persecution on Dalit Christians is systemic within the church, he writes:

> The perceptions that creep into and finally dominate theological education, ministerial training, and Church perspective, are conducive to the maintenance of the status quo...the official theology of the churches tends to be influenced by the ideology of these higher castes trained in the climate of indifference to the realities of the socio-cultural factors.[84]

Caste has therefore penetrated the churches in India, in the same way patriarchy and racism have infiltrated the praxis of the world Church throughout history. The contextual and epistemological birth of Dalit Theology, came as a response to such oppressions.[85] Dalit theological methodology was therefore influenced and precipitated by the theological movements of the 1970s that concentrated on the church of the poor – and yet vitally dependent on the

---

80   Indian Liberation Theology with its focus on communitarian praxis focused faith resonated with the ethos of the Indian poor, this was particularly the case for Dalits and Tribals. See, Wilfred, *On the Banks of the Ganges*: 90 – 94.

81   Nirmal is considered as the Father of Dalit Theology, based upon his paper originally called *Toward a Shudra Theology* which before its publication he renamed *Toward a Dalit Theology.* See, J. Jayakiran Sebastian, "Creative Exploration: Arvind P. Nirmal's Ongoing Contribution to Christian Theology," *Bangalore Theological Forum* 31:2 (1999):44–52.

82   See, Human Rights Watch, *Hidden Apartheid Caste Discrimination against India's "Untouchables"* (CHRC&GJ, 2007), 76.

83   See, James Massey, *Dalits in India: Religion as a Source of Bondage or Liberation with Special Reference to Christians* (New Delhi: Manohar Publishers, 1995), 82.

84   Saral K. Chatterji, "Why Dalit Theology," in *A Reader in Dalit Theology*, ed. Arvind P. Nirmal, (Chennai: Gurukal Lutheran Theological College and Research Institute, 1994), 28.

85   Nirmal addressed this by highlighting that the Indian Chriistian theologians refused to consider the fact that the Indian Church was made up mainly of those belonging to scheduled castes. Yet their theology lacked credibility for the Indian Church as it did not offer a model of liberation from their daily oppressions. See, Arvind P. Nirmal, "Towards a Christian Dalit Theology," in *Indigenous People: Dalits: Dalit Issues in Today's Theological Debate*, ed. James Massey (Delhi: ISPCK, 1994), 217.

Dalit experience.[86] It is therefore shaped by what Rajkumar describes as "emic-perspective" in other words, "the existential realities of Dalits, their conceptions of God, the nature of their experiences and aspirations as well as the conceptual worldview of Dalits Christians, which they share with Dalits of other faiths."[87] Dalit Theology has therefore presented itself as being counter-cultural and counter-theological, as it stands in opposition to elite theologies, because it is narrated and is shaped by the pain-pathos and protest of the Dalit. Fundamentally it seeks to bring about subjective and reflective spaces of discourse that initiate liberative action for the oppressed Dalit people. In order to do so Nirmal argues that, "counter-theologies or people's theologies, therefore, need to be on their guard and need to shut off the influences of the dominant theological tradition."[88] Dalit Liberation Theology is therefore derived not from the dogmatics of the colonialist missionaries or the orthodoxy of Brahminical Hinduism but from the struggles of a persecuted and marginalised people. Felix Wilfred describes such contextual theologies as coming from the "dusty soil" of India, stating:

> It is the same dusty soil from where any serious discourse about the mystery of the world, the human and the Divine should begin. For the religious traditions, too often accustomed to begin from heaven to enlighten the earth, attuned to move from the inner to the outer, the call to start from the earth to discover the Ultimate, to move from the outer to the inner world represents a powerful challenge, it signifies a fresh methodological and hermeneutical point of departure.[89]

Dalit Theology does not focus on the systematics of church doctrine, but instead on the brokenness of the Dalit experience. It does not conform to western rationality, analysis and praxis, and challenges the boundaries between theology and ideology in its attempts to explore the life experiences of both Dalit Christians and non-Christian Dalits. It does so in order to "become an

---

86   The fathers of Dalit theology, including Nirmal, advocated a need for the methodology of Dalit theology to be fundamentally exclusive to the Dalit people, as a means of protecting the theology from being co-opted by caste Hinduism or high-caste Christianity and colonialism. Contemporary Dalit theologians are however moving away from a theology of exclusivism, enabling greater interreligious and interrelatedness in Dalit theological discourse. Thereby allowing non-Dalits, who are profoundly committed to Dalit liberation to contribute to Dalit theological discourse.

87   Rajkumar, *Dalit Theology and Dalit Liberation,* 62.

88   Arvind P. Nirmal, "Towards a Christian Dalit Theology", 58–59.

89   Felix Wilfred, *From the Dusty Soil: Contextual Reinterpretation of Christianity,* (Chennai: Department of Christian Studies, University of Madras, 1995), vii.

endeavour for establishing a coherent, dynamic thought and action, action-reflection is the need to go for this theology-ideology continuum."[90] This is because Dalit Theology stems from the bodily experiences of all Dalits and is constructed from their humiliation, oppression, indignation and harassment at the hands of caste hegemony. Its foundation is the collective memories of the pain-pathos of thousands of years of degradation intertwined with the desire for liberation and the hope for justice and the search for the fullness of life that has been denied to them.

A theology of Dalitness therefore forces traditional theologies to examine their imperialistic methods of missiology. It questions a heavenly Godhead that appears exempt from the lives of the poor and downtrodden. It challenges the Church and the dogmatics of Christianity to witness the wounds of caste discrimination, economic deprivation and class division. Using a hermeneutical methodology shaped by the suffering of the Dalit people it thereby seeks bodily liberation in the here and now. Such a theologising is born out of the experiences of the poor—the manual scavengers, the "agricultural labourers"[91] —and all who struggle for their daily survival as a result of their Dalit identity. The truth of such suffering becomes the hermeneutical lens through which the Dalit Christ is contemplated and realised.

6 Jesus Is Dalit: The Dukkha of the Dalits Is One with Christ

Dalit theological discourse evolves through dialogical encounters with Dalit communities and endeavours to deconstruct dominant theologies in order to invoke a theology of resistance and liberation for the Dalit people. Furthermore, it is based upon the premise that "a non-dalit deity cannot be the god of the Dalits."[92] Dalit theologising therefore applies a hermeneutics of suspicion to Biblical texts and rejects dominant discourses of Christianity in order to adopt a Christology that is developed from the perspective of the most downtrodden. [93] Two Biblical paradigms in particular play a key part in such the-

---

90   John Mohan Razu, "Contours and Trajectories of Dalit Theology" in *Dalit and Minjung Theologies: A* Dialogue, eds. Samson Prabhakar et al. (Bangalore: BTESSC/SATHRI, 2008), 48.

91   Felix Wilfred, *From the Dusty Soil,* vii.

92   Arvind P. Nirmal, "A Dialogue with Dalit Literature," in *Towards a Dalit Theology*, ed. M. E. Prabhakar (New Delhi: ISPCK, 1988), 80.

93   Much like Latin American Liberation Theology, the image of Jesus is transformed from the Western blue eyed, blonde haired, white Christ, who calls for the allegiance of his followers and yet remains on a distant heavenly throne, to the Jesus, son of man, who walks

ologising—the Deuteronomic Creed (Dt 26: 5–12) and the Suffering Servant (Is 52: 13–53). The Exodus paradigm of the Deuteronomic Creed manifests the "outcastes" search for the promised land. It resonates with the identity of the marginalised Dalits, who have no land in the here and now. And offers hope and liberation for the oppressed, God's chosen people.[94] Further, the Creed exhibits the historical consciousness of an oppressed people and reveals that a relationship with God is no longer only for the Brahmins. The God of the Old Testament is therefore revealed as a servant God, who knows the pathos of the Dalits. As "to speak of a Servant-God, therefore, is to recognise and identify Him as a truly Dalit Deity."[95] The Suffering Servant paradigm affirms the Dalitness of God and shapes the Christological reflections of Dalit theological discourse.

Christ is therefore accepted as part of a Dalit counter-cultural theologising that seeks to challenge caste-oppression, and in doing so Jesus Himself is acknowledged as a Dalit. The Dalitness of Jesus Christ is realised in his genealogy which includes Tamar, and Rahab, who would be considered as "outcastes". His Dalitness is further elucidated by his circle of "outcaste" associates, "the gentiles, the sinners, the tax collectors, the publicans and so on."[96] Dalit Christology therefore centres on the incarnation of God and His choosing to take on a "polluted" identity thereby participating in the pain-pathos of the oppressed. In doing so, Jesus radically enters a world of untouchability to form a praxis of unreserved touchability. Christological reflections are therefore shaped by the *Duhkha* (suffering) of the Dalit people. Nirmal explicates Dalit Christology as follows:

> He is a servant God – a God who serves. Services to others have always been the privilege of Dalit communities in India…Let us remember the fact that in Dalits we have peoples who are *avarnas* – those below the Shudras. Their servitude is even more pathetic than that of the Shudras. Against this background the amazing claim of a Christian Dalit Theology will be that the God of the Dalits, the self-existent, the *Svayambhu* does not create others to do sevile work, but does servile work Himself. Servitude is innate in the God of the Dalits. Servitude is the *sva-dharma*

---

with the poor and oppressed, and stands in solidarity with the marginalised and rejected. See, Gustavo Gutierrez, *A Theology of Liberation* (New York: Orbis Books, 1973).

94   See, Nirmal, "Towards a Christian Dalit Theology," 60.

95   Nirmal, "Towards a Christian Dalit Theology," 64.

96   K. P. Kuruvila, *The Word Became Flesh: A Christological Paradigm for Doing Theology in India* (Delhi: ISPCK, 2002), 180.

of the God; and since we the Indian Dalits are this God's people, service has been our lot and our privilege.[97]

Witnessing Christ as the servant God relocates the Divine into uncomfortable and sometimes indecent spaces, where, as Clarke remarks, God becomes identified with "polluted professions (that is, scavengers and the washerman, who epitomise polluting occupations, become images of the Divine in the world) that encountering God and embracing Dalits become synonymous."[98] It is here that Dalit Theology becomes applicable to the lives of the contemporary *devadāsīs* and Dalit sex workers.[99] We see this in Christ's "polluted" identity, that is often revealed within Scripture by the women of the texts who dare to defy the boundaries of social convention in order to expose the "Dalitness" of Christ and challenge patriarchy. Take for example Luke 8:43–48, where the woman who had been haemorrhaging for twelve years, who, in the context of the Hindu purity laws would be considered impure based upon her bleeding, takes it upon herself to touch the cloak of Christ. In doing so she is healed, and as a result "the power" is said to have gone out of Jesus. When considering the text through the Dalit hermeneutical lens, Christ can be considered as becoming polluted in the process, losing power to help the faithful outcaste. The story narrates how as Jesus was making his way through the crowds, a woman who had been subject to bleeding for 12 years, and who doctors had failed to heal, came behind Christ and touched the edge of his cloak, and immediately her bleeding stopped (Luke 8: 42–48). Jesus then searches for the person who has touched him and taken power from him. And the woman "seeing she could not go unnoticed" comes out in trepidation, amongst the crowds of people, she

---

97   Nirmal, "Towards a Christian Dalit Theology," 224.

98   Sathianathan Clarke et al. introduction, in *Dalit Theology in the Twenty-First Century: Discordant Voices, Dicerning Pathways* (New Delhi: Oxford University Press, 2010), 30.

99   Though not named amongst the examples of professions given by Clarke, the vast majority of sex workers in India are Dalits, and sex work remains one of the most isolated forms of labour performed mostly by women with little economic autonomy by not naming prostitution amongst the examples of Dalit occupations, the male Dalit theologians become a part of the patriarchal structural violence that allows for the continued exploitation of women and girls by normalising gender differences and legitimising male dominance by not giving these women a voice. See, Prabha Kotiswaran, "Law, Sex Work and Activism in India," in *Routledge Handbook of Gender in South Asia* ed. Leela Fernandes (New York: Routledge, 2014), 88–89.

In agreement with Carey and Farao, it is a form of structural violence where women are treated as "property, exploited for economic gain, or treated as a commodity." Therefore, silencing their voices in Dalit Christology only serves to further marginalise the bodies of Dalit women. See, Carey and Farao, "Galtung's Unified Theory of Violence", 89.

announces it is she who touched him, and that she had been instantly healed."
Christ announced that it was her faith that healed her.

The woman's body becomes symbolic within the text as a site of struggle
and shame, she remains silent, she bleeds, she breaks down social barriers of
purity, by touching the cloak of the man they call the son of God, such bodily
actions in women's religious lives cannot be emphasized enough. Because it
is the agency of the woman who claims authority in her declaration that it is
she who has touched the cloak of Christ, displaying ultimate faith, she claims
power – a ritual power of healing. She like Dalit women Christians today, has
negotiated her faith in the midst of her life. And what she displays is ultimately
her relationship with Christ, a relationship shaped by "vulnerability, justice,
truth and love" a relationship that is both personal and political.[100] These
actions are particularly important when we consider the bleeding woman as a
woman who has existed on the boundaries of her faith community, as someone deemed impure for both her gender and bodily bleeding – and therefore
shamed into a feeling of socio-religious un-belonging, and yet she transgresses
the fixed boundaries by touching the cloak of Christ, who feels his own power
taken from him.

Considering Scripture through the lens of the Dalit body, particularly the
body of Dalit women who have been shamed and marginalised for their gender, caste and imposed 'impure' status, is a means by which Dalit theology
problematises colonial Christianity. As the living bodies of the Dalits, their
religiosity, identity, and shamed existence, enables a profound reinterpretation and restoration of suppressed religious narratives, one of the ways in
which this is most apparent is through the re-reading of Scripture, as will be
discussed in the following chapter. Dalit theology seeks to challenge the dominant models of Christianity that are often guilty of shaming those who transgress the boundaries of religious belonging, who challenge the status quo, and
does so by acknowledging that in the gospels it is often those who have been
marginalised by the religious elites and in their shamed bodies enter sacred
spaces to touch the body of Christ that are rewarded for their faithful resistance. Whether it be the sex worker at Christ's feet, or widows who throw back
their coins, or the bleeding women who enter sacred spaces to touch the cloak
of Christ, they are the ones who Christ recognises for their faith, they are the
ones who transgress fixed notions of belonging, and are representatives on
earth of the shamed and broken body of Christ.

---

100   Ada Maria Isasi-Diaz and Yolanda Tarango, Hispanic Women: Prophetic Voice in the
       Church (San Francisco: Harper & Row, 1988), 2.

For Dalit theologians, Jesus' ultimate Dalitness is realised on the cross, as it is on the cross that Jesus underwent absolute abandonment, brokenness and God-forsakenness. Such suffering is at the heart of the Dalit 'untouchable' and 'outcaste' experience. As it here that Jesus cries out, "My God, my God why have you forsaken me", such emotive abandonment mirrors the daily existential experiences and consciousness of the Dalit people, who like Christ have experienced "rejection, mockery, contempt, suffering, torture, and death under the dominant political and religious powers."[101] It is by partaking in such suffering that Jesus becomes a Dalit and "is another example of Dalit Christology based on the epistemological premise of pain and pathos."[102] It is because of such pain-pathos that Dalit theologising is "Jesus-centric", as "the exalted and cosmic dimensions of Christ are not explored; instead, the quite mundane suffering and serving Jesus becomes more than sufficient for explicating Dalit Theology."[103] God's liberating presence in the Dalit Jesus is therefore present in the social existence of the oppressed Dalit people. As the Dalit Jesus stands in opposition to the high-caste deities of the Hindus and the suffering of the broken people is characterised instead as redemptive suffering, as Jesus Christ as God participates fully in Dalitness. The incarnation is at the centre of Dalit Christology as God chooses to take on Himself the situation of the oppressed so as to redeem humanity. It is the cosmic dimensions of Jesus Christ that the Dalits find hope in the promise that their suffering is not eternal.

Yet the practical efficacy of Dalit Theology has been questioned by contemporary contextual theologians, due to it failing to actualise liberation for the Dalit people. This has caused a revaluation in Dalit theologies of liberation that has led to the questioning of the methodology used. Clarke for example suggests that there are dangers in concentrating the identity of the Christian Dalit consciousness on the Deuternomic Creed. He states:

> There are no miraculous signs clearly disrupting the seas; there is no drowning of the violating and violent ones who exploit and destroy the poor and the Dalits. To put it as starkly as possible, the dictum of God's 'preferential option for the poor' has remained quite sterile in terms of

---

101   Muriel Orevillo-Montenegro, *The Jesus of Asian Women* (New Delhi: Logos Press, 2009), 16.

102   Rajkumar, *Dalit Theology and Dalit Liberation,* 53.

103   Sathianathan Clarke, "Dalit Theology: An Introductory and Interpretive Theological Exposition," in *Dalit Theology in the Twenty-First Century: Discordant Voices, Dicerning Pathways,* eds. Satianathan Clarke et al. (New Delhi: Oxford University Press, 2010), 32.

practical, concrete improvements in the structures of society for the good
of the poor.[104]

Clarke therefore suggests that there needs to be a liberative praxis for social
transformation in the here and now in Dalit theological discourse, as a means
of escaping the motif of a wandering people who are simply awaiting change.
Peniel Rajkumar also critiques Dalit theological discourse for being too reliant
on the pain-pathos narrative. Noting that:

> An alternative framework for Dalit imagination of God will be one which
> is characterised by not only pathos, but will encompass elements of pro-
> test and resistance, which will place stress on questioning the perpetua-
> tion of the present status quo where Dalits are enslaved into accepting a
> slavish identity and which will be characterised by a radical discontinuity
> with the prevailing models.[105]

Clarke and Rajkumar therefore suggest that Dalit Theology move towards an
agenda of protest and encourage greater dialogue with other practical theologies of liberation. They therefore challenge the exclusive nature of Dalit Theology to instead become more inclusive, in order to recover and re-member
aspects of the Dalit identity that have only just begun to be incorporated into
Dalit Christian Theology, inclusive of Dalit religiosity.

7   Dalit Religiosity in Dalit Christian Theological Discourse

Dalit Theology proclaims a need to "guard itself against becoming co-opted by
the homogenizing propensities of elite theology."[106] Thereby implementing a
distinctively countercultural discourse that is based directly on Dalit experiences that create decolonised spaces for theologising on Dalit subjectivity. As
a result, Christian Dalit Theology has seemingly "uncritically accepted defini-
tional boundaries that distinguish religious practices of one religious group
from another's, viewing them as mutually exclusive," particularly in the case

---

104   Satianathan Clarke, "Dalits Overcoming Violation and Violence: A Contest Between Over-
      powering and Empowering Identities in Changing India," *The Ecumenical Review* Vol. 54,
      Issue 3 (2002): 285–86.
105   Rajkumar, *Dalit Theology and Dalit Liberation*, 68.
106   Clarke, "Dalit Theology: An Introductory and Interpretive", 20.

of Christianity and Hinduism.[107] Yet Dalit Theology also claims a need to be indigenously rooted and countercultural, in doing so Dalit theologians work towards re-mythologising and reincorporating Dalit worship styles and aspects of Dalit village religiosity into Dalit Christian praxis. As Hans Ucko remarks:

> There is a vast amount of folk songs, stories and myths that speak of Dalit protest, conflict and persecution by caste Hindus. This culture, which in itself is an example of anti-Brahminical counter-culture, remains as oral traditions in the worship and cult practices of the Dalits... Dalit theologians refer to Buddha, Kabir, Nanak and most recently Ambedkar as striking examples of Dalit protest. The true identity of the Dalits must go through a recovery and exposure of the suppressed past, a philosophy of 'the land is ours' over against the later Aryan conquerors.[108]

These aspects of the Dalit identity had been denied to them by the Christian missionaries as "mission policy and upper-caste hegemony prevented Dalits from outwardly bringing the empowering aspects of village symbolic culture to their new religion."[109] Mosse suggests that this has created a dilemma for the churches in India "which are attempting to 'inculturate' in the context of a firm commitment to social justice and have a membership which is overwhelmingly low-caste (or tribal)."[110] Furthermore many Dalit Christians maintain that local cultural traditions endure a praxis of caste-based hierarchies that isolate the oppressed and accommodate ideologies of Brahminism, thereby continuing to marginalise Dalits. Mosse suggests that Dalit theology "emerges out of this dilemma."[111] Such a dilemma is visible in the works of the Dalit theologian Satianathan Clarke who advocates a need for Dalit theology to focus on the historic identity of the Dalits that is intertwined with Dalit village religiosity, and engage with the "internalised religious world" of the Dalit consciousness.[112]

Clarke calls this "re-collecting" and "re-membering" the inclusive dimensions of the Dalit religious world.[113] He suggests that the "resistive and

---

107   Meredith B. McGuire, "Lived Religion: Faith and Practice in Everyday Life, Rethinking Religious Identity, Commitment, and Hybridity," *Oxford Scholarship Online* (2008): 2.

108   Hans Ucko, *The People and the People of God: Minjung and Dalit Theology in Interaction with Jewish-Christian Dialogue* (London: Transaction Publishers, 2002), 119.

109   Sherinian, *Tamil Folk Music,* 25.

110   David Mosse, "The Politics of Religious Synthesis: Roman Catholicism and Hindu Village Society in Tamil Nadu, India," in *Syncretism/Anti-Syncretism: The Politics of Religious Synthesis,* eds. Rosalind Shaw et al. (London: Routledge, 1994), 93.

111   Ibid, 93.

112   See, Clarke, *Dalits and Christianity: Subaltern Religion,* 46.

113   Ibid, 2.

constructive aspects of the dalit worldview" inclusive of what he refers to as the "symbols" of the goddess and the Dalit dappu drum, need to be comprehended and reflected upon within the context of caste dominant societies as sources of empowerment within Dalit theological discourse.[114] For Clarke the drum used by the Dalit communities in South India is a sacred symbol[115] that needs to be re-membered and renewed in Dalit Christianity as it reveals the "subaltern-based orality" of the Dalit people. He argues that whilst it has been used as an instrument of oppression to expose the Dalit "outcaste" identity, it also expresses the Dalit community relationship with God. He states: "it is a drum that invites all human beings to dismantle the respective borders that characterise their kingdoms and celebrate the borderless kingdom of God. Just as sound is available to all irrespective of boundaries, the kingdom call goes out to all people – first to the Dalits and then to the caste communities."[116] Therefore the drum, being a symbol of "collective expression and experience of the divine" holds the potential to be a powerful instrument of resistance against caste hegemony in a Dalit Theology of liberation. Clarke's Dalit Christology therefore identifies Christ as the drum for the Dalit people, as the drum is a symbol of both suffering and liberation. This methodology of Dalit Christology is used to recognise "semiotic elements" within Dalit communities in order to "decontextualize them from relationships of subordination and thus produce dalit culture and art."[117] Clarke maintains that by doing so he is a giving a voice to those who have been silenced within theological discourse.[118]

According to Clarke the Dalit goddess *Ellaiyamman* also holds liberative potential in Dalit Theology as she belongs to the Dalit people and "no doubt she lives among the outcaste and works constantly for their welfare. But her powers are also imposing and incredible. Her *Shakti* (energy and power) is cosmic: she controls nature, demons, spirits, human beings, and at times, even gods."[119] Unlike in Hindu pantheon, the goddess of the Dalits remains unmarried and is herself an "outcaste". However, despite considering the liberative potential of the Dalit village goddess, Clarke resolves to favour the symbol of the drum

---

114   Sathianathan Clarke, "Subalterns, Identity Politics and Christian Theology in India," in *Christian Theology in Asia,* ed. Sebastian C. H. Kim (Cambridge: Cambridge University Press, 2008), 284.

115   The drum is used by Paraiyar communities in South India where they are required to play the instrument at high caste weddings and funerals.

116   Clarke, *Dalits and Christianity: Subaltern Religion,* 205.

117   See, David Mosse, *The Saint in the Banyan Tree: Christianity and Caste Society in India* (California: University of California Press, 2012), 222.

118   Clarke, *Dalits and Christianity,* 185.

119   Ibid, 186.

in his theologising over the goddess, maintaining that the drum is "safer and more neutral" than the goddess. Clarke is "ambivalent about the appropriateness of using a goddess symbol in Christian theology" furthermore he argues that "any use of the goddess would require a careful study of her relation to Dalit women and feminist theology" which he admits, he is not prepared to undertake.[120] However, by dismissing the goddess he further marginalises a vital aspect of Dalit village worship and resistance, and as a result silences the devotees of the goddess in his Dalit Theology of liberation. Furthermore, both the liberative and oppressive powers of the goddess in relation to female empowerment go unexplored, and his choice of the drum as a tool for theological discourse over the divine Dalit feminine, privileges the Dalit male over the Dalit female in his Dalit theologising.[121]

Rajkumar however maintains that Clarke's theologising "corrects the misapprehension and misconception that Dalit religion is demonic by exposing the Christic presence in the religious traditions of the Dalits."[122] Yet by forcing Christ on to Dalit religiosity, is Clarke not guilty of repeating the missiological pattern of colonialism as he denies the goddess her right to liberate the Dalit people? In doing so, Clarke's theologising echoes that of Karl Rahner's approach to other world religions, where interreligious, inclusive, transcedental Christology exposes the anthropological potential in theologising through dialogue with other religious traditions.[123] Yet Clarke's theologising appears to remain within the realms of "normative theology" where "Jesus constitutes the *final*, the *definitive*, the *full* and therefore the *normative* revelation of God"[124] as the goddess of the Dalits is reduced to a "symbol." Clarke's Dalit Christology is theocentric and normative, as salvation is not restricted to knowledge of Christ, but remains dependent upon Jesus Christ. Like Rahner, Clarke appears

---

120   See, Tracy Sayuki Tiemeier, "Comparative Theology as a Theology of Liberation," in *The New Comparative Theology: Interreligious Insights from the Next Generation,* ed. Francis X. Clooney. S. J. (London: T&T Clark, 2010), 137.

121   Tiemeier, "Comparative Theology as a Theology of Liberation," 137.

122   Rajkumar, *Dalit Theology and Dalit Liberation,* 48.

123   Rahner suggest that Jesus Christ is the "culmination of salvation in human history", noting: "Only in Jesus Christ did the divine and the human reach an absolute and indissoluble unity; only in the self-revelation of Jesus is this unity also historically present..." Jesus Christ is therefore the culmination of salvation, yet such salvation must be available throughout history, "Rahner argues that faith and salvation is graspable in a latent, un-systematic form for every human being *qua* his or her humanity..."See, Jonas Adelin Jorgensen, *Jesus Imandars and Christ Bhaktas: Two Case Studies of Interreligious Hermeneutics and Identity in Global Christianity* (Frankfurt: Peter Lang, 2008), 29.

124   See, Paul F. Knitter, "Theocentric Christology: Defended and Transcended," in *Journal of Ecumenical Studies* 24 (1987): 41–52.

to be presenting a "searching Christology" that focuses on the dynamism of human experience, where emphasis lies on hope, and transcendence, and "an irrepressible and restless searching" for what Rahner refers to as the "saviour-figure"[125] this for Clarke is the "Dalit Christ." In doing so Clarke silences the goddess of the Dalits, resulting in the silencing of the matriarchal Dalit religiosity, by replacing a female deity with a male one. In agreement with the Indian theologian Samartha "no religion, including Christianity, can claim "finality". This is not to say that Clarke does not take the Dalit religious world seriously in his theology of Dalit liberation, but appears to succumb to what Samartha refers to as "Christomonism" that absolutizes Jesus by turning him into "a kind of cult figure over against other religious figures."[126] Whilst Clarke does not entirely disregard the goddess of the Dalits, he reduces her to a symbol, as for Clarke it is only Jesus who will truly liberate the Dalit people.

The Indian composer and theologian James Theophilius Appavoo, who theologises in solidarity with the Dalits, like Clarke explores the indigenous religious praxis of the Dalit communities, however he chooses to focus instead on the transformative power of Dalit folk music. Appavoo maintains that as the religions, myths and history of the Dalits have been degraded by the dominant hegemonies and considered as ignorant and superstitious, there is a need to reclaim them for the Dalit people. Explicating this need, he notes: "all aspects of our culture are pejoratively spoken of. Our deities are called devils, demons, and evil spirits. Our communication paradigms are called unscientific, primitive, and illogical. These oppressions have made Dalits internalize the oppressors culture."[127] Appavoo retaliates by seeking to regain an identity-specific Dalit religiosity through a "re-creative transmission process," that involves using Christian folk songs and fully sung liturgy, in vernacular Tamil language, in order to create a truly indigenous Dalit Theology. As Sherinian describes, he indigenises "Indian Christianity to make it continually locally relevant and reflective of their religious as well as social experience."[128] Sherinian argues that whilst Clarke ignored the "early roots of Dalit theology expressed through music and even the medium of Karnatak music...because of their compliance with upper-caste Hindu-influenced or sanskritized theology,"[129] Appavoo

125   See, Dermot A. Lane, *Stepping Stones to Other Religions: A Christian Theology of Inter-Religious Dialogue* (New York: Orbis Books, 2011), 157.

126   Stanley J. Samartha, *Courage for Dialogue: Ecumenical Issues in Interreligious Relationships* (Geneva: WCC, 1981).27.

127   J. T. Appavoo, "Communication for Dalit Liberation: A Search for an Appropriate Communication Model" (Master of Theology Thesis., Edinburgh University,1993), 33.

128   Sherinian, *Tamil Folk Music*, 4.

129   Ibid, 24.

regains it. He does so by advocating that village folk culture is relevant and necessary for Dalit worship, ritual and theology.

Like Clarke, Appavoo incorporates the drum into his indigenous religious praxis, but also includes the *urumi* which is an instrument associated with the village goddess.[130] In doing so Appavoo seeks to transform the religious status of the Dalits by empowering them "within Indian Christianity to resist the values of the local elite and missionaries who consider their music and its message an unworthy form of Christian music and theology."[131] His emphasis is therefore on liberating the Dalit people by emancipating their spiritual, cultural and psychological world. He uses radical language that dramatically transforms Christian worship and liturgy as he characterises God, not as man, but as "the bi-gendered parent", *pettavarē*, Jesus as *mūttavar* (the older brother) and the Holy Spirit as the sun, and "teacher of solidarity".[132] He therefore uses language that Dalit village communities can instantly connect with and regains aspects of Dalit religiosity that enable the cultural resources of the Dalits to be utilised in order to interpret Christian scripture and produce liberative motifs in Christian worship.[133]

Whilst Clarke privileges re-thinking of the conceptual, Appavoo instead focuses on praxis in his theological discourse, yet both essentially work towards the liberation of Dalit people through healing and mobilising. Appavoo however appears to transcend normative Christian theologising by integrating the Dalit goddess into his practical theological discourse, as he attempts to reclaim the divine feminine as a source of empowerment for Dalit women. Yet despite engaging with concepts such as a "bi-gendered" Godhead, he fails to journey beyond the heteronormative hegemony of the church. Though he grapples with the resistive power of the village goddess, his focus is instead on the collective resistance of Dalit communities through the sharing of resources, in particular the sharing of food that he refers to as *oru olai*, and of which he incorporates in to the praxis of the Eucharist.[134] His the(a)ology goes further than Clarke's "emancipatory theography", as he "uses the divine power of Dalit drums, and thus the aural power of the Dalit goddess herself, to articulate folk rhythms through his Dalit Christian liturgies and songs as the sounded means to communication with the Divine and to communicate a liberating Dalit

---

130   Ibid, 46.
131   Ibid, 46
132   Sherinian, *Tamil Folk Music*, 123.
133   See, James Elisha, "Liberative Motifs in the Dalit Religion," *Bangalore Theological Forum*, Vol. 34, no. 2 (2002): 78–88.
134   Sherinian, *Tamil Folk Music*, 154.

identity."[135] He therefore transforms the patriarchal language of the Church and permits a more inclusive liturgy that aims to empower Dalit women.

However, Appavoo like Clarke, remains bound by the limitations of Church decency and acceptance. Therefore, his theology of the goddess is limited, as Appavoo favours the communal meal aspect of Dalit village life. Appavoo's intention is to make Christ relevant to the Dalit people and to find a space in the Indian Church for the Dalits that acts as a direct challenge to high-caste Christianity and where the Dalits become the mediators of Christ. However, the mediators appear to be constructed by essentialising the Dalit experience and no space is offered for the Dalits whose brokenness could act as a challenge to the heteronormativity of the Church and Dalit Theology, as is the case for the Dalit *devadāsīs*. Despite Appavoo's theological discourse being arguably more subversive then other Dalit theologians, his theologising remains consciously praxis based and yet pertains to heteronormative theological discourse, despite challenging the masculinity of the Godhead. As a result, the Dalit *devadāsīs* and village sex workers are kept in what Isherwood and Althaus-Reid refer to as "theological closets", as their narratives are hidden from theological discourse and their voices and pathos remain on the margins.[136]

Rajkumar maintains that Dalit Theology has contemplated the cultural resources of the Dalits within its discourses, inclusive of Dalit folk religion, folklore, religions, literature and song, in order to articulate a Dalit liberation theology.[137] Yet Dalit theologians also appear to have become subconsciously complicit with the devaluation of Dalit village folk culture by marginalising the goddess in theological discourses. They have therefore succumb to the protestant missionary agenda, where, "their village goddess religion was 'heathen,' and with the upper-caste ideology that village culture (folk music) was 'degraded'".[138] Dalit theologians including Clarke, and Appavoo have explored the liberative potential of Dalit religiosity within Dalit Liberation Theology and yet have focused more on the emancipatory theography, music, the Dalit Dappu Drum, and mythology, then they have on the liberative

135   Ibid, 156.
136   Marcella Althaus-Reid and Lisa Isherwood, introduction to *The Sexual Theologian: Essays on Sex, God and PoliticsI*, eds. Marcella Althaus-Reid and Lisa Isherwood (London: T&T Clark, 2004), 6.
137   Ayrookuziel "delves into the religion and culture of various Dalit communities and identifies the following resistive features within them: gods and goddesses who condemn caste and preach a religion of common human values; rituals denouncing cast; many anti-brahminical proverbs; evidences to show that Dalit communities 'had proprietary rights and priestly privileges associated with gods and temples which are now under caste control." See, Rajkumar, *Dalit Theology and Dalit Liberation*, 46.
138   Sherinian, *Tamil Folk Music*, 40.

potential of the goddess herself. The religion of the Dalits as Kumar describes, still involves the worship of "natural elements like trees and stones and they revere mountains, thus keeping alive their tribal totemic and mystic material-istic culture."[139] Yet for the Dalit theologians it appears that incorporating such religious praxis into a Dalit Christian theologising would be too problematic. The problem therefore arises as the Dalit theologians self-determine what constitutes as "acceptable or appropriate knowledge"[140] within Dalit worship and religion. Thereby limiting the process of interreligious dialogue and fur-ther silencing the voices of marginalised aspects of Dalit communities. The re-calling and re-membering is therefore limited as to what the Dalit theologians deem decent enough to include within a Dalit Theology of liberation and the goddess of the Dalits is degraded once again as being unworthy of relevance within Dalit theological discourse, thereby dismissing the Dalit feminine in the Divine.

8   Gendered Bodies and Multiple Marginalities in Dalit Theology

Yet vitally it is the voices of Dalit women that are indispensable if Dalit Theol-ogy is to bring about real change for the Dalit people. As within Dalit theological discourse the voices of Dalit women remain marginalised. And until the socio-political, religious, and economic oppression of Dalit women is addressed, Dalit Theology will lack relevance for the Dalit women in their search for lib-eration. Dalit Theology must therefore address the extent to which caste is gen-dered, and the manner in which patriarchy and caste have been used to control and oppress the bodies of women. Chakravarti supports this notion, stating that "neither land, nor ritual quality, that is the purity of caste, can be ensured without closely guarding women who form the pivot of the entire structure."[141] Such 'guarding' of women has involved the control of women's bodies, that is a characteristic of all patriarchal societies, where there exists a necessity to con-trol the sexuality of women. Within India, this further coincides with the need to maintain caste regulations and purity. For the high-caste women who are more "confined" by purity regulations, their sexual subordination is controlled through marriage and motherhood. As the *Manu* states: "*Women were created for the express purpose of giving birth, hence they are worthy of worship, the light*

---

139   B. M. Leela Kumar "The Untouchable "Dalits,"" 17.
140   Rajkumar also describes the need to focus on the appropriate symbols of the Dalit com-munities. See, Rajkumar, *Dalit Theology and Dalit Liberation*, 49.
141   Chakravarti, *Gendering Caste*, 66.

of the house."(X.26) A woman is only considered of relevance in a so-called 'pure' state, when she is confined to the home and the producer of offspring. A belief that is not isolated to Hindu thought, Aristotle for example argued that "Women's main function is reproduction. The man via his semen always provides the soul of the offspring, while the female via her menstrual discharge provides the matter."[142] Aristotle like the *Manu*, believed women to be fundamentally inferior to men, like slaves they had a role to play within society, that of marriage, reproduction and maintaining the social order, yet they should always be considered inferior to and therefore ruled by men.

The subordination of women in India is historically and religiously outlined and conditioned by the hegemony of religious sanctification, apparent within the Hindu scriptures. The *Manusmriti* for example, defines both low-castes and women as impure, polluting, and subject to detailed regulation. The sinful nature of women is said to be a vital aspect of their socially degraded positioning. Chakravarti notes that within the *Mahabharata* (XIII.38.30) "women have been sinful from the very beginning when the creator first made the five gross elements, and he gave shape to men and women. At the time of creation the original Manu (IX.17) allotted to women the habit of lying, wasting time, an indiscriminate love of ornaments, anger, meanness, and treachery, and bad conduct."[143] Women by their very nature are therefore considered to be sinful, destructive and in desperate need of controlling. It is for this reason that Manu maintains that the husband must be the guard of his wife, in order to secure the purity of his offspring and prevent his wife from being sexually promiscuous, which is deemed an intrinsic attribute of her womanhood. Control over female sexuality is crucial in order to maintain caste hegemony, this is done through endogamy. Women are therefore considered to be the property of men to be used for reproductive labour. High caste women are the subjects of more rigid control. As James Elisha Taneti states, the higher the caste of women in the hierarchy, the more stringent the restrictions on its women are. Thus, the women in the bottom of the social ladder had greater freedom, as their sexual interactions did not necessarily alter their status."[144] It is for this reason that arranged marriages continue to be common practice as a means of continuing the male lineage – the *vansa*. The woman becomes the property of the man, used as an instrument to continue the male line. Such endogamous practices

---

142   Aristotle, *Politics*, quoted in *Women in Western Political Thought*, ed. Susan Moller Okin (New York: Princeton University Press, 1979), 81- 82.
143   Chakravarti, *Gendering Caste,* 70.
144   James Elisha Taneti, *Caste, Gender, and Christianity in Colonial India: Telugu Women in Mission* (New York: Palgrave Macmillan, 2013), 19.

are outlined in the *Dharmaśāstra,* where Rama refuses to marry Surpanakaha based upon his *kṣatriya* caste status and her Brahmin caste status.[145]

The policing of marriages by family and community members continues to be rampant across India today, and used as a means of maintaining the caste order, it is estimated that approximately 90 per cent of all marriages are arranged by family members.[146] The result of breaking caste boundaries by resisting or rebelling against such marriages often results in violence and honour killings. Therefore, despite the outlawing of caste discrimination in India, marriage and the control over the sexuality of women is one of the most powerful means by which traditional caste norms continue to be implemented. Further, the patrilineal and patriarchal structure of Indian society determines that males hold the dominant role in all social and economic spheres. As such there exists a strong preference for sons, as daughters are often considered a liability to their family in the marriage process, particularly when taking the economic implications of her dowry into consideration.[147]

How then do we contemplate God in the midst of such realities? Indian Christian theological discourse has often been guilty of excluding the voices of the most marginalised, along with accepting colonial Christological discourses, and being culpable of becoming Sancritised by implementing Brahminical hegemonies, inclusive of conceptions of purity and pollution, on to Christianity in India. Whilst Dalit Theological discourse has been guilty of being dominated by men and has overlooked the experiences of Dalit women. Marcella Althaus-Reid applied the same critique to the liberation theologians of Latin America, stating, "liberationists produced a discourse of the native woman, successfully sold as 'the poor mother'...fitting in with the patriarchal romantic idea of womanhood...it was never the poor woman who was fighting to be ordained as a minister in her church, nor the poor mother trying to get

---

145   R. K. Narayan, *The Ramayana* (Delhi: Vision Books, 1987), 52.

146   See, Steve Derne, "The (Limited) Effect of Cultural Globalisation in India: Implications for Culture Theory," *Poetics 33* (2005): 45.

147   A recent study by the National Council of Women revealed that of 560 recent cases of honour killings in India, 83 per cent of the victims were murdered due to intercaste-marriage, the study further notes that many cases were the result of high-caste women rebelling against the system and marrying men of lower castes and that their families were for the vast majority of cases the perpetrators of the violence. Such statistics reveal not only the rigidity of caste continuing to dominate the private sphere but also the agency of women in challenging the caste order, and their willingness to lose their own higher-caste status for the sake of love. However, for their families and communities this would mean the destruction of purity and honour, such shame is unfathomable for the majority of families. See, Tulika Jaiswal, *Indian Arranged Marriages: A Social Psychological Perspective* (New York: Routledge, 2014), 15.

an abortion or struggling, not against capitalism, but against abusive Christian men in her family."[148] It is the real stories of Dalit women, their embodied narratives of faith, abuse, violence and resistance, that must be heard if God is to be contemplated in honesty, as such contemplations must be shaped by the bodies of those who endure the struggles imposed by the powers of casteism, racism, sexism, and colonialism. The following chapter will offer spaces for such struggles to be voiced, by reflecting on Dalit women's experiences and Dalit womanist theological discourse.

---

148   Marcella Althaus-Reid, *Indecent Theology: Theological Perversions in Sex, Gender and Politics* (London: Routledge, 2000), 34.

CHAPTER 3

A Body Theology of the Thrice Marginalised

A Dalit woman named Bhukli Devi from the Samastipur District of Bihar was paraded naked by Bhumihar Brahmins after being accused of stealing four potatoes from a field. After she was publically humiliated the men raped and killed her, they then inserted her sari into her vagina. This act was said to symbolise the 'impurity' of her womb.[1]

∴

The stripping, parading, raping, and murdering, and then the further destruction of Bhukli Devi's reproductive organs, are violent, hideous acts that are committed as a means of reinstating caste and patriarchal hegemonies against the bodies of Dalit women. It is based upon such daily atrocities that Dalit women profess a need to bring the "silent to voice".[2] Dalit feminist and womanist theologising is therefore understood against the patriarchal assertion of men and the caste violence perpetrated against the bodies of Dalit women, in the forms of rape, harassment, abuse, objectification, murder and the denial to the fullness of life.[3] This chapter will explore the ways in which the body and the Dalit women's experiences are central to the theologising of Dalit women, as they seek to challenge the "perpetual discrimination and marginalisation" Dalit women experience and calls for a "Dalit feminist biblical standpoint that seeks to provide a forum where the issues of Dalit women can emerge and be

1   Nira Yuval-Davis, *The Situated Politics of Belonging* (London: Sage Publications, 2006), 139.
2   Monica Jyotsna Melanchthon, "The Servant in the Book of Judith: Interpreting her Silence, Telling her Story" in *Dalit Theology in the Twenty-first Century: Discordant Voices, Discerning Pathways*, eds. Sathianathan Clarke et al. (New Delhi: Oxford University Press, 2010), 231.
3   Dalit feminist theologians have criticised Dalit theological discourse for ignoring such existential realities of Dalit women, and being fundamentally anthropocentric, androcentric and patriarchal in their theological discourse. Furthermore, it does embody the pathos of violence against Dalit women. They argue that the master-narrative of patriarchal Dalit theology that is shaped by the image of the male Suffering Servant is "not liberating to Dalit women." See, Orevillo-Montenegro, *The Jesus of Asian Women*, 16; Sureka Nelavala "Liberation Beyond Borders: Dalit Feminist Hermeneutics and Four Gospel Women," (PhD diss., Drew University, 2008).

© KONINKLIJKE BRILL NV, LEIDEN, 2021 | DOI: 10.1163/9789004450080_004

discussed."[4] It will look to the ways in which a Dalit womanist theologising may enable the space for the voices of the Dalit women who have otherwise remained silenced in Dalit contemplations on God. Bhukli Devi's story though shocking, is not uncommon, her public humiliation, the shaming of her body, the rape and murder that concludes with the symbolic act of further destroying her vagina and womb, is indicative of the violent, casteist, misogynistic hatred that dominates Indian society. The rape and murder of Bhukli, a Dalit woman, cannot be ignored in the call for Dalit liberation and Dalit solidarity. Because this is a story that epitomises the grotesque injustices that Dalit women's bodies finds themselves struggling against – casteism, patriarchy, racism, classism, purity, honour, colonialism – the ideologies that inform and reinforce the notion that Dalit women's bodies are worthless and somehow deserving of such acts of terror. In a culture dominated by purity and impurity and honour and shame, it is the rapist and murderers that must be shamed, and to so do theologically enables a journeying towards true solidarity with Bhukli, as we begin to contemplate where God is when such violent acts of terror are committed against the bodies of Dalit women.

1   Dalit Women Resistance: Ja Bhim!

Dalit women in India have been at the forefront of the campaign for social, economic and political equality, as thousands have joined together, including those who have been raped and vilified, to take to the streets in protest and voice their anger at the government and the systems of impunity that have allowed caste and gender violations to occur. These women are not just fighting for themselves but for the generations before them and for the women of the future who because of their gender, caste, and class, are the oppressed. One such campaign, known as *Dalit Mahila Swabhiman Yatra*,[5] took its message across continents, seeking solidarity. One Dalit woman on the march who remained nameless, speaking at SOAS University, said:

---

4   Nelavala "Liberation Beyond Borders, 23.

5   The All Indian Dalit Mahila Adhikar Manch (AIDMAM) launched *the Dalit Mahila Swabhiman Yatra* (Dalit Women's Self-Determination March) in 2012 in Haryana, the yātrā has continued, and can be followed on social media using #DalitWomenFight. See, Sonia J. Cheruvillil, "Dalit Women, Sexual Violence and the Geography of Caste: A Journey towards Liberation – An Interview with Asha Kowtal and Thenmozhi Soundararajan," *The Feminist Wire*, May, 1, 2014. http://www.thefeministwire.com/2014/05/dalit-women-sexual-violence/.

I have been abused with filthy language, I have been denied the right to work in certain jobs despite being qualified, I have had my body touched and violated by high caste men, and now I am saying enough is enough. I am a Dalit woman and I am proud. I have the right to be respected, and I have the right to be treated with dignity, and I have the right to get justice. Ja Bhim![6]

Dalit women's resistance movements have therefore been challenging practices of untouchability and redefining ideals of Indian womanhood by narrating their struggles and expressing counter-hegemonic discourses of protest that adhere to the teachings of Ambedkar, by highlighting how all should be entitled to a decent standard of life, to justice, and to an education. For Partha Chatterjee, such protests are a result of civil society within India being restricted to just a small section of society, the rich and those with capital, the others, those in protest, form what he refers to as "political society". The Dalit women's movements are considered to be a part of the "political society". Chatterjee suggests that whilst such movements cannot be entirely ignored by the state, the problem within society is that despite the passionate protests against caste and gender discrimination, "there is little conscious effort to view these agitations as directed towards a fundamental transformation of the structures of political power, as they were in the days of nationalist and socialist mobilalisations."[7] As Rege remarks, according to Chatterjee's framework, movements such as the *Dalit women's Self-Respect Yatra*, would be "dismissed as western inspired, orientalist, for they utilised aspects of colonial policies and western ideologies as resources."[8] Therefore, whilst Dalit women have gained an autonomous national and international public voice, there is still the threat that their struggles will remain structurally ignored.

However, the Dalit women's movements within India have been utilising a variety of mediums available to them, inclusive of poetry, protest, social media, and international pleas of solidarity, in order to mobilise others to challenge and destroy structures of injustice. Take for example the following poem by the Dalit feminist poet Meena Kandasamy:

> *I'll weep to you about*
> *My landlord, and with*

---

6 I was a delegate at the conference that took place as part of the *Dalit Mahila Swabhiman Yatra* (Dalit Women's Self-Determination March) on 16 May 2014.

7 Partha Chatterjee, "Democracy and Economic Transformation in India," *Economic & Political Weekly* (April 2008): 61.

8 See, Sharmila Rege, "Dalit W omen Talk Differently: A Critique of 'Difference' and Towards a Dalit Feminist Standpoint Position," *Economic and Political Weekly* (2008): WS41.

My mature gestures—
You will understand:
The torn sari, dishevelled hair
Stifled cries and meek submission.
I am not untouchable then.[9]

As Kandasamy highlights, Dalit women have been deemed expendable due to the untouchable status and the judiciary system that persistently fails them. Kandasamy uses poetry as a means of protest, her words do not shy away from the violent indecency of the sex crimes committed against the bodies of Dalit women, and capture the hypocrisy of a caste system that deems Dalit women 'impure' and 'untouchable' whilst men continue to touch and harass them against their will. Ethnographic research in the states of Tamil Nadu and Andhra Pradesh exposed me to the social biases as well as the militant Dalit women activists who refused to tolerate discrimination and took pride in their Dalit identity. One such story came from Ruth Devi, a Dalit woman from Tamil Nadu who had been gang-raped in her village whilst working in a field near her home. Despite surviving the brutal attack her husband had left her because he felt shamed by the indecency of what had happened to her. Ruth had sought legal justice for the atrocity committed against her, yet her appeal repeatedly fell on deaf ears. Today Ruth continues to seek justice against the perpetrators, with fellow Dalit women she stands outside police stations chanting for justice to be served. Ruth like thousands of other Dalit women who have experienced such violence has joined the struggle for justice and continues to show resilience in the face of caste and gender persecution.[10] Such violence is not unusual, as Munemma who was raped by a landlord from a village near where she lived, questions:

> *I don't know why I was born as a woman? What did I do? Why should I face all this violence? Why do all these other [caste] women not face the same violence? Is it because of their caste status, their money? I feel like dying.*"

It is based upon such discourses of oppression that the concept of Dalit womanism is shaped, as Cynthia Stephen describes:

---

9   Meena Kandasamy, "Narration," in *Touch*, ed. Meena Kandasamy (New Delhi: Peacock Books, 2006), 56–57.
10   Dalit Women's Self-Repect, interview, Madurai, December 10, 2013.
11   Irudayam, Mangubhai and Lee, *Dalit Women Speak Out*, 348.

With a visceral rejection of the oxymoronic term Dalit feminism I feel the best way to go for us is to call our struggle Dalit womanism, and to acknowledge that the language that feminism speaks is, in our experience, also one of dominance which we have been struggling against.[12]

Dalit women have also challenged the hegemonic patriarchy that exists within the domains of male Dalit resistance movements, noting that their voices are too often silenced within protests and literary scenes. They note that at conferences, in academia and institutions, Dalit men dominate at the expense of the radical voice of the Dalit womanist. For Gopal Guru this is a clear indicator that this dissent highlights that class and caste identity must be explored alongside gender, as "Dalit men are reproducing the same mechanisms against their women which their high caste adversaries had used to dominate them."[13] The Dalit writer, Bama, in *Sangati*, also highlights how caste engulfs the praxis of other faiths, not just Hinduism:

Sothipillai shouted angrily: *"just look at what goes on in our church as well. It is our women who sweep the church and keep it clean. Women from other castes stand to one side until we have finished and then march in grandly and sit down before anyone else. I have stood it for as long as I could, and at last I went and complained to the nuns. And do you know what they said? It seems we will gain merit by sweeping the church and that God will bless us specially."*[14]

Dalit women Christians often continue to be marginalised by caste and class praxis, as conversion from Hinduism has not always enabled absolute emancipation from the shackles of existing ideologies of prejudice. [15] Bauman for

---

12   "Feminism and Dalit Women in India," CounterCurrents, accessed February, 17, 2015, http://www.countercurrents.org/stephen16i109.html.

13   Guru, "Dalit Women Talk Differently": 2549.

14   Bama, *Sangati,* trans. Lakshmi Holmström (Delhi: OUP India, 2009), 23.

15   Yet whilst Dalit and low caste women were often disregarded and degraded by both the Indian elite and Imperial British rule, it could however be argued that the Christian missionaries of the British Empire offered empowerment for all Indian women through education, despite this being motivated by the desire to convert the Indian masses. Christianity in India became a vehicle of social mobility for the Dalits and low-castes, as both women and men who were previously denied access to an education were provided schooling by the missionaries. Chakravarti uses the example of the 'breast-cloth' controversy of the shanars in the Travancore region to capture this point. When the shanars converted to Christianity they attempted to resist social purity laws by demanding that their women cover-up their breasts, a right previously reserved for the upper-caste women who were

example has argued that conversions to Christianity for Dalit women have often led to "an adoption of norms of consonant with upper-caste Hinduism and Victorian Christian values."[16] This is visible in the extent to which missionary efforts sought to control the womanhood and bodies of Dalit women, visible in the speech made the Dalit Christian convert, Mohini Das, who spoke at the All India Depressed Classes Association in Lucknow in 1936, stating, "wherever His [Jesus's] teachings took root the condition of women began to alter. She became not just a glorified courtesan and housekeeper, but a homemaker, a companion to her husband and a fit mother for bringing up his children."[17] The patriarchal language is evident throughout the speech, as is the need to adhere to high-caste and Victorian ideals of womanhood, that are deemed to be decent and godly. However according to Gupta, Dalit women converted to Christianity as part of an "affair of desire", where Dalit women challenged caste and religious boundaries, enabling a "transformative politics of religious rights."[18] They did so through a rebellious religiosity, where Dalit women were described as worshipping Christ often alongside household gods, whilst resisting the stigmatisation of caste and gender discrimination often imposed on Dalit women by making them dress in a certain way, leading the women who converted to dress in the style of Victorian women, so that they could no longer be degraded by the high-caste women.[19] In order transgress oppressive social orders apparent with Hinduism, many Dalit women therefore found hope, education and some level of liberation in Christianity, and from this transformative hope a Dalit Christian theology from the bodies of women developed, where the language of resistance and the desire for dignity and liberation is encountered.

---

depicted as virtuous. Chakravarti notes however that the shanars were not interested in covering the breasts of their women in a western style, but instead wanted their women to dress in the same manner as the high-caste women. The issue here went beyond the question of sexual morality as taught by the Christian missionaries and instead was an attempt to contest the social hierarchy over purity and chastity through the Sankritisation of low-caste women. See, Chakravarti, *Gendering Caste,* 119–120.

16   See, Charu Gupta, "The Intimate Desires: Dalit Women and Religious Conversions in Colonial India", *The Journal of Asian Studies,* Vol. 73. No. 3 (2014): 661–687, 662.

17   Mohini Das, speaking at the All India Depressed Classes Association, with a speech entitled, "What Womanhood Owes Christ", in Gupta, "The Intimate Desires: Dalit Women and Religious Conversions in Colonial India", *The Journal of Asian Studies,* Vol. 73. No. 3 (2014): 668.

18   Gupta, "The Intimate Desires: Dalit Women and Religious Conversions in Colonial India", 662.

19   See, Gupta, "The Intimate Desires: Dalit Women and Religious Conversions in Colonial India": 661–687.

2   The Voice of Dalit Women in Dalit Theology

The Christian theology of Dalit women is a practical theology it aims to pro-mote the liberation and well-being of the whole Dalit community, whilst tak-ing into account the social, economic, cultural and psychological dimensions that are intertwined with the gender and caste politics of Dalit women. The Dalit feminist perspective therefore challenges Dalit theological discourse and Dalit movements as a whole, to analyse and address the caste-dynamics of oppression alongside patriarchy. It does so by calling for a re-reading of Scrip-ture in order to make the text relevant to the lives of Dalit women and enable the narratives of the Bible to speak to the experiences of Dalit women. As Sureka Nelavala describes: "Dalit feminist biblical interpretation authenticates and allows the life situations of Dalit women and their stories to be in active conversation with the text. Similarly, the text has a particular message and rel-evance to the contexts and questions of Dalit reality."[20] By enabling the experi-ences of Dalit women to be the primary source of reflection and contemplation in Dalit Theology it becomes a Dalit womanist theologising[21] – where those who are marginalised because of their gender, race, caste and class become the voices of protest and resistance. Violence against Dalit women therefore becomes the hermeneutical lens through which Christ is contemplated. Dalit womanist theology therefore explores the multifaceted aspects of oppression by becoming a body theology, as it is shaped by the countless scars imposed on

---

20   Surekha Nelavala, "Inclusivity and Distinctions: The Future of Dalit Feminist Biblical Studies," in *New Feminist Christianity: Many Voices, Many Views* eds. Mary E. Hunt et al. (Woodstock, Vermont: Skylight Paths, 2010), 105.

21   Womanist theology is a practical theologising that responds to the experiences of African American women. The term was originally coined by the African-American author Alice Walker, who describes its meaning as "femaleness that is characterised by an inquisitive-ness that seeks to understand that which is essential to know oneself; Sees personhood as defying social constructions. Womanism invites us to question perceptions of human sexuality that contradict our sense of unconditional acceptance; encourages us to cel-ebrate life in its totality...; Demands a deeper, more intense critique relative to the multi-ple dimensions of Black women's lives, individually and collectively." See, Katie Geneva Cannon, Emilie M. Townes, and Angela D. Sims, *Womanist Theological Ethics: A Reader* (Louisville, Kentucky: Westminster John Knox Press, 2011), xvi;
Womanist theologies go beyond feminist theology as they maintain a commitment to the interwoven dimensions of oppression experienced by women of colour – inclusive of social, cultural, religious, race and caste dynamics. As Monica Coleman remarks, "as a form of liberation theology, womanist theologies aim for freedom of oppressed peoples and creatures. More specifically, womanist theologies add the goals of survival, quality of life, and wholeness to black theology's goals of liberation and justice." See, Monica A. Coleman, *Making a Way Out of No Way: A Womanist Theology* (Minneapolis: Fortress Press, 2008), 11.

to the flesh of the Dalit people by the divergent systems of hegemony. When describing body theology, the feminist theologians Lisa Isherwood and Marcella Althaus-Reid, note that it acts as a direct challenge to traditional theology as it forces theology "to look again at the way in which the human person is understood and to overcome the dualism that carries within it a large dose of negativity about the way in which we express our humanness through our flesh."[22] Dalit womanist theologising is therefore done through the hermeneutics of the flesh of the most marginalised.

3   The Dalit Womanist Christ

The Dalit feminist theologian, Evangeline Anderson-Rajkumar, outlines the contours of such theologising by narrating the experiences of persecuted women alongside the suffering of Christ. She begins with the story of Kausar Bano, a Muslim woman who was crucified by the Hindutva forces in the Gujarat massacre of 2002. Bano's husband narrates the brutal murder of his wife and unborn child, stating: "They pulled my wife out of my arms, slit her stomach with a sword and paraded the baby on the tip of a sword. I think I heard my child cry. Then they poured petrol on both of them and lit them. I hid behind a five-feet wall and witnessed what happened to my wife and child. Then I ran for the fear of my life."[23] Anderson-Rajkumar goes on to describe the tale of a nameless pregnant black woman who was hung to a tree, burnt alive, mocked whilst screaming in pain and had her abdomen ripped open. The baby inside her was torn out and killed.[24] She then follows the account of this atrocity by narrating the pathos of Jesus – who prior to his death was paraded, humiliated and mocked. Anderson-Rajkumar aims to bring to the forefront of Dalit Christology the pain-pathos of the tortured flesh of women – who have been violated, humiliated and murdered, as a result of their sex, religion, race, caste and class. She states:

> While the experiences of violence of the two women are not because of [what] they themselves did, the experience of violence by Jesus was because of what he chose to do. While the two women represented the "negative other" and therefore became the targets of violence, Jesus

---

22   Lisa Isherwood and Marcella Althaus-Reid, introduction in *Controversies in Body Theology*, eds. Marcella ALthaus-Reid et al. (London: SCM Press, 2008), 3.
23   Evangeline Anderson-Rajkumar, "Politicising the Body: A Feminist Christology" (paper presented at the theological colloquium Asian Faces of Christ, Delhi, March, 20, 2004).
24   Ibid.

suffered violence consciously, as a consequence for his struggle for justice. While the narrations of the experiences of the two women are not called scripture, nor ascribed with "authority," the passage from Mathew is. Does this mean that we cannot place the text of Jesus' crucifixion in juxtaposition with "women's bodies" as other "texts"?[25]

Anderson-Rajkumar outlines how the bodies of the women are sites of hatred "that are converted into sites of violence."[26] The pregnant status of the women is considered a threat to the higher-castes, the racists, and all ideologies that seek to control and subjugate the marginalised. Therefore, for Anderson-Rajkumar, the womb becomes a vital space of counter-cultural theologising. She notes that "if the wombs are considered as a threat to the survival of the caste system, then it is precisely there that we need to search for alternative modes of counter-theology and speech."[27] The brutality of the killing of these women and the destruction of their unborn children intends to cement the hegemony of patriarchy, racism and casteism on to this generation and prevent the existence of future generations.[28] By narrating their brutal murder alongside that of Christ's, Anderson-Rajkumar makes the bodies of oppressed women the reference points for theologising.

It is the suffering of Jesus alongside his association with the marginalised outcastes that means that Christ is not only found in the experiences of persecuted women but is Himself oppressed. It is because of the shared experiences of oppression, violence and suffering that Jesus is God for the Dalit womanist. And it is through the resurrection, that Jesus becomes the liberator for Dalit women. The task therefore of the Dalit womanist theologian is to illustrate the struggles of the oppressed communities against structures of evil, and relate the people's pathos to God's will to liberate the downtrodden. In order to do so, theologians must make the gospel message clear in the context of the marginalised, so that God's people know that God has journeyed with the oppressed. Dalit women therefore "draw upon the teachings of the Bible and God's direct revelation in their lives for their understandings of God."[29] By asserting that the struggle of Dalit women is God's struggle, and that the story of Jesus becomes

---

25   Anderson-Rajkumar, "Politicising the Body: A Feminist Christology."
26   Evangeline Anderson-Rajkumar, "Turning Bodies Inside Out", 207.
27   Ibid, 210.
28   Ibid, 211.
29   Monica A. Coleman, *Making a Way Out of No Way: A Womanist Theology* (Minneapolis: Fortress Press, 2008), 14.

the story of the oppressed through the "faith made possible by the grace of His presence with us."[30]

Whilst Anderson-Rajkumar relates the violence of Dalit women directly to the crucifixion of Jesus in order to portray a Dalit womanist Christology, she does not apply the Dalit cultural strengths – such as religiosity, music, and dance – to her Dalit theologising, and therefore to a certain degree fails to present a Dalit identity-specific theology. The risk of not incorporating such aspects of the Dalit identity is that it denies opportunities for cultural resistance and personal autonomy in the search for liberation. As Roja Singh remarks, "an inversion of the colonising discourses re-member Dalit women with their culture. What religion and hegemonic institutions had demonised is recovered as subversive strategies to claim their dignity."[31] Further, the maleness of Jesus remains a constant, as whilst we are made aware that Jesus suffers, is humiliated, tortured and is crucified, the focus on the women's narratives is the violence committed directly against their femininity. The masculinity of Jesus remains intact. Yet the women are violently raped, their wombs are destroyed and their unborn babies killed. These are experiences that a God made incarnate into a male body cannot relate to. In agreement with the Dalit feminist theologian Gabrielle Dietrich, "we may not gain much if we address God as father and mother as long as the division of labour between mothers and fathers in day-to-day life remains unchallenged."[32] To add to this, whilst rape and sexual violence and the destruction of female flesh remains a prominent feature of day-to-day life for Dalit women, can a male God, who as Anderson-Rajkumar describes, experiences violence "because of what he chooses to do"[33], truly know the pathos of the flesh of Dalit women?

4   Dalit Feminist/Womanist Hermeneutics

For the Dalit theologian, Monica Jyotsna Melanchthon, it is through a hermeneutics of suspicion that focuses on the silenced within the narratives of Scripture that marginalised women can be made visible. Melanchthon outlines how subaltern feminist interpretation, "while giving voice to the silent,

---

30   See, James H. Cone, *God of the Oppressed* (New York: The Seabury Press, 1975), 104.

31   See, Roja Singh, "Bama's Critical-Constructive Narratives: Interweaving Resisting Visible Bodies and Emanicipatory Audacious Voice as TEXTure for Dalit Women's Freedom," in *Dalit Theology in the Twenty-first Century*, 228.

32   Gabrielle Dietrich, *Reflections on the Women's Movement in India: Religion, Ecology, Development.* (New Delhi: Horizon India Books, 1993), 3.

33   Anderson-Rajkumar, "Politicising the Body: A Feminist Christology."

also rethinks history and agency. It regards women's activities and social relations as central, and it is concerned with sets of cultural and political practices
that cut across all domains of the social."[34] In order to outline her subaltern
Dalit feminist interpretation she re-reads the Apocryphal book of Judith in
the Old Testament.[35] Her concentration is not however on the character of
Judith – a beautiful, wealthy Jewish woman, but instead on the servant in the
text. Using the methodology of Badri Narayan's study of Dalit women heroes
she focuses on the "unnamed woman", the maid servant who journeys with
Judith in her mission to save Bethulia.[36] Narayan's investigative study into Dalit
women heroes brings "to the fore the manner in which oppressed communities rewrite or recreate history and myth; they reinvent the past in order to
give new meaning to reality arrogate a better future."[37] It is based upon the
marginalised communities re-writing of myths within the context of subaltern
community struggle for identity, that Melanchthon's exploration of the book
of Judith attempts to expose the narrative of the silent maid. She highlights
how the maid is referred to at least thirteen times and "was in charge of all
[she] Judith possessed" (8:10). She was responsible for cleaning and caring for
Judith (10:2) and with Judith she travelled to Bethulia (10:6). On their journey it
is both Judith and the maid who are met by Holofernes' patrol and taken into
custody (10:11). Despite the maid being with Judith in her ordeal, Melanchthon
notes that "Judith alone answers all the questions posed and the maid is not
mentioned again during all the time the text recounts Judith's introduction to
Holofernes and the camp."[38] The maid is cited again when standing at Judith's
bedchamber and after Judith has chopped off the head of Holofernes she

34 Monica Jyotsna Melanchthon, "The Servant in the Book of Judith", 232.
35 Judith is a wealthy widow (8:4–8), described as being faithful and devout, "no one spoke
ill of her, for she feared God with great devotion (8:8). She sought justice for her people,
whom she rebukes for their lack of faith in the Lord (8:9–35). She implements her plot to
seek justice for her Jewish people against Holofernes and uses her beauty to her advan-
tage (10:4). On route to Holofernes she is captured by the Assyrian's – she deliberately lies
to them by telling them that she is fleeing from her fellow Hebrews who were planning
on handing her over to Holofernes. Distracted by her beauty, they lead her and her maid
to the tent of Holofernes under the protection of the Assyrian patrol (10–11). Holofernes
believes her story, and compliments her wisdom and beauty, considering a gift from God
(11:22). Judith and her maid then become his guest (12). Judith is able to murder Holofernes as she chops off his head whilst he is drunk (13:3), her maid helps in the process
by standing by the bedpost and later hiding the bed as they return to Bethulia. Their brav-
ery and wisdom led to the fleeing of the Assyrians and protection of the Hebrew people
whilst Judith lived.
36 Melanchthon, "The Servant in the Book of Judith", 235.
37 Ibid, 234.
38 Ibid, 236.

hands it to the maid. Judith is the main protagonist of the text, remembered and celebrated up until and beyond her death. Whilst the nameless maid is forgotten, although before Judith's death, Judith sets her free (16:23).

For Melanchthon the few details the reader is given of the maid are highly relevant – she is clearly trusted and respected, and yet despite her role is given little mention by either the male author or Biblical scholars. By refusing to acknowledge her presence, her role, class, occupation and identity are ignored. Yet for Melanchthon her character "is perhaps the most haunting and therefore deserving of our attention...not only is she silent, but she has become almost invisible within traditional interpretations of the book." She argues that it is therefore the responsibility of the Dalit feminist theologian to identify her and bring voice to the silenced, as the maid takes on the role of the Dalit women.[39] Melanchthon does so by attempting to piece together aspects of the maid's historical narrative that are missing from the text, thereby re-writing or re-mythologising the book of Judith. She maintains that the intelligence and loyalty of the maid, whom she names Habra, is apparent in the confidence and trust placed on her by Judith. This friendship, according to Melanchthon, "transcended class, age and ethnicity," and the silenced hero in the narrative is the maid.[40] By re-mythologising the narrative of the silent maid, Melanchthon intends to engender Dalit women's identity by highlighting the agency of the silenced as they struggle against systems of evil throughout history. She states:

> Constructing a myth about Habra that challenges the community to reflect on her role in the saving of the nation might bring to the fore traits and qualities, identified through her actions, which could be used for the sake of the marginalised. Reconstructing Habra would provide the marginalised communities with a hero, perhaps a role model.

Melanchthon's Dalit feminist hermeneutics offers a powerful reconstruction of the text that identifies with the Dalit struggle for identity and power, as the maid takes on a central role in the liberation of the Hebrew people. Through the methodology of re-mythologising in order to present a Dalit woman hero in Habra, Melanchthon portrays a character who though silenced, is brave, loyal and respected, and crosses the boundaries of her servant status to be a confidante of Judith and help to bring down the oppressors of the Hebrews. Yet it is vital to remember that she herself remains a servant until the death of her master, and is bound by the social hegemonies of patriarchy and colonialism,

---

39   Ibid, 236.
40   Ibid, 238.

as a result a more pronounced hermeneutic of suspicion is needed in my opinion, if the text is to be considered as a narrative of resistance.[41] Whilst Melanchthon's interpretation exposes the silenced in the master narrative and attempts to "recover, reinvent, and reconstruct the alterity of the marginalised" by re-reading the story to offer a history, context and identity to the silenced maid, her interpretation is confined to focusing on the faithful, loyal, and obedient aspects of the maid's identity – who is essentially bound to her master Judith.

Furthermore, the religious identity of the maid has also been denied to her, as we hear only of the God of Judith. Dalit women have also experienced such oppression by the destruction of their religiosity by both Brahminical Hinduism, and imperial Christianity. The roles that the maid performs within the text must also be read with a greater hermeneutic of suspicion, bearing in mind the structures of purity and pollution that have condemned Dalit women to their oppressed status. For example, after Judith has chopped off the head of Holofernes, "she went out and gave Holofernes' head to her maid, who placed it in her food bag" (12:9). We know that Judith herself is strict in her obedience to the purity laws of Leviticus, as she stresses the need to bathe every evening (12:7), and "by observing the dietary laws and by bathing every night, Judith remains for certain in the status of cultic purity, and thus she can utter her prayers to the Lord (12:8)."[42] Judith becomes unclean when she chops off the head of Holofernes, yet according to Hieke, the act was a form of cultic sacrifice to God and as an act of Holy War she can be purified through the sprinkling of water (Num 31: 19), she is therefore able to maintain her purity. However, the maid, who did not kill in order to offer the sacrifice is forced to take the blooded carcass head of an infidel and put it in her food bag, thereby polluting herself and her food. The purity laws of the Torah are clear, that "all who touch a corpse, the body of a human being who has died, and do not purify themselves, defile the tabernacle of the Lord; such persons shall be cut off from Israel" (Num 19:13). Thus the maid is polluted by Judith's actions, and whilst we are made aware of Judith purifying herself, we are not informed of the maid doing so, thereby cementing her status as an impure outcaste – this was done not by choice but command.

Musa Dube further suggests that Judith operates within the framework of patriarchy, noting how "a feminist reader thus realises that Judith may have

---

41   Melanchthon, "The Servant in the Book of Judith," 247.
42   Thomas Hieke, "Torah in Judith. Dietary Laws, Purity and Other Torah Issues in the Book of Judith," in *A Pious Seductress: Studies in the Book of Judith,* ed. Geza G. Xeravits (Berlin: Walter de Gruyter, 2012), 102.

offered public resistance against collaboration with imperialism, but she makes no such challenge against patriarchy."[43] Dube basis her analysis on Judith's failure to question the male leadership of her people and whilst she held the wisdom and respect to overthrow the patriarchal hegemonies of the Hebrews, she withdraws "from public space to the private" and is buried in her husband's grave."[44] Such Biblical narratives should therefore be read with greater caution and suspicion if they are to be considered as mythic narratives of Dalit heroine resistance. As the Dalit womanist must also ask why Judith waited until she was on her deathbed to free her loyal maid. By questioning the actions of the main female protagonist, the text can be further applied to the contemporary battle for Dalit women's liberation. As it could be argued that Judith appears to be taking on the role of the white feminist and the Brahmin woman – as she remains focused on her own plight and that of her fellow Hebrews. The woman who she relies upon, she keeps as her servant until her death; so whilst the liberation of the Hebrews is considered urgent, her maid who is further marginalised by her class, caste or colour, must wait to be freed.

Melanchthon's Dalit feminist hermeneutics opens the door for new ways of challenging Biblical texts by reflecting on the marginalised characters within the narratives. She uses the methodological tool of re-mythologising Biblical narratives in order to offer a voice to the silent woman heroines and in doing so she emphasises the silenced history of Dalit women in their fight for liberation. Melanchthon notes that much like in Dalit mythology, in the story of Judith, "what is glorified is her 'patriotism, femininity, loyalty towards the husband, religiosity,' which would suit the ideology of the dominant communities."[45] However, as Melanchthon points out, the texts "significance lies in their telling, writing, and celebrating, and the manner in which the stories meet the needs, desires, and expectations of Dalits/oppressed—whether imagined, nationalist, or otherwise."[46] When reading the text with a hermeneutic of suspicion from the perspective of Dalit women's bodies what comes to life in the story of Judith is how the bodies of women are used in a colonial context, as well as in the relationship between servant and master, and are victimised by the laws of purity. Such readings of Scripture are dialogical and pluralistic as they offer divergent meanings, "this dialogue occurs in several directions: coloniser and colonised, colonial and postcolonial, rich and poor, powerful and

---

43   Musa W. Dube, "Rahab Says Hello to Judith: A Decolonializing Feminist Reading," in *The Postcolonial Biblical Reader,* ed. R. S. Sugirtharajah (Oxford: Blackwell Publishing, 2006), 154.

44   Ibid, 154.

45   Melanchthon, "The Servant in the Book of Judith", 244.

46   Ibid, 241.

impotent, those in the centre and those on the margins, male and female, and different and ethnic groups."[47] For Melanchthon, the Dalitness of the narrative is exposed in the silenced body of the maid, as by re-mythologising her narrative the formerly silenced finds a voice, the Dalitness is therefore the starting point of her hermeneutics. However, problems with such dialogues occur with the non-liberative elements of the myths, traditions, biblical narratives and characters, and with the ideologies of subjugation apparent within the narratives that remain unchallenged.

5   The Missing Voice of the Indecent in Dalit Theology

Dalit theological hermeneutics is context-specific and fundamentally praxis focused in its seeking liberation for the Dalit people. Through the methodological approach of re-telling and re-reading Biblical texts in order to address the shared oppression of Dalits or other marginalised people, Dalit hermeneutics seeks to offer a voice to the silenced. Dalit Feminist Theology therefore attempts to "give visibility to their oppressive stories, and to listen to the voice of the oppressed, while approaching the oppressors' visibility with suspicion."[48] Yet what has become apparent in such dialogue is the focus on the so-called morally decent oppressed and the failure to offer a platform for the voices of the most marginalised Dalit women, who have been further socially excluded as a result of imperialistic moral agendas, patriarchal ideologies and religiously imposed praxis' of bodily subjugation. This includes the Dalit sex workers, the contemporary Dalit *devadāsīs*, and all those who exist outside of the realms of the sexually "decent" oppressed. Within Dalit theological dialogue the women whose sexuality has determined their livelihood and oppression have not been called upon as prophets of witness in Dalit theological discourse. As to date no Dalit Theology has addressed the Dalit sex workers, or the contemporary *devadāsīs*, choosing instead to remain within the realms of the "decent" within Dalit liberation theologising. The destabilising aspects of Dalit theological discourse are as a result limited, as the bodies of women whose sexuality has determined their social status exist outside of the dialogical circle of Dalit theological discourse. Yet in the face of rape, sexual exploitation, caste violence on gendered bodies, social persecution against the children of sacred sex workers,

---

47   Leo G. Perdue, *Reconstructing Old Testament Theology: After the Collapse of History* (Minneapolis: Fortrress Press, 2005), 302.

48   Surekha Nelavala, "Reading the 'Sinful Woman' in Luke 7:36–50 from a Dalit Feminist Perspective" in *Dalit Theology in the Twenty-first Century: Discordant Voices, Discerning Pathways*, eds. Satianathan Clarke et al. (New York: Oxford University Press, 2010), 263.

enforced marriages, and all that has served to denigrate the bodies of Dalit women, determines that we cannot stay silent on the apparent silence of God.

For Marcella Althaus-Reid, "what has been excluded from Liberation Theology has been the result of a selective process of contexts of poverty and experiences of marginalisation", the same can be said for Dalit Theology.[49] The Dalit theologian has walked through the slums and the villages without paying attention to the rebellious Dalits who continue to worship their dangerous deities and who sell their bodies for sex to feed their children in the name of their goddess.[50] It cannot be ignored that Christianity was the religion of the colonisers who imposed upon the colonised their moral order. Nor can it be ignored that the bodies of many Dalit women have been further impacted and degraded by the Christian Church as a result of social, political and economic constraints imposed by notions of ideal womanhood. As the Church in India has brought with it "a discourse of respectability and sexuality [which] tended to narrow the already restricted range of behaviours and choices deemed appropriate for women."[51] Many Dalit women still converted to Christianity with the "intent to undermine the caste, class, and gender ideologies that justified oppression."[52] However, the subversiveness of the historic Dalit identity has at times been lost as colonial patriarchal dogmatics have been normalised by the Indian Church. Marriage for example has become a necessary means of rehabilitation for those sacred sex workers who accept Christ, and as Maraschin notes, through such practices the Church has "limited the rich possibilities of human sexuality and condemned practices which did not fit its dogmatic theology."[53]

The narratives of the contemporary *devadāsīs* do however hold the potential to act as a prophetic voice that could destabilise the theologies and dogmatics that have degraded the bodies of women. It is in such lived experiences

---

49   Marcella Althaus-Reid, *Indecent Theology: Theological Perversions in Sex, Gender and Politics* (New York: Routledge, 2000), 4.

50   During my time working alongside Dalit Christian women with the Church in South India it was clear that Dalit Christian within the Church looked down on the Dalit women who had not converted, particularly the *devadāsīs*, who they viewed with disdain, referring to them as "ignorant", "prostitutes" or "dirty". Thus taking on the language of the high-castes and the Victorian missionaries. Christian morality with regards to ideal womanhood has created a new level oppression for Dalit women. The gender dimension is addressed with regards to further oppression imposed on to Dalit women for their caste and gender, yet the rigidity of morality has inflicted further scars on to the bodies of the Dalit women who are not considered 'decent'.

51   Eliza Kent, *Converting Women: Gender and Protestant Christianity in Colonial South India* (Oxford, Oxford University Press, 2004), 5.

52   Sherinian, *Tamil Folk Music as Dalit*, 29.

53   Jaci Maraschin, "Worship and the Excluded," in *Liberation Theology and Sexuality*, ed. Marcella Althaus-Reid (London: SCM Press, 2009), 174.

of the poor that the God of life is revealed. Therefore, a theologising in the brothels amidst the sacred sex workers must be born out of the moments in Dalit history that challenge religious and political discourses of authority that have further silenced the bodies of women. Furthermore, a Dalit feminist hermeneutics of suspicion must be applied to all contours of theological discourse in order to move beyond binary thinking. Yet as is the case in Liberation Theology, Dalit Theology has been guilty of failing to deconstruct the moral order "which is based on a heterosexual construction of reality" as imposed by the colonialists.[54] The brothels of the sacred sex worker remain a hybrid space – being a place of work, family and religiosity – that is missing from Dalit theological discourses. Dalit Feminist Theology must therefore "transgress its own boundaries and outlaw itself" if it is to be true to the marginalised experiences of the subaltern.[55] This requires what the Latin American feminist theologian Marcella Althaus-Reid refers to as an "indecent theology", meaning "a positive theology which aims to uncover, unmask, and unclothe that false hermeneutics which considers itself as 'decent', and, as such, proper and benefitting for women especially in sexual matters."[56] Such a theologising would enable the pathos of the bodily experiences of the *devadāsīs* to shape a Dalit feminist epistemology and radical Dalit hermeneutics.

Employing the voice of the Dalit sacred sex workers in Dalit theological dialogue forces a hermeneutical shift to the indecent, as it allows the bodies of women whose sexuality, religiosity and livelihoods, that exist outside of the realms of the decent, to be the foundation on which a Christology is shaped. The feminist theologian Lisa Isherwood addresses the desire to enable such voices to be heard by questioning:

> What would they say, these silenced and maligned vaginas that have borne the force of clerical and theological wrath for centuries? Now is the time to find an honest voice uncorrupted by theological niceties. The

---

54   See, Marcella Althaus-Reid's critique of Liberation theology where she calls for the feminist theologian to "undress the mythical layers of multiple oppression in Latin America" as the same critique can be applied to Dalit feminist theology, that whilst addressing caste discrimination must also witness the multiple layers of colonialism and patriarchy that have enforced their moral orders on to the bodies of Dalit women. Resulting in marriage and sexual control and decency being idealised as the only accepted forms of religious social practice. See, Marcella Althaus-Reid, *Indecent Theology*, 2.

55   See, Marcella Althaus-Reid, "'A Saint and a Church for Twenty Dollars': Sending Radical Orthodoxy to Ayacucho," in *Interpreting the Postmodern: Responses to "Radical Orthodoxy"*, eds. Rosemary Radford Ruether et al. (New York: T&T Clark, 2006), 113.

56   Marcella Althaus-Reid, *From Feminist Theology to Indecent Theology* (London: SCM Press, 2004), 83.

vicar is coming to tea: get out the bondage gear, not the cucumber sand-
wiches and let's do theology. But what would yours say? I bet it wouldn't
be 'Hail Mary'. How about 'Hail Holy Queen', what gender...lies behind
those innocent words? A heterosexual woman getting close and theological with a gay man in drag or not? A heterosexual man dressed as
Cleopatra for a night? A stone butch looking for all the world like Princess
Di or Ivana Trump? The list is endless. What wonderful theology these
people could produce if they took Marcella's [Althaus-Reid] advice and
went to bed for a week and then wrote the 'Song of Songs'.[57]

Such theologising crosses the boundaries of imposed ideals of womanhood
that have been highly sacralised through patriarchal readings of Scripture. It
does so by allowing the bodies of the most marginalised women to be prophetic by uncovering hidden spaces of theological revelation. Applying such
a theology to a Dalit feminist discourse would enable the missing voice of the
Dalit sacred sex worker to create a sexualised yet holy theological space for
reflecting on new representations of God.

Whilst Anderson-Rajkumar presents a Dalit womanist theology that applies
the bodily experiences of violence committed against women as a result of
caste and patriarchy, her Christology does little to bring about change in the
here and now from the daily oppressions of Dalit women whose experiences
of a male Christ have only furthered their daily suffering. Take for example the
words of the dedicated *Mathamma,* who stated:

> *I am told to accept Christ but Christ does not accept me. The church will not
> let me and my children be baptised, I am not welcome to come to church ser-
> vices, I am not welcome because I am prostitute, so the goddess Mathamma
> will release her wrath because I have accepted Christ, and the Church still
> does not welcome me because I am a sex worker, what hope is there for me?*[58]

Applying such narratives to Dalit feminist Christological reflections diversifies the womanist discourse in order to locate the revelatory capacity of the
oppressed through acts of indecency, resistance, and counter-cultural religiosity. A Dalit womanist theologising that comes directly from the body must
not be afraid of being "indecent" – after all what is decent about rape, sexual
violence, the slashing of wombs and the ripping out of foetus'? It is only by

---

57   Lisa Isherwood, "Indecent Theology: What F–ing Difference Does it Make?" *Feminist The-
      ology* 11/2 (2003): 147, accessed April 15, 2015, doi: 10.1177/096673500301100203.
58   Bama, interview, Madurai, Tamilnadu, November, 11, 2014.

allowing such voices to be prophetic within theological discourse that the most marginalised of women will find hope in the salvific grace of God.

Furthermore, applying an "indecent" lens to Dalit feminist hermeneutics that takes into consideration the suffering of the contemporary sacred sex workers, enables the text to take on new meanings – enthused by a more indecent and liberating theological *yātrā*. Take for example Melanchthon's study of Judith, the sexuality, femininity and masculinity of the narrative are brought to light when re-read through the lens of the "indecent" marginalised sacred sex worker. After all the book of Judith is a narrative that is shaped by the sexuality of women as it portrays the complex interaction of psychological, social, cultural and biological influences on women as sexual beings. This is made apparent in Holoferenes' plans to get Judith drunk and rape her, as he states: "Go and persuade the Hebrew woman who is in your care to join us to eat and drink with us. For it would be a disgrace if we let such a woman go without having intercourse with her. If we do not seduce her, she will laugh at us" (12:11–12). Holoferenes' masculinity is under threat of humiliation if he does not have sexual control over Judith's body. Yet Judith uses her own body against him, in order to entice, seduce, distract and kill Holoferenes. The contemporary *devadāsīs* are also faced with the persistent threat of rape, from their Landlords, the villagers and the high-caste men. In their suffering their bodies become prophetic as the threat of rape speaks of dominion, whilst they use their bodies in order to survive, much in the same way Judith is forced to use hers. Judith and the maid use their sexuality in order to perform a terrorist act of murder against the imperial threat to Israel, actions that are "allowed under the duress of circumstances if they serve a good cause."[59]

Let us also re-consider the relationship between Judith and her maid, as who is to say that their relationship was not itself sexual and that together they mocked patriarchy by using the sexual weaknesses of men against them? When re-read through a queer lens[60] the women support each other, Judith has no need to re-marry because of the bond she has with her maid, and together they take on forces of patriarchy. Thus offering a critique to the heteronormativity of the marriage metaphor that is also used by the contemporary Church and reform movements to attempt to control and rehabilitate the bodies of the

---

59   Michael Wojciechowski, "Moral Teaching of the Book of Judith," in *A Pious Seductress: Studies in the Book of Judith*, ed. Geza G. Xeravits (Berlin: Walter de Gruyter, 2012), 92.
60   Using Marcella Althaus-Reid's definition of queer, "queer is a word which originially meant 'transverse' or 'oblique' and it is used in a positive way. Queer theory celebrates diversity, the crossing of borders and Imprecise frontiers. It liberates the assumed reference of theology and therefore liberates Godself from assumptions and ideological justifications." See, Althaus-Reid, *From Feminist*, 143.

contemporary sacred sex workers. Though Biblical scholars have consistently pursued the case of "moral" decency and purity on to the body of Judith, as the widow who "knew" no other man and was buried in her husband's grave, portrayed as a born again virgin[61] – a Dalit *devadāsī* re-reading could expose a more radical tale. One in which sexuality is not considered sinful but instead empowering. Feminist scholars have also been guilty of imprinting on to the character of Judith a "pure" and "decent" depiction, for instance Athalya Brenner-Idan writes, "let us face it, she resembles greatly the largely a-sexual, even though not unemotional, saviour Superwoman of modern comics...such figures do wear seductive clothes and are depicted as having strong emotions, as well as power. They appear sexy...like Judith, do they seem to promise, but, appearances aside, never deliver?"[62] The apparent chastity of Judith is presented as her ultimate strength. Yet when such biblical texts are read from the perspective of women who use their sexuality as a means of providing for their family, surviving and as part of a religious order, the text is transformed and the sexuality of the women together becomes a formidable force of resistance.

When applying the missing voices of the marginalised Dalit sacred sex workers and the "indecent" poor to Dalit hermeneutics and theological discourses, the interconnection between ideologies of patriarchy, casteism and sexual control are exposed. As it in the historic and contemporary identities of the *devadāsīs* that the socio-political and economic subjugation of Dalit women is made most apparent. For example, Cynthia Stephen outlines the implications of the degraded role of the *devadāsī*, noting the social and economic repercussions of caste and gender violence:

> The religious establishment, allying with the political powers of the locality, grabs leadership of the local religious power centre and through this takes control of the rites, rituals, offerings and thereby the economic surplus of the people of the area...The subaltern traditions thus fall under the total sway of the Brahminical forces with little hope of change.[63]

A theological *yātrā* with the contemporary sacred sex workers, requires that Dalit Theology become "indecent", as by doing so it is able to challenge "the

---

61   See, Angelo Passaro, *Family and Kinship in the Deuterocanonical and Cognate Literature* (Berlin: Walter de Gruyter, 2013), 280.

62   Athalya Brenner-Idan, "Clothing Seduces: Did You Think It Was Naked Flesh That Did It?" in *A Feminist Companion to Tobit and Judith*, eds. Athalya Brenner-Idan et al. (London: Bloomsbury,2015), 223–224.

63   Cynthia Stephen, "A Name of Our Own: Subaltern Women's Perspectives on Gender and Religion," *Journal of Dharma* 36, 4 (2011): 419.

heteronormative foundation of society and heterosexist assumptions that undergird much of traditional theology"[64], thereby enabling Dalit women, inclusive of the sacred sex workers to become a prophetic voice. In doing so the Dalit womanist theologian becomes a "decolonializing partner, in search of liberation"[65] as "it is the silent voice that gets resurrected as powerful Speech, Voice, and Song while theologising."[66] Dalit women's experiences are fundamentally unique and shaped by divergent trajectories of oppression; and subjective to a diversity of religions, regions, and languages. It is by incorporating the voices, that in the case of the contemporary sacred sex workers are also moulded by sexual violence, rape, sexually transmitted diseases and village religiosity, that a Dalit Theology of liberation shaped by the bodily scars of the most marginalised is born.

6   Boundary Crossing with the Sexual Stories of the Oppressed

The Dalit *devadāsīs* present the Dalit liberationist movements with complex and profound sexual stories where a lived religiosity is encountered that combines the erotic with the divine and in doing so crosses the boundaries imposed by religious institutions and dogmatics. As despite the Indian caste system and other systems of patriarchal control, inclusive of the church, seeking to retain control over the sexuality of women through endogamy, moral codes of decency, and other such acts of sexual control and violence, the *devadāsīs* represent a challenge to such systems of patriarchy and violence against women, as many are not afraid to voice their narratives of oppression that challenge enforced models of decency. A passing comment made by one *devadāsī* over a meal one day highlights this point, she stated: *"At the time the man will say he wants to marry you, but you know he just wants sex, and I wouldn't want to marry him anyway, I want his money and him gone."* The woman in many ways attempts to take control of her sexuality, she knows how the community view her, she has lived with the communal shaming from both men and women who have condemned her to the margins of her community and purposefully discriminated against her, and yet she is resistant to conform to the norms of the society around her. The sexual stories of the *devadāsīs* can evoke unease, particularly for Dalit women and reformist movements who seek to 'liberate'

---

64   See, Kwok Pui-lan, "Changing Identities and Narratives: Postcolonial Theologies," in *Complex Identities in a Shifting World: One God, Many Stories,* ed. Pamela Couture, Robert Mager et al. (Zurich: LIT, 2015), 121.

65   Dube, "Rahab Says Hello to Judith", 148.

66   Anderson-Rajkumar, "Turning Bodies Inside Out", 209.

the dedicated women through marriage and into the confines of 'decent' womanhood. Yet their narratives of transgressive feminine sexuality and religiosity challenge the Dalit consciousness to become aware of the way in which marriage and decency is used to further shame and control the bodies of women. Such embodied stories of sexuality and protest are also visible in the stories and language of the Dalit liberationist writers, that are often disruptive of the colonial Indian feminine, and use the bodies of Dalit women to challenge caste and class norms. Whilst embodied writing is apparent in Dalit Womanist theology, the sexual narratives and subversive and obscene language that is visible throughout the work of Dalit women's writing is not visible in Dalit Christian Theologising. Take for example the work of the Dalit writer Bami, in her book *Sangati*, a Dalit woman called Raakkamma stands up to her drunk and violent husband in public, stating:

> How dare you kick me, you low-life? Your hand will get leprosy! How dare you pull my hair? Disgusting man, only fit to drink a woman's farts! Instead of drinking toddy everyday, why don't you drink your son's urine? Why don't you drink my monthly blood?[67]

Such language, according to Hubel, is deployed by Dalit women writers in order to "combat and repel" Indian feminine norms supported by middle class and high-caste women.[68] It is indecent and honest, as the woman speaks from an embodied experience of a battered Dalit woman who has been at the receiving end of misogyny and caste violence. She does not filter her words for the comfort of the listener and nor should she, she seeks to shame her oppressor and wants the community that has enabled the shame to hear her words. We find in the narratives of Dalit women tales of domestic violence, caste violence, sexism, discrimination, sex, and rape, to ignore such realities is to disregard the daily lives of the oppressed. To overlook the language of the oppressed is to disregard the words of protest and resistance that offer the potential to challenge socially constructed gendered norms. Hubel remarks that in the poetry of the *devadāsī*s a similar language is used, where "fear, shyness, simplicity, and modesty are simply not valued." In contrast to the feminine norms of middle class, high-caste and Christian women, "complex forms of irony, intense eroticism

---

67   Bama, *Sangati: Events*. Trans. Holmström L. (New Delhi: Oxford University Press, 2008), 61.
68   Teresa Hubel, "Tracking obscenities: Dalit women, devadasis, and the linguistically sexual", *The Journal of Commonwealth Literature*, Vol. 54 (2019): 52–69, 64.

and sexual daring, and a bold self-confidence" are apparent.[69] Visible in the poem *A Courtesan to her lover*, by Ksetrayya:

> Who was that woman
> sleeping in the space between you and me?
> Muvva Gopāla, you sly one:
> I heard her bangles jingle.
> Thinking it was you, I reached out for a hug.
> Those big breasts collided with mine.
> That seemed a little strange,
> but I didn't make a fuss...
> Who was that woman?[70]

The *devadāsī* courtesan in the poem transgresses the boundaries of sexual behaviour, she speaks of engaging in a queer sexuality where breasts collide, and she appears more intrigued by the woman with whom she shares her bed than Muvva Gopāla. The poem displays a form of sexuality that has been silenced since the advent of modern India. In the process of such silencing the complexity of the sexual narratives of women and the oppressed often goes ignored. Yet the narratives of contemporary Dalit women, including that of the *devadāsīs* disrupt the notion that the sexual narratives of the oppressed are somehow monolithic. Audre Lorde suggests though that the "erotic is not only about the power of one's own sexual energy, but instead includes and goes well beyond it to a site of knowledge production and energy that is alternative to regimes of the state and received culture."[71] As with all aspects of life there may be experiences of liberation and resistance apparent within the erotic lives of Dalit women that offer alternative ways of knowing and uncover new truths about the divine.

It is for this reason that Dalit poets such as Meena Kandasamy have spoken out so powerfully against the patriarchal forces within Indian society that seek to control the sexuality of women through marriage, shame and decency, where femininity is judged by a woman's respectability, her politeness and submissiveness. Kandasamy writes:

69 Hubel, "Tracking obscenities: Dalit women, devadasis, and the linguistically sexual: 65.
70 Kṣetrayya, A courtesan to her lover", in *When God is a Customer: Telegu Courtesan Songs by Kṣetrayya and Others* by Ramanujan et al. (Berkley, CA: University of California Press, 1994), 73–74.
71 See, Jafari S. Allen, *Venceremos? The Erotics of Black Self-Making in Cuba* (London: Duke University Press, 2011), 192.

Your society always makes
The spoon-feeding-the-man
The pot-and-pan banging,
The-sweeping-the-floor
The masochist slave
And other submissive women
As goddess.[72]

The 'brothel' of the *devadāsī*, the place in which she sleeps and has sex with her patrons, is also the place in which she often to prays to the goddess, and to Jesus – in the case of the *devadāsīs* who have also found hope in Christ. God is present in such places, and God is present each time the *devadāsī* has sex.[73] The presence of God in the brothels of the sacred sex workers has been missing from the writings of Dalit women's theology, just as the lived experiences of sex workers has been silenced by feminist liberation theologians in general. Lauren Mogrow highlights this point, stating, "feminist liberation theology (and sexual theology) could be located closer to women's actual lives, through listening to the voices and stories of sex workers and taking seriously both the structural and feminist critiques offered."[74] A hermeneutics of suspicion that applies the silenced voices of the *devadāsīs* in a Christian theologising challenges accepted ideas about womanhood, as by applying narratives of the erotic it is possible to oppose colonial ideals of womanhood, and cultivate spaces for contemplating God that transgress the fixed boundaries of gendered decency and sexuality.

In agreement with David Joy there remains a need to "decolonise" the Church in India as the colonial elements remain poignant within the religious activities and engagement of Indian Christians. Joy maintains that there is therefore a need to reconstruct the "identity of the church in a postcolonial context but re-constructing the identity of the church in a postcolonial context is not an easy task as it has so many stages and barriers."[75] Yet this is vital if Dalit Theology is to resonate with the most marginalised of Dalit experiences. As so

---

72   Meena Kandasamy, *Touch* (Mumbai: Peacock Books, 2006), 130.

73   In agreement with Thia Cooper, "each time we have sex. God is present." See, Thia Cooper, *A Christian Guide to Liberating Desire, Sex, Partnership, Work, and Reproduction*, (Palgrave Macmillan, 2017), 1.

74   Lauren Mogrow, *Missionary Positions: A Postcolonial Feminist Perspective on Sex Work and Faith-Based Outreach from Australia* (Leiden: Brill, 2017), 74.

75   David Joy, "Decolonizing the Bible, Church, and Jesus: A Search for an Alternate Reading Space for the Postcolonial Context," in *Decolonizing the Body of Christ: Theology and Theory After Empire?* eds. David Joy et al. (New York: Palgrave Macmillan, 2012), 20.

far the Dalit Christ does not appear to have stood outside of heteronormative frameworks or journeyed into indecent spaces. Furthermore, despite goddess worship being central to religious beliefs in India, Dalit Christian Theology has not "engaged the goddess traditions in its attempts to make sense of the Christian faith."[76] In agreement with Marcella Althaus-Reid, "the problem remains and Christianity has been and still remains the religion that was imposed on the Other."[77] Dalit Theology must therefore confront the bodies of the Dalits that have been marginalised by colonialism as well as caste and patriarchy. The contemporary Dalit *devadāsīs* therefore emerge as new theological subjects in Dalit theological discourse. A journeying with Dalit Theology into the brothels of the sacred sex workers requires enabling sex workers, village prostitutes, trafficked *joginis*, and reformed *Devadāsīs*, to become the lens through which Christ is contemplated and Scripture is interpreted. As their bodily struggles destabilise the homogeneity of the Church and force us to witness evils of caste and patriarchal violence. Such narratives also reveal the need to contemplate the hybridity and multiple religious belonging of sub-Dalit caste groups, in order to engage in a truly indigenous, subaltern Dalit Theology of resistance.

---

76   Ibid, 142.
77   Althaus-Reid, *From Feminist Theology*, 104.

CHAPTER 4

Liberating Scriptures Whores with the *Devadāsīs*

> *I will direct my indignation against you, in order that they may deal with you in fury. They shall cut off your nose and your ears, and your survivors shall fall by the sword... and the nakedness of your whorings shall be exposed. Your lewdness and your whorings shall have brought this upon you, because you played the whore with the nations, and polluted yourself with the idols.*
> EZEKIEL, 23: 25–31

•••

> *"They pounced upon the girl and tried to rape her. When she resisted, they tied a black dupatta on her eyes and chopped off her nose, ears and hands with an axe. They also tried to gag her...The three then fled threatening her with dire consequences if she told anybody about the incident."* They did this because she was a woman, and a Dalit and therefore considered polluting.[1]

∶∶

In this chapter, using the methodology of Dalit womanist hermeneutics, I will explore and re-read Biblical passages that condemn, marginalise, destroy, violate, rape and mutilate the bodies of women – whilst labelling them "whores", "prostitutes", "concubines" and "harlots". As when read from what the

---

1 This is just one of thousands of cases of violence committed against Dalit women in India. There are striking similarities between the metaphorical language used in Ezekiel to prophesise against the dangers of idolatry and the lived reality of the incident committed against a Dalit girl in Kanpur. The cutting off of body parts, the destruction of the woman's sexuality through nudity and rape and the threat of more to come. Such castigations and violence is committed because of their "polluted" status. See, Faiz Rahman Siddiqui, "Dalit Girl Mutilated for Resisting Rape in UP," *The Times of India*, February 7, 2011, accessed April, 15, 2015. http://timesofindia.indiatimes.com/india/Dalit-girl-mutilated-for-resisting-rape-in-UP/articleshow/7439907.cms.

liberation theologian, Jon Sobrino, refers to as the *Sitz im Tod*[2], of the brothels of South India, such texts capture the embedded ideologies that continue to be the foundation for the sexual control and condemnation of women today. Whether metaphorical or literal, I will highlight how such Biblical texts have impacted theologies and moral constructs by attempting to define and control the sexuality of women. Such androcentric scriptural passages parallel centuries of oppression on women, whose bodies have been corrupted, controlled and raped by patriarchy, racism, colonialism and casteism. By re-reading the "whores" of Scripture, through the lens of the contemporary *devadāsīs*, an attempt is made to liberate the tortured bodies of women both within the text and outside of it, by giving the silenced women a voice. As the existential bodily scars of the *devadāsīs*, expose the lived reality of the prophetic patriarchal language that has justified centuries of gender-based oppression. This chapter will therefore seek to challenge the socio-political influences and religious dogmatics, that reinforce such violence and oppression on to the bodies of the *devadāsīs*, whilst grappling with the marginalised sex workers, "concubines" and "whores" of Scripture, who throughout remain voiceless and stigmatised. As the profoundly ostracised voices of the contemporary *devadāsīs* require a re-reading and re-invention of the myths, religions and hegemonic structures that have forced them into their current state in order to attempt to overcome their situation of oppression.

The patriarchal construction of gendered metaphors within Biblical texts that have symbolised women as 'evil temptresses', 'villainous whores', and 'exploitative prostitutes', have created dangerous ideological frameworks that have haunted the identities of women throughout the generations. As have the passages that include the silenced concubines and prostitutes – who are violently destroyed by the hands of men. Exploring such texts from the social context of the Dalit women, who from childhood have been forced into sex work, labelled as 'harlots', 'concubines', 'whores' and 'prostitutes' makes visible the shared phenomenon of enforced marginalisation and silenced torment, that has ridiculed and chastised the bodies of women in diverse ages and contexts. Social reform movements in India "captured the *devadāsī* and defined her as immoral, hence repugnant to society,"[3] whilst the British colonial Christian missionaries using the Anglicized term '*nautch girl*', categorised the women as sacred, sexualised, temple harlots that were symbolic of idolatry, shamefulness

---

2 Jon Sobrino originally coined the term *Sitz im Tod*, yet it was later used by Stenstorm in reference to the death dealing powers against women. See, Stichele, "Re-membering the Whore," 118.

3 Epp, "Violating the Sacred?" 110.

and indecency, which they believed to also be central elements of the Hindu religion.[4] Christian Biblical texts,[5] coinciding with missionary interpretations of Indian womanhood, and Hindu Scriptural texts such as the *Manu*[6] have marginalised and vilified the bodies of women, whilst condemning and chastising the bodies of sex workers.[7]

The denunciation of sex workers within the Bible is expressed most violently in the deployment of the whore metaphor, where murder, rape, mutilation, burning and other acts of brutality are described as adequate responses to the disobedient "whore" (Isa. 1:21, 23:15–18; Hos. 1–4; Mic. 1.7; Am. 7:17; Jer: 3:1–10; Nah. 3:4–7; Ezek. 16 and 23, Rev.17–19). In a patriarchal society such imagery cannot be isolated from the hegemonic context in which it functions as "inscribed in these metaphors are androcentric views on women, sexuality, and power in gender relations."[8] Yet, Musa Dube maintains that to date feminist Biblical scholars have attempted to evade the narratives of the sex workers and abused women of Scripture. Dube notes that "the overall impact of these feminist readings is to silence the agency of the sex workers, to erase the historical presence of sex workers in sacred texts and to distance sex workers from the historical Jesus, primarily because feminist readers are heavily invested in the patriarchal construction of decency in sexual morality and family."[9] However, such Biblical texts cannot be deemed innocent given the horror of the violence described in the prophetic threats and taking in to consideration the physical, emotional and sexual violence that women continue to face today.

---

4   Ibid, 133.
5   Christian missionaries in India promoted the social purity movement that maintained that the devadāsīs were dancing girls who were prostitutes. See, Thurston, *Castes and Tribes*, 127.
6   The *Manu*, the first law-giver...not only equated women with *śūdras*, their seductive qualities necessitating constant dependence on sons, fathers and husbands, but he also held prostitutes in great disfavour (Manu, ix, 259; iv, 209, 211, 219, 220; v.90); Magazine and newspapers including *The Indian Spectator* on 25 June 1886, refers to prostitutes as "loathsome nuisance who offended the eye and ear wherever they were liked." See, Epp, "Violating the Sacred": 120.
7   Epp, "Violating the Sacred": 88.
8   Caroline Vander Stichele, "Re-membering the Whore: The Fate of Babylon According to Revelation 17:6," in *A Feminist Companion to the Apocalypse of John,* ed. Amy-Jill Levine et al. (London: T&T Clark, 2009), 114.
9   Musa Dube, "Review of Avaren Ipsen, Sex Working and the Bible, London: Equinox 2009," *Religion and Gender* Vol. 2, No. 2 (2012): 361; For Ussher, women's sexuality has been portrayed as being both "fatal and flawed-paradoxically framed either as absent, within the archetype of the asexual pure Madonna, or as all-encompassing and dangerously omnipotent, an image represented most clearly by the witch or whore. Jane M. Ussher, "The Construction of Female Sexual Problems: Regulating Sex, Regulating Women," in *Psychological Perspectives on Sexual Problems: New Directions in Theory and Practice,* eds. Jane M. Ussher et al. (London: Routledge, 1993), 10–11.

The narratives are therefore exceptionally dangerous as they are rooted in existing views held by religious powers with regards to women who break normative patterns of sexual morality, in particular the sex workers.

1   Bringing Metaphors to Life through Dalit Womanist Hermeneutics

A Dalit womanist hermeneutic of suspicion acts as a direct challenge to dominant Western traditional Christian theologies and Biblical readings that have influenced the subordination of women. As Ivy Singh describes: "it emerges in a context in which they suffer, struggle and cry to find out where God is. In this struggle, they feel that a Father God or a brother God or a male God or a God who has been pictured as taking care of humans cannot help. But a God who understands and participates in people's struggles collectively can be worthy of worship."[10] Dalit womanist interpretation is counter-cultural and identity specific, it removes the layers of patriarchal suppression and colonial impositions from the text in order to make visible the silenced identity of the most marginalised people apparent within the narratives, because they are the characters that Dalits can relate to, as they are the 'broken ones'. It is for this reason that Dalit womanist interpretation attempts to do as Monica Jyotsna Melanchthon states, and "construct new texts that could play a significant role in the Dalit struggle for identity, power, and resistance against caste hegemony."[11] The problem is however, that to date Dalit feminist hermeneutics has avoided issues of sexuality particularly relating to prostitution, despite a large number of Dalit women being embedded within *dhanda* (sex work). Yet Dalit feminist hermeneutics necessitates the use of real life situations of Dalit women as being a vital tool for interpretation of Scriptural texts, where the pain-pathos of the Dalit women's experiences must be central.[12]

Melanchthon writes: "every Dalit reading of the Bible forcefully claims an approach that is vested in the pain and prejudices of being discriminated against."[13] This is particularly the case when exploring texts such as Ezekiel 23, where gender oppression and the alienation of women's bodies shape the

10   Ivy Singh, "Eco-feminism as a Paradigm Shift in Theology" *Indian Journal of Theology* 45/1&2 (2003): 15.
11   Monica Jyotsna Melanchthon, "The Servant in the Book of Judith: Interpreting her Silence", 247.
12   See, Nelavala, "Liberation Beyond Borders": 24.
13   Monica Melanchthon, "Indian Dalit Women and the Bible: Hermeneutical and Methodological Reflections," in *Gender, Religion and Diversity: Cross-Cultural Perspectives,* eds. Ursula King et al. (New York: Continuum, 2004), 223.

narrative of the text. As the bodies of women are used as metaphors to expose heinous punishments upon the sinful and disobedient. Yet some feminist scholars, inclusive of Elizabeth Schüssler Fiorenza, have maintained that the gendered metaphorical language of the "whores" in the Ezekiel 23, like that of the whore of Babylon in the Book of Revelation, "would be completely misconstrued if understood as referring to the actual behaviour of individual women," thus excusing these "whores" of Scripture as literary figures.[14] Keller however notes that whether metaphorical or not, "there is no veiling the way this vision of justice boils down to the burning and devouring of a woman's body."[15] This is particularly the case when re-reading and re-interpreting the "whores" of scripture through a Dalit womanist lens, as the abuse and violence narrated is echoed on a daily basis in the slums, cities and villages of India, where Dalit women's bodies become the template on which lessons on caste, patriarchy and pollution are preached and enforced.

Therefore, the dangers of such language cannot be ignored, as within these Biblical narratives it is God who is the perpetrator of the violence that is committed against the personified and gendered body of Israel. The metaphors are brought to life when the narratives are read through a postcolonial lens as "both colonizing power and decolonizing power are unthinkingly male, and the strife between the two powers is waged over the territory of the female."[16] For the contemporary sacred sex worker it is the political movements, religious hierarchies, caste orders, colonial powers and patriarchal forces that battle over their bodies. As subalterns they exist outside of the mainstream of power and their protests, cries, and anguished voices are silenced. Much like the "whore" in the book of Revelation, they are the "sexually oppressed women" who the postcolonial theologian Jean K. Kim argues are "caught in a no-win situation between foreign and native men".[17] A textual critique of Scriptures violent gendered metaphors by the most marginalised of Dalit women, will therefore aim to expose the bodily realities of the text, from one sexually abused body to another. It does so through an "indecenting process", where the reader is forced to come back "to the authentic, everyday life experiences" of the oppressed and "bring back the sense of reality, and not the common-sense reality politics

---

14   Elizabeth Schüssler Fiorenza, *Revelation: Vision of a Just World* (Minneapolis: Fortress Press, 1991), 96.
15   Catherine Keller, *Apocalypse Now and Then: A Feminist Guide to the End of the World* (Minneapolis: Fortress Press, 2005), 76.
16   Jean K. Kim, "'Uncovering her Wickedness': An Intercontextual Reading of Revelation 17 From A Postcolonial Feminist Perspective," *Journal for the Study of the New Testament* 73 (1999): 62.
17   Kim, "'Uncovering her Wickedness': 61.

denounced by Gramsci which constructs not only objectivity but subjectivity."[18] Advocating for the non-literalising of the text only serves to exclude the literal bodily implications that this language has on women whose own narratives echo that of the persecuted "whores" of scripture.

2   Through the Lens of the *Devadāsī* to the Bodies of Oholah and Oholibah

Ezekiel 23 describes the violent, eroticised relationship between YHWH and the personified nations of Jerusalem and Samaria by using the gendered metaphors of the two sisters, Ololah and Olohlibah. Oholah and Oholibah are the personified rival kingdoms, who are besotted with the foreign nations Egypt, Assyria and Babylon. The name Oholah translates as "her tent" and Oholibah as "my tent is in her", according to Streete, the names are metaphors for female genitals. The text serves as a warning against idolatry and is portrayed through the violent abuse of women's bodies at the hands of men.[19] The women within the narrative are depicted as "whores" who are violently degraded, raped and tortured. The abuse is divinely justified as the prophet Ezekiel presents the text as a divine speech from YHWH (23:1). The two sisters are described as coming from one mother (23:2), yet no reference is made to a father. The reader is informed that as children, "they played the whore...their breasts were caressed, and their virgin bosoms fondled" (23:3). From childhood they became the wives of YHWH (23:4), their virginity was taken from them, and they were labelled "whores". From the very beginning of this chapter there is nothing decent about this Biblical text, it uses sexual violence, paedophilia, and therefore enforced prostitution, rape and sexual abuse as a means of describing two idolatrous nations that are divinely condemned.

The feminisation of the rebellious cities and enemy states is not unusual in Old Testament texts. The idolatrous subject is frequently presented as the "unfaithful wife" or "whore". Hosea for example compares the city of Samaria, "to a sexually dispossessed wife who is cursed with nakedness, and prevented by her husband from further illicit contact with her lovers (Hos. 2.1–13)."[20] As the postcolonial scholar Gale Yee maintains, the sister 'whores' of Ezekiel are "sexual metaphors" and "symbolic alibis" depicted by the patriarchal male

---

18   Althaus-Reid, *Indecent* Theology, 71.
19   Gail Corrington Streete, *The Strange Woman: Power and Sex in the Bible* (Westminster, John Knox Press, 1997), 94.
20   Kim, "'Uncovering her Wickedness', 70.

elites "who wield political, economic and social power," in the context of colonial threat which later led to the conquest and exile of the elites.[21] Ezekiel
presents Jerusalem and Samaria as sexual deviants, describing how they have
whored themselves and betrayed their loyal husband in pursuit of their lovers.
The punishment for such adultery will be violent and extreme as a result of
their uncontrollable sexuality. Whilst a socio-economic and political critique
is exceptionally relevant to the text, the gender violence that is fundamental to
the whore metaphor cannot be ignored. Nor can it be excused as metaphorical
language. As Kim remarks, "metaphors originate in a socio-cultural context,
and reinforce the status quo of the established order of the society."[22] Furthermore the contemporary situation is one in which the epidemic of violence
against women is widespread across all societies. Therefore, there are implications of such metaphors when taking into consideration patriarchal abuses
against the bodies of women that permeate in the contemporary world.

The implications of the text are realised when the narratives of the women
whose bodies have been tortured in such a manner bring Oholah and Oholibah to life. As instantly similarities are drawn when considering the narratives of the *Mathamma devadāsīs*, where their children have no fathers, they
are said to only come from the mother, and like Oholah and Oholibah they
belong to the divine through marriage. Further, their sexual exploitation and
bodily degradation began when they were children, and as a result they are
considered "whores" for the rest of their lives. Take for example the narrative
of Prici who was offered to the goddess *Mathamma* when she was just a few
months old. Prici was dedicated to the goddess as her family faced extreme
poverty. Her mother had also served as a dedicated *Mathamma*. In describing her tribulations, she said: "*I was raped by my landlord from when I was just
10 years old. It was his right, so he told me.*" He took her virginity because he
wanted her to know that she was his property. By the time Prici was 16, the
Landlord lost interest in her, he gave her away to traffickers and Prici ended up
in the brothels of Chennai.[23] From childhood the *devadāsīs*, like Oholah and
Oholibah are married to the divine, their virginity is taken from them, their
identities become moulded by the hegemonies of power as they become the
sacred prostitutes of the village.

YHWH takes the sisters as his wives, "Oholah is Samaria, and Oholibah is
Jerusalem" (23:4), as van Dijk-Hemmes notes, in the midst of their marginalised

---

21   Pui-lan Kwok, *Postcolonial Imagination and Feminist Theology* (Westminster, John Knox
        Press, 2005), 81.
22   Kim, "'Uncovering her Wickedness': 70.
23   Prici, interview, Chennai, December, 16, 2014.

and defiled identities, "after having been required to look at themselves as depraved since the very beginning of their history, they now shamefully have to acknowledge that YHWH was nevertheless willing to take the risk of a marriage relationship with them,"[24] as well as having children with them (23:4). There are striking similarities between the narrative of Ezekiel 23 and the lived experience of the *devadāsīs*. In dedication the *devadāsīs* are married to the goddess, becoming her property; if she is un-loyal in the marriage she will face the wrath of the divine, for Olohah and Oholibah their disloyalty was their sexual relations with foreign lovers and their 'lusting' (23:5). The Dalit *devadāsīs* too, can be punished for sexual relations outside of their caste restrictions that are controlled by high-caste men.[25] According to Levitical code (Lev. 18:18), marriage to the sisters would be forbidden, just as marriage to *devadāsīs* is forbidden based upon religious traditions.[26] Yet for the contemporary *devadāsīs* marriage is also used by the reformist movements as a means of controlling the women's sexuality in order to force the women into adhering to heterosexual patterns of moral decency. For many contemporary *devadāsīs*, being the wives of God, has resulted in divinely justified domestic violence and sexual abuse, just as it did for the sister 'prostitutes' of Ezekiel. As the prophet describes, "both women are degraded and publicly humiliated in order to stress that their sexuality is and ought to be an object of male possession and control."[27] The sexuality of Oholah is deemed uncontrollable as she cannot help but be tempted by the exotic foreign colonialists who are clothed in wealth and splendour, Assyria's finest "handsome young men" (23:6–7). As a result, she is said to 'defile' herself by sexually satisfying these high ranking foreigners (23:7).

What is of particular interest here is the use of the verb *tāmē* (23:7), meaning "to become "unclean" and "defiled". Yee notes that "purity and defilement... extend to other relations with the nations, who are the racial/ ethnic 'other' of Israel...Personal relational defilement between the genders and communal

---

24   Fokkelien Van Dijk-Hemmes, "The Metaphorization of Woman in Prophetic Speech: An Analysis of Ezekiel XXIII," *Vetus Testamentum* Vol. 43, Fasc. 2 (1993): 165.
25   Marriage is also used as a patriarchal tool of the social reformists who maintain that *devadāsīs* are immoral women who can only be reformed and controlled through traditional, heterosexual, monogamous marriages are the only means of removing the *devadāsī* system. Indian feminists have been guilty of legitimising patriarchal notions of the family, "using quasi-feminist arguments" to maintain that monogamous, heterosexual traditional understandings of marriage can be used to control the sexuality of women, under the assumption that prostitutes need freeing from their role as sex workers. See, Van Dijk-Hemmes, "The Metaphorization of Woman, ":165.
26   See, Streete, *The Strange Woman*, 94.
27   Van Dijk-Hemmes, "The Metaphorization of Woman,": 165.

political defilement among the nations became interchangeable."[28] When read through the Dalit feminist lens, the defiled, "unclean whore", is a reminder of the persistent branding affiliated to the Dalit woman's "untouchable", "impure" societal status. The Dalit body is considered a ritually impure and polluting matter, that has led to the "torture, rape and murder" of those who resist such purity laws.[29] For the Dalit *devadāsī* who from childhood has had her sexual partners determined for her, the text depicts her embodied struggles. The *devadāsī* cannot have sexual relations with the men they desire, if she does, she risks offending the goddess and the high caste men, disobedience against her divinely ordained sacred 'prostitute' status will force her body to be further chastised. The Dalit *devadāsī* is deemed "untouchable", "defiled" and "impure", yet her embodied sexuality, her "tent", is very much touchable when the male powers desire it. The Dalit feminist theologian, Evangeline Anderson Rajkumar, describes women's bodies as the locations of hatred which are converted into "sites of violence."[30] Oholibah experiences such violence as a result of the jealous wrath of YHWH, as the lust turns to loathing (23:29) for both YHWH and the men of Babylon, and so they deface her, chop off her nose, kill her children and strip her naked (23:25).

The feminist postcolonial theologian, Kwok Pui-lan, maintains that the violence and "the pornography of these texts should be coded not simply as another form of patriarchal violence, but as colonial ethnic conflict framed as a sexualised encounter."[31] When placed into the context of the Dalit women, the "priestly elite" of Ezekiel become the colonialized high-caste men, and the Christian missionaries, as well as the reformers all of whom have sought to control the sexuality of the *devadāsīs*. Kwok Pui-lan notes how "the woman was used as a trope for the land and the nation, and sexual images became tropes for colonial dominance."[32] The description that follows of the *devadāsīs*, is shaped by the moral agenda of Christian British imperialism imposed on to the mind-sets of the colonialized and elaborates on their vilified depiction:

> Bashfulness, timidity, simplicity and delicacy are four ornaments of women; but if they are found in a dancing girl her occupation is gone and

---

28   Gale A. Yee, *Poor Banished Children of Eve: Woman as Evil in the Hebrew Bible* (Minneapolis: Fortress Press, 2003), 125.

29   See, Anand Teltumbde, *Khairlanji, A Strange and Bitter Crop* (New Delhi: Navayana, 2008), 16–21.

30   Anderson-Rajkumar, "Turning Bodies Inside Out," 206–208.

31   Yee, *Poor Banished Children of Eve*, 111.

32   Kwok Pui-lan, *Postcolonial Imagination and Feminist Theology*, 81.

she must starve...Our rulers being English people, they must not know the deception practised by the prostitutes...[33]

The children of Oholah and Oholibah, remain nameless and voiceless throughout the text, though they are punished for the apparent 'sins' of their mothers, "they shall seize your sons and your daughters, and your survivors shall be devoured by fire" (23:25). The identity and agency of the children is lost amid violence and condemnation. Similarly, Epp argues that "all *devadāsī* children, who have god as their father, face an identity question: are we *devaru makkalu* (children of god) or *sule makkalu* (children of prostitutes)?"[34] The children of the *devadāsīs* are frequently persecuted and marginalised based upon their lost identities.

The Dalit identity that resonates with the oppressed is witnessed in the bodies of the ones whom YHWH delivers into the hands of those who hate them, leaving them naked and bare, the "polluted" ones (23:28–30). For the Dalit feminist, Dalit women are those who are: "naïve, mostly illiterate, hardworking, ignorant, and poor, who experience untouchability, marginalisation, and discrimination in every aspect of their lives, yet cannot voice, analyse or use their struggle to develop a theory and to find their way to liberation."[35] The Dalit woman is forced to remember her societal positioning through the rigidity of caste violence that violates her body through caste, gender and economic based oppressions and sexual abuse. Like Dalit women, Oholibah too must be vehemently reminded of her sins and outcaste status, she is "forced to drink from her 'sister's cup,' the destruction of Samaria, a cup that is filled with scorn, derision, drunkenness, and sorrow. Oholibah will not only drink it but drain in, gnaw its broken pieces, and tear out her own breast (23:34), the breasts 'pressed' so fondly by her quondam lovers. All this is retaliation for her 'whorings' (23:35)."[36] Social constructs bound by patriarchy reiterate their control over the bodies of women through systems of evil, whether through casteism, racism, classism, economic or sexual exploitation. Drinking from her "sister's cup", leads to the self-mutilation of Oholibah tearing out her breasts, as an act of self-hatred of the female form. As Yee remarks, "Ezekiel reinforces the blame laid on her in v 30, and scapegoats the nation's sins upon her hacked up body. She herself obliterates the bodily sites of her erotic pleasure and guilt."[37]

---

33   Yatharardhavasini, quoted in Priyadarshini Vijaisri *Recasting the Devadasi: Patterns of Sacred Prostitution in Colonial India,* 151–152.
34   Epp "'Violating the Sacred': 24.
35   Nelavala, *Liberation Beyond Borders,* 25.
36   Streete, *The Strange Woman,* 95.
37   Yee, *Poor Banished Children of Eve,* 133.

Ezekiel is using rhetoric that directly attacks female sexuality, agency and identity, whilst justifying exploitation, rape and gender violence. Whether metaphorical or symbolic, when read in the light of the existential realities of sexually abused Dalit *devadāsīs*, the female figures used to exemplify this apparently 'deserving' bodily violence are brought to life. Furthermore, the dangers of such gender violence in Holy Scripture become apparent when read alongside the contemporary gender and caste-based oppression of Dalit women. The means by which the sexually passive, silenced, and condemned women can achieve liberation is only through the voicing of such narratives as a means of protest and resistance, thereby demanding justice, whilst exposing the injustices of the dominant forces. The gendered metaphorical language of prophetic literature, as Weems suggests; "teach us how to imagine what has previously remained unimaginable. In this case, the battered, promiscuous wife in the books of Hosea, Jeremiah, and Ezekiel makes rape, mutilation, and sexual humiliation defensible forms of retaliating against wives accused of sexual infidelity."[38] Therefore, "the imagining of woman as something else betrays habits of definition within a frame of reference that is dominated by the interests and the perceptions of the 'first' sex."[39] Using the Dalit feminist hermeneutical methodology of applying the lived experiences of the contemporary *devadāsīs*[40] to the text, makes conscious the ongoing exploitation of the women in order to move towards a Dalit Theology of protest. As it is the voices of the women who have been at the underside of history that have the potential to shame the hegemonic patriarchal forces that have chastised and abused their bodies.[41] By doing so, the *devadāsīs* help liberate the women of

---

38 Renita Weems, *Battered Love: Marriage, Sex, and Violence in the Hebrew Prophets* (OBT: Minneapolis: Fortress, 1995), 98.

39 This quote is taken from the Introduction to the Utrech Interfaculty Women's Studies Research Program, "Women between Control and Transition" and re-quoted in Van Dijk-Hemmes, "The Metaphorization of Woman", 162.

40 It is also vital to take into consideration the expressed agency of the dedicated *devadāsī Mathammas*, as expressed in the previous section, the "very fabric of the self of the devadāsīs must be taken into account because this is what shaped their way of living in and their attachment to the devadāsī tradition. See, Bernhard Ortmann, "Body Constructions Among Devadasi and Dalit Children," in *Body, Emotion and Mind: Embodying the Experiences in Indo-European Encounters,* eds. Martin Tamcke et al. (Berlin: LIT Verlagm, 2013), 12–13.

41 A clear example of such resistance can be witnessed in the recent *Dalit Women Self-Respect Yatra* movement, where Dalit women have marched and protested in India to fight against caste and gender discrimination, they are marching as an example to other women to resist dominant forces of evil. They have visited sites of gang-rape, voiced cases of rape, murder and abuse and they are demanding direct action. See, "Dalit Women in India Stage Month-Long March for Justice," International Dalit Solidarity Network,

Scripture, who have become symbols of evils, from the shackles of patriarchy – by standing in solidarity as contemporary victims of 'divinely' justified oppression. This is the irruption of the prostitute, where the silenced and sexually exploited bodies are given a voice, a voice that does not re-read the text under the pretence that metaphorical rape and abuse is some-how acceptable, but challenges the language of the prophets with a body theology shaped by the scars of sexual abuse, rape, the hacking off of breasts, the tearing out of wombs, and all other forms of bodily exploitation.

The prophetic texts of Ezekiel legitimatises the bodily fate of women by openly acting as warnings to all women to "take warning and not commit lewdness...they shall repay you for your lewdness, and you shall bear the penalty for your sinful idolatry; and you shall know that I am the Lord God" (23:48–49). Without rejecting, refuting and re-reading such passages from the perspectives of the women who have experienced such atrocities, theologies of liberation run the risk of further marginalising the contemporary realities of the bodily oppressions that are apparent within the text and outside of it. Re-reading the text of Ezekiel 23 with a preferential option for the Dalit *devadāsīs*, means taking the side of the disembodied female "whores" who are voiceless within the text. It challenges centuries of androcentric Biblical exegesis' that have justified patriarchal oppressions enacted on to the bodies of women. Such readings require, as Musa Dube argues, "suspicion of the patriarchal sexual morality of in/decency and for constructing liberating sex worker readings of the Bible."[42] A Dalit womanist interpretation deconstructs the text by applying the lived reality of the *devadāsīs* as a powerful tool of interpretation, in order to give the bodies of Oholah and Oholibah a voice, emotions and a religious and socio-economic identity, all of which have been removed from their marginalised, refuted and rejected status.

3   Tortured Concubines and 'Christ the Decent Woman'

The Bible has been used as a political weapon to justify female subjugation, as the Church has based its doctrines on the patriarchal narratives that prevent the liberation of women from hegemonies of gender based persecution. Sex workers have been condemned as worthy of bodily destruction based upon their sexual acts outside of the realm of marriage. Yet the men who enforce

---

accessed March 19, 2014. http://idsn.org/news-resources/idsn-news/read/article/dalit-women-in-india-stage-month-long-march-for-justice/128/.

42   Dube, "Review of Avaren Ipsen": 361.

themselves on to the so-called "whores", who rip off their breasts, take their virginity and deny them of their childhoods, are handed down no punishments. The God of Ezekiel 23 is entirely separated from oppressed women, he cannot and does not feel the suffering of the raped and broken women, he distances himself from them, judges and condemns them and authorises their slaughter. This is not an innocent metaphor but one that resonates with the mentality and doctrine of the Church that has since its birth proclaimed that the sexually 'immoral' woman is a representative of evil, sinfulness and shame. Throughout Scripture the bodies of women are used in order to engrave narratives of patriarchy, where the foreign seductress, rebellious wives, harlots, and concubines are punished for being powerful, sexually rebellious, and independent women. Such violence against women is entrenched within the narratives of war, the struggles for power, and prophetic texts that proclaim the omnipotence of YHWH.

The grotesque gang raping and murdering of the Levite's concubine in the book of Judges is one such example. As Phyllis Tribble describes, the story "depicts the horrors of male power, brutality, and triumphalism; of female helplessness, abuse, and annihilation."[43] The narrative tells the tale of a concubine who we are told has played the "harlot", she leaves her 'husband', and escapes to her father's house (Judges 19). The Levite later travels to her father's house to retrieve his concubine. Yet as an "ineffectual" and poor man, he is slow in doing so (19:2).[44] When the Levite and concubine finally leave the house of their father it is dark (19:9–10), they end up in the village of Gibeah, where they are foreigners. They are offered hospitality by an Ephraimite, who is himself a foreigner of this land. On the night of their arrival a group of "depraved" men come to the house of the Ephramite and demand that the Levite come out to them so that "they may know him" (19:22). As Wootton remarks, "they want to commit the ultimate act of violence and humiliation against a man, to rape him, to pierce his body."[45] The Ephramite instead offers up his own virgin daughter and the concubine.[46] He says to the group of men: "ravish them

---

43   Phyllis Trible, *Texts of Terror: Literary-feminist Readings of Biblical Narratives* (London: SCM Press, 2002), 65.

44   Janet Wootton describes how the Levite is clearly portrayed as being an indecisive and weak character, in his taking the suggestions of his servant and inability to take control over his concubine. See, Janet Wootton, "Biblically Slicing Women," in *Controversies in Body Theology* Eds. Marcella Althuas-Reid et al. (London: SCM Press, 2009), 158–174.

45   Wootton, "Biblically Slicing Women," 161.

46   The low status of the concubine is further highlighted by the fact that the Ephramite is able to give her away without the permission of the Levite. See, Daisy L. Machado, "The Unnamed Woman: Justice, Feminists, and the Undocumented Woman," in *A Reader in*

and do whatever you want to them; but against this man do not do such a vile thing" (19:24). The women's bodies are considered available for violation and destruction. Their silence within the narrative echoes that of the silenced women throughout history who have been trafficked, sold into the sex trade, raped and tortured. Furthermore, the indignation with which the group of men treat the Levite and Ephramite men, echoes the way in which caste discrimination perpetrates itself in battles of masculinity within India. The threat of male rape should not therefore be ignored within the narrative, as Valorie Vojdik remarks:

> Like the rape of women, the rape and sexual violation of men constructs and enforces actual and symbolic gendered power on several levels… to maintain and enforce the established gender order; to weaken, demoralize, and destroy collectives of people; to construct ethnicity, national, and other forms of collective identity; and to both construct and resist the dominance of transnational and global actors…sexual violence against male victims functions to masculinize and empower the perpetrator/ collective and feminize/conquer the victim/collective. Both function as gendered tools to empower particular male groups within specific social spaces.[47]

As a form of patriarchal resistance the Ephramite man offers up the women – an act that is symbolic of the worthless positioning of women's bodies in a misogynistic society where they are used as by-products of male domination. The men then violently gang rape the concubine, they abuse and torture her body throughout the night (19:25). The atrocity committed against the concubine mirrors the narrative of one such incident in Uttar Pradesh, where one evening two teenage girls were taken from their home, the next morning the family woke to find their bodies hanging from a mango tree in the village. Throughout the night they had been gang raped, tortured and brutally murdered. Their bodies were then hung, exemplifying the fearless hegemonies of patriarchy and casteism.[48] The concubine is found lying at the door of

---

Latina Feminist Theology: Religion and Justice, eds. María Pilar Aquino, et al. (Texas: University of Texas Press, 2002), 164.

47   Valorie K. Vojdik, "Sexual Violence Against Men and Women in War: A Masculinities Approach," *Nevada Law Journal* Vol. 14 (2014): 926–927.

48   Zee Media Bureau, "Uttar Pradesh Shocker: Two Sisters Gang-Raped. Hanged from Tree; 4 Arrested," *Zee News India*, May 29, 2014, accessed February 17, 2015, http://zeenews.india. com/news/uttar-pradesh/uttar-pradesh-shocker-2-sisters-gang-raped-hanged-from-tree-4-arrested_935769.html.

the house the following morning, the master remorselessly tells her to get up. When she does not answer he throws her tortured corpse on to the back of a donkey and heads back to his home. "When he had entered his house, he took a knife, and grasping his concubine, he cut her into twelve pieces, limb by limb, and sent her throughout all the territory of Israel" (19:29).

For Trible "neither the characters nor the narrator recognizes her humanity. She is property, object, tool, and literary device. Without name, speech, or power, she has no friends to aide her in life or mourn her in death...Captured, betrayed, raped, tortured, murdered, dismembered, and scattered— this woman is the most sinned against."[49] Throughout the text the concubine remains nameless and silenced. Though she is not alone, as to her nameless body the names of the hundreds of thousands of women who throughout history have faced the horrors of domestic violence, rape, sexual abuse, neglect, torture and silencing, can be added. In her story we see that of the raped and murdered Dalit girls, the trafficked sex workers, the abused wives, the women of every age and place who know her journey all too well. And just as God appears to be missing or silent from the narrative of the concubine, we are forced to ask the question: where is God today, as women continue to face such torture, and when it is Dalit girls being kidnapped, gang-raped and hung?

The inexplicable silence of YHWH in this ancient world seems to tragically continue within the praxis of the contemporary Church, where God is kept away from conversations on gang-rape, paedophilia, enforced sex work and human trafficking. Instead theologies and doctrines either ignore or embrace the Biblical narratives where "prostitutes" are violently destroyed and women are deemed as being in need of sexually controlling. Questions therefore must be asked about the role of the Church when reflecting upon violence against women and the role of the prostitute. Thomas Aquinas for example called prostitutes a necessary evil:

They were permitted by God to prevent chaotic eruptions of sinful male lust...in other words, prostitutes protected 'good' wives from the immoral, lustful demands of their husbands. Prostitutes supposedly exhibited the sexual licentiousness inherent in all women, inherited from Eve, which good women repressed. The most 'holy' women, like the most holy men, were supposed to follow a celibate vocation.[50]

49   Phyllis Trible, *Texts of Terror*, 80–81.
50   Rita Nakashima Brock, "Marriage Troubles," *Pacific, Asian and North American Asian Women in Theology and Ministry,* accessed March 17, 2015, http://www.panaawtm.org/images/BROCK_Marriage_Trouble.doc.

It is based upon such patriarchal religious-frameworks that Christological reflections are formed and result in what Althaus-Reid argues is "Christ-the-decent-woman, making of our concept of God a permanently crippled dualistic shortcoming."[51] Patriarchal notions of sexual decency have therefore marginalised the women and men who act as a challenge to heterosexual and "decent" social frame-works, and when Christ is consumed by such hegemonies, he becomes the God of the straight man and the chaste woman.

The Churches understanding of sex workers does not appear to have progressed much since the Victorian era, where evangelical movements of the 19th century focused on saving the "fallen women", by bringing an end to their sinful ways in order to restore "decent" moral orders. As Frederickson describes: "evangelicals concerned themselves with winning souls to Christ and prostitution stood in the way of this goal. Any way they looked these women posed a danger. On the one hand, they were seen as luring men into sin and keeping men from reforming. From a different vantage point prostitutes were seen as victims of male lust in need of Christian teaching and charity to guide them to redemption."[52] Josephine Butler for example was considered a revolutionist and feminist of her time, and declared a commitment to the needs of prostitutes, deeming them as victims in need of support. Yet when describing the sex workers who did not accept the errors of their ways and refused to participate in the body of Christ, she writes: "fine flaunting courtesans who are carried away by vanity, and obtain high prices from rich profligate men, [who] less deserve our pity in their present phase of life; only that we know then to be on the fatal slope down."[53] Yet for those willing to accept Christ, she maintained they could be saved by the grace of God.

Such missiological praxis' echoes that of the Church in South India today, where, as one Dalit *devadāsī* remarked:

> I am told to accept Christ, but Christ does not accept me. The church will not let me and my children be baptised, I am not welcome to come to church services, I am not welcome because I am prostitute, so the goddess Mathamma will release her wrath because I have accepted Christ, and the Church still does not welcome me because I am a sex worker, what hope is there for me?[54]

51   Marcella Althaus-Reid, *From Feminist Theology*, 90.
52   Kristine Wardle Frederickson, "Josephine E. Butler and Christianity in the British Victorian Feminist Movement" (PhD diss., University of Utah, 2008), 359.
53   Frederickson "Josephine E. Butler and Christianity," 375.
54   Bama, interview, Madurai, Tamilnadu, November, 11, 2014.

For Althaus-Reid it is not the Bible but "it is the eyes of the reader that are responsible for the construction of the imagined Christian woman's body..."[55] As it is through the lens of patriarchy that women are imagined as ideal when sexually constrained and silenced, as can be witnessed in the reform programmes imposed on to the bodies of the *devadāsīs*, that have sought to enforce models of femininity and domestication on to both the *devadāsīs* and the goddess herself.[56] As on one ex- *devadāsī* named Pratima argues:

> There was no value for us as human beings [worthy of respect]. No human being derives value from being a devadasi. Now we cover our heads with the end of our sari and work into the evening in the fields, earning twenty rupees. There is value in that. We are beautiful and the people call to us, amma [mother]...they regard us with respect. [57]

The bodies of the *devadāsīs* have been devalued to the extent that many believe that they themselves as *devadāsīs* are not worthy of being treated like human beings. Is this why the Levite's concubine stayed silent, had she succumb to the bullying of patriarchal hegemonies where she believed that she was deserving of the atrocities committed against her? The bodies of women become reduced to the needs and satisfactions of the dominant forces – where only as chaste mothers are they considered worthy of any respect or at least tolerance. The Dalit activists and reform movements have reinforced this message through the marrying off of *devadāsīs*. Whilst there has been progress in the conditions of the lives of dedicated women, as Ramberg notes, "they also sever ties between humans and gods and eradicate the modes of life they produce. One kind of abandonment has been exchanged for another, or one kind of belonging for another kind of belonging."[58] God herself however has been missing from the churches focus on sex workers as She has been marginal to the debate. This has resulted in theologies that dismiss the bodily experiences of prostitutes whilst forcing a misogynistic moral order on to the bodies of women. A theological yātrā is therefore required in order to contemplate God

---

55   Althaus-Reid, *From Feminist Theology*, 99.
56   Ramberg highlights how "within discourses of reform she is figured as a goddess who neither claims nor enters the bodies of those she desires...but rather as a devi who merely requires a devotional and chaste orientation of the heart." Thereby transforming the perception of the goddess in order to make her a "decent" deity. See, Lucinda Ramberg, *Given to the* Goddess, 102.
57   Ramberg, *Given to the Goddess*, 105.
58   Ibid, 141.

in the Brothels with the bodies of the sacred sex workers. It is here that we may meet the Christ who is on the side of the "indecent" and oppressed.

4   The Prostitute at Christ's Feet with Her Matted Hair: A Model of Resistance

A woman, known for being sinful, walked in unannounced and uninvited to the house of Simon, one of the Pharisees, bringing with her a jar of ointment. She stood behind the man they call the son of God, and wept at his feet, she then bathed his feet with her tears, and dried them with her hair. She went on to kiss his feet and anoint them with her ointment (Luke 7:36–38). Who is this sinful nameless woman? For many scholars she is considered to be a prostitute, as she enters the public arena[59] to attend a banquet[60], and as Corley remarks, "the combination of the term 'sinner' with her identification as a woman known in the city makes it more than likely that Luke intends for his readers to identify her as a prostitute, or more colloquially, a 'streetwalker' or 'public woman'. She is known for her sexual promiscuity."[61] Her long unbound hair, used to wipe the feet of Christ is also said to be evidential of her prostitute status as "in the ancient tradition and in conservative societies, it is commonly presumed as shameful and unacceptable for women to have unbound hair in public."[62] For Martin Hugo Cordova Quero, she has come to be understood by many to be a prostitute who is now "remembered as the crying woman", who has become "an archetype for those who repent and seek salvation in Jesus." This is as a result of what Foucault refers to as the *normalising gaze*, where the sinful woman becomes the decent woman, turning her back

---

59   The labelling of the woman as a public sinner, "reflects the dichotomy between the public and the private realsm, the social separation between men and women." See, Nuria Calduch-Benages, *The Perfume of the Gospel: Jesus' Encounters with Women* (Roma: Pontificio Istituto Biblico, 2012), 55.

60   Kathleen Corley maintains that respectable women would remain within the private sphere and the public was reserved for men or sinful women, namely prostitutes. She argues that the woman in Luke 7 is most likely a prostitute due to the other people Jesus dined with, the "tax collectors and sinners", and that the description offered and the actions she performs including the erotic bathing of the feet insinuate that she is a prostitute. See, Kathleen E. Corley, *Private Women, Public Meals: Social Conflict in the Synoptic Tradition* (Michigan: Henderickson Publishers, 1993), 26.

61   Corley, *Private Women, Public Meals*, 124.

62   Nelavala, "Liberation Beyond Borders", 147.

on sexual immorality.[63] Yet when read through the hermeneutical lens of the Dalit sacred sex worker, the text exposes new models of resistance and mediums of prophecy and liberation.

If we are to accept that the unnamed sinful woman is a prostitute then as Ipsen describes her body would have been the "only means of obtaining adequate sustenance" as was the case "for the masses of unattached, unskilled, non-owning women and their dependents, displaced in the harsh colonial economy..."[64] As a woman in the city, who has sinned (7:37), her body then becomes the first act of resistance within the text, as she "sins" in order to survive in a patriarchal and colonialized context. In the same way in which the bodies of poor women today are sexually exploited in the market economy of global capitalism. By presenting that same body before the religious leaders, the unnamed woman forces them to behold her existence. Their discomfort can be realised in the reaction of the "decent" Biblical scholars, Christian theologies and doctrines that have instantly declared her a sinner, not the sinned against. Feminist Biblical scholarship is also guilty of further marginalising the woman by attempting to make her "decent". The feminist theologian Monica Ottermann's reading of Luke 7:36–50 for example suggests that Luke is "androcentric, macho, and Christocentric" as he "dirtied the memory and the good reputation of the woman of Bethany."[65] Thus the feminist theologian aims to cleanse the unnamed woman of her suspected "sinful" nature at the expense of sex workers and all who exist outside of the "normalising" gaze of the hegemonic powers.

The second act of resistance within the text is the unnamed, marginalised woman entering the home of the Pharisee, uninvited (7:37–38). As Calduch-Benages remarks, "our protagonist is not worried about the titles of marginalisation in her confrontations and introduces herself at the banquet in a typically masculine setting. She asks where Jesus is and goes directly to him. She wants to meet him. Transgressing all the strict social rules, she takes the risk of being repudiated, misunderstood, deprecated and condemned."[66] Read through the lens of Dalit women, this is an act of protest and resistance, as

---

63   Martin Hugo Cordova Quero, "The Prostitutes Also Go into the Kingdom of God: A Queer
      Reading of Mary of Magdala," in *Liberation Theology and Sexuality,* eds. Marcella Althaus-
      Reid et al. (Hampshire: Ashgate Publishing, 2006), 86.
64   Avaren Ipsen, *Sex Working and the Bible,* 128.
65   Werner Kahl, "Growing Together: Challenges and Chances in the Encounter of Critical
      and Intuitive Interpreters of the Bible," in *Reading Other-wise: Socially Engaged Biblical
      Scholars Reading with their Local Communitie*s, ed. Gerald O. West (Atlanta: Society of
      Biblical Literature, 2007), 150.
66   Calduch-Benages, *The Perfume of the Gospel,* 57.

it echoes the means by which Dalit women have been protesting against the cultures of violence, caste discrimination and atrocities committed against them. As Dalit women activists have been travelling across India, entering court rooms, temples, villages and places in which such violence has been perpetrated or ignored, in order to stand before religious leaders and legal systems and demand justice. The women, uninvited, are entering the places of authority, presenting before the Pharisees of their context, their bodies and their narratives of oppression and demanding justice in the here and now.[67] As a woman, deemed polluted, existing on the margins of society, the unnamed woman enters the house of the religious elites, the "Brahmins" of her context. In doing so she uses her body to challenge the social hegemonies of patriarchy and break the boundaries of purity, pollution and decency. She carries with her "alabaster ointment" (7:37) – she becomes the cleanser.

She stands behind Jesus, at his feet weeping (7:38). The third act of resistance through protest. Traditionally Biblical scholars have determined that her tears are a sign of her repentance, "so that we may read it and take this woman as an example for us in weeping for our sins."[68] Yet read through the lens of the downtrodden they appear to be tears of protest. Unlike in Matthew, where the "decent" woman pours expensive oil on the head of Jesus (Mt 26:7), the "indecent" untouchable woman in Luke positions herself at his feet. In the four-tier Hindu society according to the Manu, feet are symbolic of the place of the *śūdra*s, below them are the Dalits, the Brahmins represent the head, "the Khatri the arms, the Vaish the stomach...The Shudras were thus the perennial victims of this heinous social injustice"[69] and the Dalits have suffered even worse. Though she remains silent throughout, her cries of protest for the downtrodden are enough to bathe the feet of Jesus, thereby drenching the symbolic place of the Dalits. The cries of the unnamed woman sobbing at the feet of the incarnate God then come to symbolise the tears of the subjugated and all the women whose tears of oppression have gone unheard. The unnamed woman has come to Jesus because she has faith in him and believes he will hear the suffering of her people.

---

67   The Dalit Women's Self-Respect *Yatra* aims to the break the silence on caste discrimination and bring an end to cultures of impunity. See, Rucha Chitnis, "Meet the Indian Women Trying to Take Down 'Caste Apartheid,'" *Yes! Magazine*, October 26, 2015, accessed November 26, 2015. http://www.pri.org/stories/2015-10-26/meet-indian-women-trying-take-down-caste-apartheid.

68   See, H. H. Pope Shenouda II, *The Life of Repentance and Purity* (Sydney, Australia: C.O.P.T, 1990), 341.

69   Gurusaran Singh Saran, *The Wheel Eternal* (Pennsylvania: Red Lead Press, 2013), 73.

She then dries his feet with her unbound hair, and continues to kiss and anoint them (7:38). When read through the lens of the Dalit *devadāsīs*, the unbound hair is of even greater significance, as the matted hair of the *devadāsīs* is considered a sign of her divine status and calling – and also a further cause of social stigmatisation. As Ramberg notes, "magical hair marks the bodies of some *Yellemma* women, called by the *devi* away from family life and endowed with the capacity to heal afflictions and disperse the blessings of fertility and well-being in their communities. These capacities and powers are locked up in their hair as a sign of their renunciation of conjugal sexuality and their primary attachment to this hot devi..."[70] Barbara Reid also highlights how Paul maintains that women should braid or bind up their hair "for the sake of propriety and so that they would not be mistakenly identified with ecstatic worshipers of oriental divinities for whom dishevelled hair was a sign of true prophecy."[71] Reid suggests that Luke's intention is not to present the "sinful woman" as a prophet, like that of the woman in Mark (14:3–9) but instead it "has lost all prophetic significance; it is a gesture of love."[72] Although I would argue that the woman is prophetic – as she exposes the inadequacies of the Pharisees, protests against the social orders and challenges Christ to witness her brokenness.[73]

The physical actions of the woman are of great significance, for Hyunju:

> This detailed depiction of her movement is startling as it brings to the fore the physicality of a woman. Tears, hair, lips, and hands work together as her body language to express something precious in her heart and mind... The usual interpretation of her gestures tends to ignore or avoid any discussion of its undeniably erotic dimension. In the patriarchal and dualistic worldview that overshadows the eyes of exegetes, emotion belongs to the inferior order, physicality is suspicious and touch is feared as something dangerous.[74]

---

70   Lucinda Ramberg, *Given to the Goddess*, 100–101.
71   Barbara Reid, *Choosing the Better Part?: Women in the Gospel of Luke* (Minnesota: The Liturgical Press, 1996), 120.
72   Reid, *Choosing the Better Part?*, 120.
73   The letting down of her hair could also be an act of grief, as described by Cosgrove, in the ancient Mediterranean world, her unbound her could be representative of a "grieving ritual". See, Charles H. Cosgrove, "A Woman's Unbound Hair in the Greco-Roman World, with Special Reference to the Story of the 'Sinful Woman' in Luke 7:36–50," *Journal of Biblical Literature* Vol. 124, No. 4 (2005): 683.
74   Hyunju Bae, "The Moments of Divine Eros in Luke 7:36–50," in *Religion, Ecology & Gender: East-West Perspectives*, eds. Sigurd Bergmann et al. (Berlin: LIT Verlag, 2009), 41–42.

The unnamed woman is now empowered by her own sexuality and femininity, as her body takes a central role throughout the narrative. She shames the inadequate Pharisees through her tears and hair (7:44). Despite traditional exegetes attempting to disempower the woman by "giving her a place seen appropriate to women: the crying figure pleading for salvation"[75], she is the agent of her own liberation, whilst Christ forgives her, he celebrates her faith and her great love. He does not castigate her, nor does he tell her to go away and sin no more.

The narrative of the unnamed woman in Luke has produced "both empowering and oppressive readings, and has prompted a variety of interpretations."[76] The majority of Biblical commentaries have focused on the saving grace of Christ and ignored the agency of the unnamed woman, noting as Jeffrey Siker states that "far from not being a prophet, Jesus engages in prophetic critique of a religious teacher and leader who is quick to judge another but fails to see his own failings..."[77] For N. T. Wright, "Jesus turns the tables on the Pharisee. *He* is the one who is guilty of poor hospitality – almost as much of a social blunder as the woman's letting down of her hair...for Luke, true faith is what happens when someone looks at Jesus and discovers God's forgiveness..."[78] In doing so, Siker, Wright and others have dismissed the role of the unnamed woman entirely – as all credit is attributed to Christ, and the unnamed woman who dared to cross the boundaries of purity and break the rules of social convention, in order to place her marginalised body before Christ and cry the tears of the subjugated remains ignored. As an active agent "the anointing woman even prefigures Jesus' own footwashing of his disciples (John 13:1–20)."[79] This is a display of what Hyunju Bae refers to as divine eros, where the powerless becomes empowered: "By interacting with a marginalised woman in mutuality, Jesus grants political empowerment to her. He accepts her gift, and welcomes her as she herself welcomes him. Jesus 'reciprocates the reception she had given him.'"[80] For Marcella Althaus-Reid systematic and even Liberation Theology "has made Christ participate in the female identity's definition of being either a *puta* or a decent woman."[81] Yet Jesus welcomes the unnamed woman in the manner in which she portrays herself – allowing no other to define her.

---

75   Cordova Quero, "The Prostitutes Also Go into the Kingdom of God", 87.

76   Bae, "The Moments of Divine Eros in Luke 7:36–50": 41.

77   See, Jeffrey S. Siker, *Jesus, Sin and Perfection in Early Christianity* (New York: Cambridge University Press, 2015), 161.

78   N. T. Wright, *Luke for Everyone* (London: Society for Promoting Christian Knowledge, 2001), 35.

79   Bae, "The Moments of Divine Eros in Luke 7:36–50", 43.

80   Ibid, 45.

81   Althaus-Reid, *From Feminist Theology*, 89.

The tears of the woman are the means by which in her silence she expresses her protests against the systems that have forced her body to exist on the margins of society as an "indecent" woman or *"puta".* Reflecting on the unnamed woman in Luke through the lens of Dalit women enables new Christological reflections, where "the sinner and the prostitute become... a metonym of the sexually ostracized and economically exploited people with whom Jesus can be theorized as feeling at home."[82] Together both the unnamed woman and Jesus shape a model of resistance against oppressive structures of decency.

5   From Sinful Woman to Prophetic 'Prostitute': A Theology from
       Indecent Bodies

The unnamed woman, the silenced slaughtered concubine, the tortured harlots, and the all other persecuted women both in and out of Scripture challenge traditional theologies to focus on the bodies of the most marginalised of women, and demand that we ask where is God in the midst of such atrocities? The Dalit theologian George Zachariah's re-reading of the parable of the Prodigal Son, addresses this question by focusing on the prostitutes within the text. He notes that "the prostituted women are those who are, like Dalit women, socially ostracized" by colonialism, hegemonic orders of morality and religiosity.[83] The parable does not however focus on the systematic evils that have stigmatised and ostracised the bodies of the prostitutes, instead "it exhibits excitement over the *metanoia* of the son but says little about the system that dehumanises him." Zachariah therefore asks the question of whether "salvation is a rescue operation of young rich men from 'sinful' women" and "is there a Father who is concerned with systems that make women prostitutes and is committed to redeeming those systems and its victims?"[84] It is for this reason that Indecent Theology demands a recognition of the interconnectedness of theology, politics and economy, in order to unveil the God who manifests herself in communities of the marginalised, as "all political theories are sexual theories with theological frames of support."[85] Whilst violence against women

---

See, Margaret D. Kamitsuka, *Feminist Theology and the Challenge of Difference* (Oxford: Oxford University Press, 2007), 108.

83   Monica Jyotsna Melanchthon,"Unleashing the Power Within: The Bible and Dalits," in *The Future of the Biblical Past: Envisioning Biblical Studies on a Global Key,* eds. Roland Boer, Fernando Segovia (London: Society of Biblical Literature, 2012), 57.

84   Quoted by Melanchthon, "Unleashing the Power Within: The Bible and Dalits," 57.

85   Althaus-Reid, *Indecent* Theology, 176.

and the torturing and raping of their bodies continues to be a widespread phenomenon across all societies, a theology must be contemplated that does not support but destabilises the oppressive social systems that have endorsed and enabled the subjugation of women. Because as Mario Aguilar maintains, "any human being who is being tortured today is a son or daughter of God created in her image, thus synchronic questions about the presence or absence of God must be asked regardless of the indecency of the moment of torture."[86] Asking such questions whilst taking into consideration the lived experiences of the contemporary Dalit sacred sex workers requires addressing the theological and structural powers that have enabled such torture to occur. By doing so we are forced to reflect on God differently, as the bodies that the theologies of hegemony have assumed evil and worthy of destruction, become the communities through which the God of the oppressed reveals herself.

Such a theologising is "born in a dialectic of secrecy and occupying a place of dis/grace"[87] because it involves walking with God in places where money is exchanged for sex, where women lie dying of disease and where villagers walk by in disgust. It requires contemplating Christ whilst praying to a goddess and wearing a *tali*, because as Aguilar writes, "God walks with us in our world of disorder, creativity and changing human relations...God is our greatest companion because he is one of us."[88] Therefore without focusing on the marginalised oppressed and the "transgressive, episodic and deviant, vague and non-definitive" moments of life, how can we reflect on the God of life?[89] For the Dalit theologian Anderson Jeremiah, Christology from a Dalit perspective needs to re-evaluate and re-situate itself "to render it appropriate for the continuing peripheral lives of the Dalits."[90] This must include the indecent lives of the Dalit sex workers whose narratives are incarnational stories worthy of a theological yātrā. Much like the harlots, concubines and 'prostitutes' of scripture, their incarnational narratives of bodily torture, oppression, exclusion and stigmatisation, become prophetic as they force the church to address the systems

---

86   Aguilar. *Religion, Torture and the Liberation of God*, 2–3.
87   Marcella Althaus-Reid, "Hard Core Queer: The Church of Dis/grace," paper read at the conference "Queering the Church," Boston University School of Theology, April 18, 2007, quoted in *Dancing Theology in Fetish Boots: Essays in Honour of Marcella Althaus*-Reid, eds. Lisa Isherwood and Mark Jordan (London: SCM Press, 2010), 1.
88   Aguilar, *Religion, Torture and the Liberation of God*, 1.
89   Althaus-Reid, "Hard Core Queer: The Church of Dis/grace," 1.
90   Anderson H. M. Jeremiah, "Exploring New Facets of Dalit Christology: Critical Interaction with J. D. Crossan's Portrayal of the Historical Jesus" in *Dalit Theology in the Twenty-first Century: Discordant Voices, Discerning Pathways* eds. Sathianathan Clarke et al. (New Delhi: Oxford University Press, 2010), 150.

that enable such violence against women to occur, and challenge constructed models of decency. In agreement with Althaus-Reid in order to contemplate a Christology from the margins "we need to consider, for instance, prostitution, sexual options and the case for women differentiating sexual pleasure from affectivity."[91] Such a theologising "puts Christian theology very firmly into bed with God in a sexually active way"[92] noting that the bodies of the sex workers are not strangers to the divine.

The tortured "harlots" and "concubines" of the Old Testament expose the grave reality that these tales are not ancient myths but contemporary truths that the Biblical scholars and patriarchal theologies have legitimised. They call into question the authority of the Church as a moral community and through the Dalit hermeneutical lens expose the inadequacies of Scriptural interpretations that ignore the bodies behind the text. In doing so the bodies of the 'harlots', 'concubines' and 'prostitutes' become prophetic as "the human Jesus who received a woman's sensual expression as a fully acceptable act is also the divine Christ. The divine affirms the body, human sexuality, excessive emotion, and the erotic in the context of prophetic liberation."[93] The same bodies through their suffering expose the injustice of systematic evils – inclusive of caste and gender persecution. This is an Indecent Dalit Theology as it is "a positive theology that aims to uncover, unmask and unclothe that false hermeneutic that considers itself 'decent' and as such, proper and befitting for women especially in sexual matters."[94] The bodies of "prostitutes" and "harlots" therefore enable an incarnational theologising that is generated from the places that the Church has traditionally sought to exclude, rehabilitate and reject. The God of the prophetic prostitutes exists outside of the binary structures of theological heteronormativity because just as Christ rejected the idealised norms of decency by choosing the prostitute over the Pharisees – the God of the marginalised is one who through the incarnation opted to be immersed into the flesh of humanity and witness the injustices of hegemonic systems of evil.

---

91   Althaus-Reid, *From Feminist Theology*, 89.

92   See, Angie Pears, *Doing Contextual Theology* (London: Routledge, 2010), 127.

93   Hyunju Bae highlights that witnessing Christ through the power of the divine eros is of key relevance to the Asian feminist context as such a Christology "would counteract the portrait of Christ the Lord that lent its support to both colonialism and patriarchal dominance in the church and society." See, Bae, "The Moments of Divine Eros in Luke," 47.

94   Marcella Althaus-Reid, "On Wearing Skirts Without Underwear: 'Indecent Theology Challenging the Liberation Theology of the Pueblo'. Poor Women Contesting," *Feminist Theology* Vol. 7, no. 20 (1999): 39, accessed December 17, 2015. doi: 10.1177/096673509900702004.

6   Liberating the "Whore" in Dalit Theological Discourse

Within Dalit theologising the Bible plays a central role as a source of empowerment as it enables the development of a Christian Dalit identity. The problem
however arises when the identity is shaped by hetero-patriarchal Christian
theologising that portrays the 'decent' woman as godly, to the detriment of the
Dalits who transgress heteronormative sexual orders. Melanchthon describes
how the "potential of biblical texts for liberation, negotiated and renegoti-
ated in the light of the Dalit experience, makes possible the discovery of God
within the Dalit social and cultural milieu and their liberation from oppressive forces."[95] As understanding God as the servant-God is central to the Dalit
theological agenda, "to speak of a servant-God, therefore, is to recognise and
identify him as a truly Dalit Deity."[96] Yet the God of the Old Testament who
appears to legitimise the torture of women and the bodily destruction of the
so-called 'sexually immoral' cannot be ignored from Dalit theological discourse whilst such atrocities committed against women continue to be perpetrated in the here and now. Bodily and psychological violence committed
against Dalit women includes domestic violence, social discrimination, sexual
abuse, assaults and harassment, murder, rape, and gang-rapes, all of which are
portrayed as prophetic narratives used in the Hebrew Bible to impose a code
of moral order on to the bodies of women. Therefore, whether metaphorical or
literal such existential narratives confront the Church and theologies with the
bodies of the women who within traditional theology have remained invisible
and voiceless and therefore demand a re-reading of Scripture. A theological
yātrā with the sacred sex workers enables us to discover God "outside the borders of decent theology, and in the context of the Other as the poor and the
excluded."[97] It is an uncomfortable and indecent journey as it contemplates a
God that allows rape and re-imagines a Christ who learns from the prophetic
tears of a prostitute.

Sathianathan Clarke maintains that "a marked feature of Dalit theology is
the dual rejection of the violence-prone gods of Hinduism who serve *dharma*
impeccably by killing Dalits and Christian notions of a God who lauds it over
creation to bring about subjection."[98] In an attempt to reject the God of violence and remain focused on the Dalit deity apparent within the broken body
of Christ,[99] Dalit Christian theology has however risked further marginalising

---

95   Melanchthon, "Unleashing the Power Within," 58.
96   Nirmal, "Towards a Christian Dalit Theology", 224.
97   Marcella Althaus-Reid, *The Queer God* (London: Routledge, 2003), 4.
98   Sathianathan Clarke, "Introductory and Interpretive Theological Exposition", 25.
99   See, Arvind P. Nirmal, "A Dialogue with Dalit Literature," 80.

the lost voices of the tortured women of scripture and outside of it, by ignoring the passages that depict the angry, violent, patriarchal God who lauds it over the bodies of 'Dalit'[100] women. The body of the Dalit sacred prostitute has become the impure 'other,' as Anderson-Rajkumar suggests, "a pure Brahmin needs an impure Dalit to construct his power and identity. An upper caste woman needs the category of 'that poor Dalit' to thank God for her status and social location. The Pharisee needed the tax collector to define his piety and purity."[101] So what of the dedicated Dalit sacred prostitute? Her voice is excluded from theologising at the intended expense of her agency. In agreement with Martín Hugo Córdova Quero "theology has historically invested huge amounts of energy into fitting the *decent* patterns of societies (supported by the so-called *orthodoxy*) and condemning those that are considered *indecent*...which also privileges a particular conception of the body."[102] As sexual outcastes, the Dalit sacred sex workers have been rejected from the epistemology of "decent" theologising as they disrupt idealistic 'moral' orders imposed on to the bodies of women. Yet their sexual stories are narratives by which we can contemplate a radical and identity-specific Dalit Christology.

Linda Epp maintains that today's *devadāsīs* are India's poet-artists who act as a challenge to Dalit reformers, who endeavour to pursue a social reformist model to remove the *devadāsī* entirely from their historically rooted religious roles. She describes how "Dalit reformers face an impossible dilemma of embracing *devadāsī* existence as theologically and/or metaphysically valid and creating a place in the world other than from the periphery."[103] A Dalit *devadāsī* theology of liberation would involve revealing the struggles for both social and spiritual emancipation that will be encountered in what Pieris refers to as the "idioms and languages of the cultures such struggles have created," and witnessing the moments of resistance and protest where the Spirit is present.[104] In order to do so "we must question the ways in which divine power has traditionally been understood as omnipotent, omniscient, unchanging and unsympathetic or non-relational power."[105] The Dalit theologian Ayrookuzhiel further suggests that in the need to be counter-cultural in the Dalit search

100   I have consciously used the term 'Dalit' here to describe the sisters of Ezekiel 23, in order to account for the oppressed, outcaste and downtrodden bodies of the women.
101   Anderson-Rajkumar, "Contours of Womanist Theology," 207.
102   Córdova Quero, "The Prostitutes Also Go into the Kingdom of God," 81.
103   Epp "Violating the Sacred," 64.
104   Aloysius Pieris *An Asian Theology of Liberation* (Edinburgh: T&T Clark, 1988), 85.
105   Carol Christ, "The Road Not Taken: The Rejection of Goddesses in Judaism and Christianity," in Patriarchs, Prophets and Other Villans, ed. Lisa Isherwood (London, Equinox Publishing, 2007), 30.

for justice and freedom, "Dalits have to go further back and find again in the deeper Indic spiritual resources, myths and songs that which can sustain them in their struggle for human dignity."[106] By doing so, Dalit Theology would enable a space for the so-called sacred prostitutes to irrupt within theological discourse and challenge Dalit Theology to explore the roots of their identity and religiosity that is embedded in the myths of the goddess. By engaging in what Mantin refers to as "Goddess-talk", which she maintains, "has a distinctive role to play in renegotiating, re-visioning and refiguring such a paradigm shift."[107] This would require re-discovering the historically rooted myths and indigenous beliefs surrounding the identity of the *devadāsīs*, because as Melanchthon argues, "there are liberative streams within religious traditions other than the Judeo-Christian tradition as well,"[108] applying such narratives to a theology of Dalit *devadāsī* liberation exposes new waves of counter-cultural resistance. Therefore, in order to truly engage with the Dalit *devadāsī*, a Dalit theologising must contemplate her lived religiosity, in order to further challenge existing epistemes and present a truly identity specific Dalit theological discourse of liberation.

---

106   Hans Ucko describes the writings of A. M. Abraham Ayrookuzhiel, see, Hans Ucko, *The People and the People of God*, 116.

107   Ruth Mantin, "Dealing with a Jealous God: Letting go of Monotheism and 'Doing' Sacrality," in *Patriarchs, Prophets and Other Villains*, ed. Lisa Isherwood (London: Equinox Publishing, 2007), 49.

108   Monica Melanchthon, "Indian Dalit Women and the Bible", 219.

CHAPTER 5

Towards an Indecent Dalit The(a)ology with the Silenced Goddess

You are the deity who expels our troubles; come rid us of evil.
You are present in the neem leaves for driving out women's afflictions.
You are present in the fire, the head of our religion.
You have lived with fame in our village, Malaipallaiyani...

• • •

You are the goddess who guards boundaries:
You protect with your spear;
You will protect us from 4408 diseases;
You will protect the Harijans from the torture of the High caste.[1]

∴

This chapter will explore the religious praxis of the Dalit village communities that is multifaceted, disordered, complex and community-specific, in order to be a subaltern and identity-specific theological discourse that is based upon the lived experiences of contemporary 'sacred sex workers'. It will reflect upon the lived religiosity of Dalit subaltern communities and the "emancipatory mythography"[2] relating to the goddesses that are grounded in praxis' of liberation for the Dalit people.[3] Such praxis and mythology challenges systematic

---

1 As quoted by Sathianathan Clarke, "this is part of an opening prayer of adoration sung by the local Paraiyar *Pucari,* K. Pallaiyasn." See, Sathianathan Clarke "Reviewing the Religion of the Paraiyar: Ellaiyamman as an Iconic Symbol of Collective Resistance and Emancipatory Mythology," in *Religions of the Marginalised: Towards a Phenomenology and the Methodology Study,* ed. Gnana Robinson (Delhi: ISPCK, 1998), 35.

2 See, Clarke, "Paraiyars Ellaiyamman as an Iconic Symbol of Collective Resistance," 35–53.

3 Despite such liberative potential there have been concentrated efforts by certain Dalit movements to disassociate with the religious past that was considered "holistically digressive", superstitious and irrational.

Christian theologies and Church dogmatics as they are born out of the experiences of the most marginalised communities and reveal profound truths about the God of the oppressed in the most "indecent" of places. This chapter will consider the Christological implications of such Dalit goddess religiosity. It will do so whilst moving towards an Indecent Dalit theological discourse, as it forces Dalit Theology to contemplate the Dalit Christ in the brothels of *Mathamma*, where Jesus becomes a goddess who understands the needs of a sex worker. Contemplating Christ from a Dalit the(a)ological[4] perspective and moving towards an indecent Dalit theological discourse challenges the theologies, which, as Ruether writes, are "built on many millennia of repressed fear of the power of female bodily processes,"[5] and enable us to engage with the hybridity of multiple religious belonging, and indecent and oppressed identities in the South Indian village.

The myths, folklores and traditions surrounding the Dalit village deities, particularly the goddesses *Mathamma* and *Yellamma* are challenging to androcentric Indian Christian theologies, as they enable an encounter with the divine feminine of Dalit religious praxis.[6] Furthermore, the religious hybridity and multiple religious belonging, that is apparent in Dalit village communities, challenges existing models of liberation theology. Along with the variant interwoven forces of oppression, inclusive of caste, gender and poverty that have forced the *devadāsīs* into their current social positioning, there needs to be a space to theologise on the place of the goddess in the lives of the *devadāsīs* and Dalit communities as a whole, as "within the Dalit world, the initial encounters of the divine are perceived and expressed as the divine feminine."[7] As the

---

4 The(a)ology refers to a 'goddess theology', otherwise referred to as Thealogy, as Isherwood and Stuart describes "Thealogy differs from Christian feminism in that it endeavours to begin its reflection in a space beyond patriarchal religion…Thealogy maintains that patriarchy has de-sacralized and demonised women's bodies and it seeks to resacralize women's bodies." See, Lisa Isherwood and Elizabeth Stuart, *Introductions in Feminist Theology* (Sheffield: Sheffield Academic Press, 1998), 79.
  See, Susan Frank Parsons, *The Cambridge Companion to Feminist Theology* (Cambridge: Cambridge University Press, 2002), 79.
5 Rosemary Ruether, "Women's Body and Blood: The Sacred and the Impure," in *Through the Devil's Gateway: Women, Religion and Taboo*, ed. A. Joseph (London: SPCK, 1990), 18–19.
6 Despite concentrated efforts to portray the goddess as an evil force that condemns child girls into a life of sexual servitude, the deity's mythological background and historic worship forms contradict the negative narratives that have embedded contemporary Mathamma's into lives of poverty, sexual abuse and caste-based discrimination.
7 Joseph Prabhakar Dayam, "Gonthemma Korika: Reimagining the Divine Feminine in Dalit Christian Theo/alogy," in *Dalit Theology in the Twenty-first Century: Discordant Voices, Discerning Pathways*, eds. Sathianathan Clarke et al. (New Delhi: Oxford University Press, 2010), 142.

Dalit theologian, Joseph Prabhakar Dayam states, Dalit theology "must be a
critical discourse on the experiences of the divine encounters mediated to
the community through the gods and goddesses."[8]Without divulging into the
context and histories of the Dalit village deities, the liberative potential of the
goddess is emitted from Dalit theological discourse and a vast proportion of
Dalit histories and identities are lost and excluded. Yet despite goddess worship being central to religious beliefs in India, Dalit theology has not "engaged
the goddess traditions in its attempts to make sense of the Christian faith."[9]
Therefore, this chapter will explore the diverse myths and beliefs operant in
the religions of the Dalit communities that create dynamic and identity-specific, liberative, caste-resistant theologies. This final chapter seeks to provide
a model of Dalit Liberation Theology that supports the need to be affirmative
to the Dalit identity yet challenges existing Dalit theological discourses to see
beyond the hetero-patriarchal gaze. It therefore aims to move Dalit Theology
towards an Indecent Dalit Theology as the sexual narratives of the oppressed
Dalit women expose worship patterns, beliefs, mythology and suffering that
challenges the normative gaze of androcentric Dalit theological discourses
and reveals prophetic movements and moments of resistance and lived theologies of liberation.

1   The Re-Birth of the Goddess in Dalit Theologising

Matriarchal goddess worship dominates rural village religiosity in South India;
the ethnologist Edgar Thurston witnessed in his 19th century studies that
each village claimed its own mother goddess, he writes: "each is supposed to
be guardian of the boundaries of the cherished. She is believed to protect its
inhabitants and its livestock from disease, disaster and famine, to promote
the fecundity of cattle and goats, and to give children."[10] The *devadāsī* institution has become intertwined with the history and worship of such deities,
however during the 1700s the *devadāsī* status was transformed, as "certain religious, social, and political developments took place that provided resources
for the transformation of the identity of the *devadasi*..." as such transformations occurred the goddesses identities were sancritised and re-imagined as
being part of a divine married couple. This resulted in the increasing stress on

---

8   Joseph Prabhakar Dayam, "Gonthemma Korika: Reimagining the Divine Feminine in
        Dalit Christian Theo/alogy," 142.
9   Ibid, 142.
10   Thurston, *Castes and Tribes of South India*, 105.

the necessity for the dedicated women to be married and female sexuality to be controlled.[11] Liddle and Joshi, note that "the concept of marriage, involving male control of female sexuality, is important for understanding how the mother goddess was incorporated into the patriarchal brahmin religion. In the villages, the old matriarchal religion was brahminised by providing orthodox male deities as husbands of the mother goddesses."[12] However, despite consistent efforts to control the religious deities of the Dalits, Clarke highlights how the goddesses of certain Dalit communities inclusive of the *Ellaiyamman* goddess of the Paraiyars refused to be colonialised by the high-castes. Instead the "Paraiyars' goddesses remain single, unmarried, and unobliged to the Hindu Gods. They refuse to be co-opted and domesticated by the larger symbols of power as represented by the Hindu gods."[13] Certain goddesses therefore remain counter-cultural and identity specific to Dalit communities.

Historically the non-Brahminical religions of the rural villagers have belonged to the Dalit people, many of whom attempted to reject Brahminical impositions on their religious beliefs. Liddle and Joshi, highlight how the rejection came as a result of the attempt to control women's sexuality, "the religious myths of the brahmins may tell the story of women's destructive power and how it was constrained by men through control of women's sexuality, but the religion of the common people tells the story of women's continuing power and resistance to male control."[14] The socio-religious identity of the women dedicated to the goddess *Mathamma* has been negatively transformed as a result of caste and colonial influences, where religious identities and divine rights embodied in the female form came to be considered as dangerous, and thus in need of controlling. Fuller maintains that as a result, the religiosity involved in *Mathamma* worship "cannot symbolise the equality and liberation of the lower castes."[15] In contrast Anandhi suggests that a self-proclaimed identity can be reclaimed through ritual traditions that oppose the 'impure' occupational rigidity of the caste system, as "the ritual space and the construction of such traditions can be important sites of reconstituting ones self-identity and producing alternative moral discourses by contesting notions

11   See, Epp "'Violating the Sacred', 126.
12   Joanna Liddle & Rama Joshi *Daughters of Independence: Gender, Caste and Class in India* (London: Zed Books, 1986), 54.
13   Clarke, "Paraiyars Ellaiyamman as an Iconci Symbol," 38.
14   Liddle & Joshi *Daughters of Independence*, 55.
15   C. J. Fuller, "The Hindu Pantheon and the Legitimation of Hierarchy", *Man*, Vol. 23, No. 1, (1998): 37

of untouchability and injustice."[16] One such example is that of the goddess
Matangi, a Dalit deity who challenges the purity laws.

Foulston refers to the Dalit goddess *Matangi* as "the outcaste goddess", as she
is associated with pollution and left-over food and is "an embodiment of inauspiciousness and the forbidden, the goddess exemplifies the transcendence of
social norms associated with Tantric practice."[17] The goddess challenges ideal
notions of Indian womanhood as well as ridiculing societal rules of purity and
pollution, "through the offering of impure substances and practices the Tantric
sadhaka aims to overcome worldly values regarding pollution..."[18] For the "outcaste" Dalit communities the deity "*Matangi* is then perceived as liberating
in nature, offering her devotees the chance of salvation through transcendence of pollution."[19] She is worshipped by those who are deemed "polluted"
and "untouchable" and rewards the polluted peripheral nature of her people
by requesting that worship styles take the form of further polluting motifs,
inclusive of the offering of left-over food. Foulston maintains that "these con-
notations of inauspiciousness and death indicate *Matangi's* connection with
the boundaries and periphery of Hindu society, key themes in Tantric practice." The goddess challenges notions of purity as she "embodies the idea of
transgression and provides a prime focus for Tantric adherents aiming to overcome aversion to social pollution in the hope of achieving religious liberation
or gaining magical powers for worldly aims."[20] The Dalit goddess *Matangi* is
therefore considered to be the goddess of the periphery, as she takes the side
of the oppressed by challenging social practices and polluting herself in the
process.

Dalit goddesses reveal liberative motifs specifically to the Dalit women,
as in the temples of *Yellemma* and *Mathamma*, the goddess in her female
form knows the emotional and physical pain and torment of her devotees.
Such religiosity is instantly challenging to androcentric Christian theologies.
In agreement with Carol Christ, the "Goddess is a symbol of the divine as
female and therefore of femaleness as divine or in the image of divinity. Reimagining divine power as Goddess has important psychological and political
consequences."[21] This is particularly the case when contemplating Christian
theologies with the dedicated Dalit sacred sex workers. As the *devadāsīs* are

---

16   Anandhi, "Gender, Caste and the Politics:" 66.
17   Lynn Foulston and Stuart Abbott, *Hindu Goddesses: Beliefs and Practices* (Brighton: Sussex
       Academic Press, 2009), 123.
18   Ibid, 123.
19   Ibid, 123.
20   Ibid, 123.
21   Carol Christ, "The Road Not Taken," 29–30.

directly associated with the divine feminine and therefore the psychological implications of journeying with the symbolism and myths relating to a female deity offers the opportunity to move away from static patriarchal images of the divine and reimagine a liberative goddess that is not physically and sexually controlled by hegemonic communities. Further, re-imaging the divine as female within Dalit Christian theological discourse is psychologically and politically critical for the women who have for centuries been dominated by a male God, that has resulted in female subservience to male power and divinely justified sexual abuse.

2 A *Tali* around Her Neck and a Bible in Her Hand: Indecent Religious Hybridity in the South Indian Village

As a dedicated sacred sex worker, the religious narrative of Mathamma Kanaganithian is disruptive to conventional constructions of Christian identity. She is a devotee to the goddess yet she has converted to Christianity and continued to wear her *tali* – a symbol of her marriage and commitment to the goddess *Mathamma*. I met Mathamma Kanaganithian in a church in Nagalapuram, a rural village in Andhra Pradesh, where she worshipped but was not allowed to be baptised as a result of her "immoral" past. When we met she described her love of Christ who had saved her and her children from the "shame" of being a practising *devadāsī*. As a dedicated Christian and goddess devotee she automatically transgresses the boundaries of colonial Christianity by remaining "married" to the goddess, as she further declared: *"I do not want to be punished by the goddess, if I take off my tali I will offend her, then I or a member of my family could become sick."* Yet alongside this she also declared her beliefs in the God Jesus, noting: *"By accepting Jesus I will be welcomed into the Kingdom of heaven, if I do not, then I go to hell…when I need food or when people try and attack me, I ask Jesus to help me, and he will feed my family and comfort me through the night when I cry."* Her religious hybridity initiates a new religious identity that is shaped by her experience of both the goddess and Christ, where she simultaneously lives with beliefs in both, and allows both Christ and the goddess to structure her meaning of life. Jesus like *Mathamma* is perceived as a village deity, owned by the Dalit community, and as a God who acts in the here and now, who protects and punishes. This adheres to Anderson Jeremiah's study of Christianity amongst the Paraiyars of South India, as he notes that "there is no discontinuity in the Paraiyar Christian's perception of gods and goddesses, but rather that there is a confluence of local Paraiyar and Christian worldviews, giving forth a highly polyphonic, highly functional and contextually relevant perception of Yesusami."[22] Jesus for the dedicated devotee of the goddess offers a means of escape from existing social orders that subjugate her bodily experience. Yet she continues to operate from a multiple religious belonging positioning as a result of her identity specific religious and spiritual locality.

Mathamma's existential religious experience is an embodiment of religious hybridity. As Homi Bhabha understands the concept of religious hybridity "not as a mere fusion of two cultures or spaces but as the creation of a third space that is characteristically different from the original two and allows both of them some level of fluidity in their identity as they relate to each other."[23] Mathamma creates a "blurred" space of religious identity and "borderless" spirituality in her love of Jesus and sustained belief in the ultimate powers of the goddess. The ministers of the church described her beliefs and that of her community with regards to the goddess as "superstitious." In doing so, the church as the dominant power degrades the Dalit religiosity and suppresses the goddess as mere "superstition". Ramberg notes that "to ask what counts as religion is to pose a question about forms of knowledge as they intersect with relations of power. Whose ways of talking to gods and spirits are designated as religion, and whose are stigmatised as superstition?"[24] In Mathamma's religious context, the Christian church appears to hold the intellectual hegemony in the same way the project of modernity during the Enlightenment period used colonialism and Christian mission to preach "morality, new humanity, justice, and happiness"[25] at the expense of the colonialized indigenous belief systems. It does so by assigning the supremacy of Christianity over and against all other religious belief systems, where the local village religiosity is stereotyped as ignorant superstition. According to Kwok Pui-Lan, "the necessity of the creation of stereotypes points to the unstable psyche of the colonisers and the contradictory nature of colonial authority...colonialism violently impinges one culture upon another, the colonial subjects have to learn a foreign tongue

22   Yesusami, is the Tamil name for Jesus that is used in Jeremiah's study of Dalit Christians in Thulasigtamam – it translates as 'God Jesus'. See, Anderson H. M. Jeremiah, *Community and Worldview among Paraiyars of South India* (London: Bloomsbury, 2013), 153.

23   See, Raj Nadella, "The Motif of Hybridity in the Story of the Canaanite Woman: Its Relevance for Multifaith Relations," in *Many Yet One? Multiple Religious Belonging* eds. Peniel Jesudason Rufus Rajkumar and Joseph Prabhakar Dayam (Geneva: WCC Publications, 2016), 111.

24   Ramberg, *Given to the Goddess*, 5.

25   See, Chris Sugden, *Seeking the Asian Face of Jesus: A Critical and Comparative Study: The Practice and Theology of Christian Social Witness in Indonesia and India 1974–1996* (New Delhi: Regnum, 1997), 389.

and the cultural idioms of their oppressors."[26] In contrast the lived religion of the Dalit communities presents a religiosity that subverts systematic belief systems, as Mathamma moves beyond and within religious boundaries in order to negotiate her identity and alter her status as a sacred sex worker and practising Christian. Kwok Pui-lan outlines the lived reality of such multiple religious belonging as follows:

> Cultural hybridity challenges the myths of purity of cultural lineage, homogeneity of identity, and monolithic understandings of national cultures. Hybridity in postcolonial discourse demystifies the power of representation, for it can function as camouflage, contest, or a space in-between so that denied knowledges can be articulated and recognised.[27]

The religious hybridity of the sacred sex worker is an embodied and lived truth where "the less visible world and the visible world" are held "together as a complete unit in which human beings and spirits interact daily."[28] In the case of Mathamma Kanaganithian as with many other Dalit Christian converts in the South Indian village, she holds her faith in the Jesus who is the God who can act to help her now. This may mean transgressing caste boundaries, receiving meals from the church, schooling her children, or escaping sexual violence – the promise of an eternal life becomes less relevant when the needs are very much in this life. Yet her bond with the goddess cannot be denied, as it was the goddess who saved her from small pox as a child, it was the goddess who she was dedicated to, and it was the goddess who had helped her provide for her children. The religious paradigm of the Dalit sacred sex workers is indecent as it exposes the sexuality, economy, caste hegemonies and patriarchy of both society and theological constructions. As in agreement with Althaus-Reid "every discourse of religious and political authority hides under its skirts suppressed knowledge in exile which is marginal and indirect speech."[29] The suppressed discourse of Mathamma Kanaganithian transgresses the boundaries of religious belonging as her religious reality is ambiguous, multifaceted and complex, and fundamentally shaped by her resistance in response to her daily suffering and needs.

---

26   Kwok-Pui-lan, "The Legacy of Cultural Hegemony in the Anglican Church" in *Beyond Colonial Anglican Communion in the Twenty-first Century* (New York: Church Publishing Incorporated, 2001), 53.
27   Ibid, 53.
28   Jeremiah, *Community and Worldview*, 152.
29   Althaus-Reid, *Indecent Theology*, 20.

Problems however arise when the church insists on an exclusive religious belonging that refuses to acknowledge or incorporate the religious identity of the Dalit community. As Prabhakar Dayam and Rajkumar remark, "there is an overwhelming insistence on rigidity and singularity in the expectations made of our religious identifications and affiliations. Such a context poses problems to those who, out of necessity, upbringing, or choice, find (spi)ritual sustenance in other religious traditions alongside Christianity and openly acknowledge that they have been 'faithed' by drinking deeply from the wells of different religious and spiritual traditions."[30] In the case of Mathamma Kanaganithian and other dedicated women, the church along with reform and rehabilitation programmes has degraded the goddess, as well as the religious praxis of the dedicated women. As one church leader stated in response to a practising *devadāsī*: "*She is a prostitute, she says she is Dalit but she is not, she is not worthy of calling herself a Dalit.*" The church leader suggests that the Dalit identity is itself exclusive and does not include those who are sexually "immoral", he thereby reproduces hierarchal structures of patriarchy that are embedded within the church and enforces them on to the gendered body of the *devadāsī*. Furthermore, the church attempts to use resources such as food and education as a means of control over the body politics of Dalit women, as conversion and the denial of the goddess become pre-requisites for gaining access to church resources and a means of escaping caste discrimination and sexual exploitation – at the expense of imposing and perpetuating a rigid moral order and westernised religiosity.

Despite attempts to control the religious behaviour of the Dalit village communities inclusive of the converted *devadāsīs*, the religious praxis of the Dalit villagers remains transgressive in their understanding and worship of Jesus. Asked where Jesus is, Mathamma responded:

> "He is with me now, next to me, just as he was when I would do bad things, he is with me when I have sex with people for the goddess, he is with when I get called bad names and when I pray to him, he always answers."[31]

The religious experiences of Christians in the South Indian village are shaped by their daily struggles. For the converted sacred sex workers this may be the

---

30   Peniel Jesudason Rufus Rajkumar and Joseph Prabhakar Dayam, introduction to *Many Yet One? Multiple Religious Belonging* (Geneva: WCC Publications, 2016), 2.

31   Mathamma Kanagarathinam, interview, Nagalapuram, Andhra Pradesh, December 12, 2014.

abuse and vilification of their body, the fear of going hungry, the need for healing from their sexual transmitted diseases, or the desire for an education for
their children as a means of escaping their socio-economic positioning. Jesus,
like the goddess, is called upon to respond to such daily tribulations. Jeremiah
also recounts how like the Dalit village deities, Jesus is considered to have the
power to punish those who displease him, for one Paraiyar Christian named
Poovamma, it is because of the way that Christians in the community are
behaving, as they are jealous, envious and quarrelsome, that she is convinced
"Yesusami has punished her community to their present status of being Paraiyars until they learn to live properly."[32] Poovamma repeats the Hindu belief that
untouchability is a divine form of punishment on to her beliefs of Jesus. This
exposes the extent to which caste violence and the concept of untouchability
is embedded into the South Indian village religiosity as it cannot be escaped
despite conversion. Even Jesus in the eyes of Poovamma becomes an orches-
trator of divinely ordered caste persecution. Such beliefs also encapsulate the
potentially inhospitable side of religious hybridity where the dominant hegemony of the divergent religious orders, be it caste, patriarchy, racism, or classism,
are used to further threaten, control and subjugate the identity of the believers.

Dalit village religiosity is fluid in the manner in which it negotiates mul-
tiple-religious realities. As the religious identities exist on what the feminist poet Gloria Anzaldúa refers to as the "borderland" of identity discourse.
Through the postcolonial lens the "border" is "reconstituted as a psychic,
social, sexual, and spiritual terrain, which creates confusion and alienation,
but also offers the possibilities of decolonising the mind and creating social
change."[33] The hybridity of their religious belonging can therefore be understood as an imposed religiosity used as a tool by the colonialisers or hegemonic
powers that have enforced upon the subaltern their divinely justified moral
orders to subjugate and oppress the 'other'; but it can also be considered as a
means by which the individual can undermine the hegemonic religious orders,
as their lived religiosity disrupts and destabilises established categories. The
hybrid narratives of the subaltern communities are therefore not confined to
normalised categories of religious identity but cross the boundaries of religious decency. The religious hybridity of the contemporary sacred sex workers
therefore requires an indecent theologising as they are "made of these con-
tradictions and contradictums" where their lived religious experiences act as

---

32   Jeremiah, *Community and Worldview*, 88.
33   Kwok, "Changing Identities and Narratives: Postcolonial Theologies," 117.

discourses of resistance against religious powers.[34]Apparent in Mathamma's declaration that Jesus is there when she has sex for money, and when she calls out to the goddess, as it confronts us with what Althaus-Reid refers to as "a powerful transgressive image of God." As we are exposed "to the nude God who emptied herself in a brothel's kenosis of sexuality, poverty and violence."[35] Witnessing God in the midst of the indecent hybridity of Mathamma's religious discourse therefore forces a theologising that is troubling to Western monistic and systematic thinking as it challenges implicit cultural and philosophical imperialism that is apparent in the praxis of the Church.

3   Jesus and the Goddess: Towards a Dalit The(a)ological Christology

Feminist theologians, such as Carol Christ, have acknowledged the difficulty in producing a systematic feminist Christology that excludes patriarchal hegemony and is relevant to the bodily realities experienced by women. She therefore reflects on a the(a)ology,[36] where the spiritual experiences of women are central. For Christ, "the need to counter the dualistic and androcentric assumptions which had determined patriarchal religions made it necessary to turn to Goddess symbolism."[37] Her the(a)ology is therefore shaped by the embodied existential stories of women who are the oppressed and represent the 'underside' of a dualistic worldview and who seek authentic selfhood.[38] She contends that in women's movements where such self-hood is sought as "quests for truth or justice or being" spirituality is a central component.[39] Similarly Dalit Feminist Theology focuses on the need to witness the spiritual and Divine self-hood apparent within the authentic narratives of the Dalit women, who represent the downtrodden of history. Thus producing embodied theologies shaped by resistant movements of Dalit women. The(a)ology shaped by counter-cultural Dalit goddess spirituality and worship holds the potential to ideologically dismantle inherent processes of subjugation inclusive of androcentric Christology

---

34   Althaus-Reid, *Indecent Theology,* 20.
35   Althaus-Reid, *The Queer God,* 95.
36   The term 'thealogy' was first used by Naomi Goldenberg "to denote feminist discourse on *thea* (the Goddess) instead of *theo* (God)." See, Melissa Raphael, *Introducing Thealogy: Discourse on the Goddess* (Sheffield: Sheffield Academic Press, 1999), 9.
37   See, Ruth Mantin, "Carol Christ: Feminist Spirituality and Narrative," in *Contemporary Spiritualities: Social and Religious Contexts,* eds. Clive Erricker and Jane Erricker, 93–113 (London: Continuum, 2001), 101.
38   Ibid, 102.
39   Ibid, 102.

and oppressive purity laws imposed by the Hindu caste system, by decentring the theological powers and experiencing God in the communal experiences of Dalit women and marginalised societies.

For a Dalit *devadāsī* Christian theologising in the case of the dedicated *Mathammas*, this would mean exposing the embodied narratives of goddess spirituality and salvaging a Christian theology that becomes relevant to Dalit women who have only experienced the marginalising potential of male-centric Christian theologies. Whilst also taking into consideration patriarchal Brahminical societal control over female deities, that has transformed the goddess mythology and worship, resulting in the fractured identities of the *devadāsīs*. Conscious and unconsciously male-centric theologies have impacted the socio-religious and communal attitudes, as Daly argues, "the use of patriarchal symbols will inevitably reinforce the power of patriarchy and the use of feminist symbols will inevitably reinforce the power of feminism."[40] The religious identities of the dedicated *Mathammas* and Dalit communities as a whole are sites of contestation and transformation that seek to challenge the dominant forces but at times become subservient to subconscious control. Clarke describes Dalit religious communities as being culturally excluded and "either marginalised or co-opted", they therefore have to be "vigilant in their endeavour to preserve their own culture and religion."[41] Re-reading the mythology of the goddess from a Dalit hermeneutic of suspicion exposes the rebellious resistance of Dalit deities that offers liberative themes for a counter-cultural Dalit feminist Christology. Take for example the myth of the goddess *Mathamma*, where the head of a Dalit woman is switched with the body of the goddess Renuka.

When read through the hermeneutical lens of the Dalit, the goddess *Mathamma* is witnessed as a central deity to the outcaste Dalit communities because of her reborn, 'untouchable' status; when her son, Paraśu Rāma, went to behead her, she clung to her 'untouchable' maid, and as a result became polluted. When she was brought back to life, the deity was incarnated into an 'untouchable' body. It is as the 'polluted' goddess that she becomes '*Amma*' or 'mother' to the Dalits. As Prabhakar Dayam describes, "for the Dalits, the divinity of the 'wholly other' lies in choosing to 'belong' to the Dalit self by becoming one with the community and getting polluted in the process...By doing so the goddess privileges 'pollution' as divine necessity in her self-disclosure."[42]

---

40   See, Ellen K. Wondra, *Humanity has Been A Holy Thing: Toward a Contemporary Feminist Christology* (Maryland: University Press of America, 1994), 31.

41   Sathianathan Clarke, "Paraiyars Ellaiyamman as an Iconci Symbol," 37.

42   Prabhakar Dayam "Gonthemma Korika," 144.

Mathamma myths also focus on the symbolic victimisation and resistance of women, as both Renuka and the 'untouchable' woman are the victims of the male antagonist who survive and go on to become a divine power and source of hope and resistance. As Vijaisri states: "the goddess is thus a source of hope to those who are ill not because she has healing powers as such, but because she ultimately adjudicates the battle of mysterious demonic forces and turns the flow of vows and curses in favour of the petitioner."[43] Clarke further highlights how the myth "reinforces the fact that formidable divine power is generated to protect and guard her subjects from all harm."[44] Christian Dalit Theology that perceives the Divine in Christ as the pained, polluted, broken and 'untouchable' One, "who became the belonged to the un-belonged"[45] must consider a critical and constructive journeying with such aspects of the divine feminine that are historically rooted in the identity and communities of Dalits where '*Amma*' is central.

Religious expressions of the divine goddess and spirituality in Dalit communities can be both transformative and at times oppressive as can be witnessed by the embodied narratives of the contemporary *devadāsīs*, they are however the place in which Christ must be contemplated as they are the spaces in which Dalit communities have their own experiences of the Divine.[46] Francis Xavier Clooney questions: "how do we learn from religious traditions other than our own? How are we to assess what happens when that learning leads to affirmation and empathy, and thereafter affects how one lives one's own life?"[47] To retort to this, when contemplating Christ amid the spiritual narratives, myths and worship traditions of the goddesses of the Dalits, the gospel is contextualised into the narratives of the people and the revelation of the incarnate Christ is witnessed on what Felix Wilfred refers to as the banks of the Ganges. As the "Ganges then, symbolises the divine passing through our lives making everything alive and flourishing; it signifies the continuous flow of divine grace right through our life and its innumerable expressions."[48] A Christian theologising that recognises the flow of the divine passing through the Dalit villages witnesses the God who is untouchable, polluted, victimised and oppressed. Jesus is God for the Dalits as "the fact of being humiliated, excluded

---

43   Paul Younger, "A Temple Festival of Mariyamman": 507.

44   Clarke, "Paraiyars Ellaiyamman as an Iconic Symbol," 37.

45   Prabhakar Dayam "Gonthemma Korika,"146.

46   Clarke, "Paraiyars Ellaiyamman as an Iconic Symbol,"50.

47   Francis Xavier Clooney, S. J. "Passionate Comparison: The Intensification of Affect in Interreligious Reading of Hindu and Christian Texts," *The Harvard Theological Review*, Vol. 98 (2005): 367.

48   Wilfred, *On the Banks of the Ganges*, xiii.

and rejected goes with the very heart of Christian faith which has shown in the rejection of Jesus, his humiliation and passion that God is a God who is on the side of the poor and marginalised."[49] Christ's incarnation, is as Prabhakar Dayam states, "a journey of knowing the human pain and getting polluted in the process of claiming the parenthood of the god/ess. Pollution is a necessity of the divine disclosure."[50] Contextualising Dalit Christology amidst the Dalit village religiosity, challenges Dalit theologising to further encounter the Jesus of resistance and rebellion, who challenges the status quo and breaks down hegemonic systems of oppression. As M. E. Prabhakar maintains "dalitness is the key to the mystery of his divine human identity,"[51] the Dalit goddess must become one with the un-belonged in order to be incorporated into the emancipatory mythology of oral Dalit traditions, just as Jesus must become truly Dalit in order to be God in the Dalit village.

4 Jesus in the South Indian Village

The gods and goddesses of the Dalit village community are unmediated, communal and can be accessed by all, as such the Dalit village encounters with Jesus are shaped by a faithful praxis that is based upon the needs of the individual or the community. For the converted *devadāsī*, Jesus responds when he is called upon, whether that be for food, comforting, disease, or rain, he is "directed by the necessities of the human being."[52]Jesus therefore becomes real for the *devadāsī* when he participates in her struggles and suffering. The religiosity of the converted goddess devotee is therefore shaped by reciprocal relationships based upon her needs, the needs of her community and the needs of the gods and goddesses who require faith and devotion. Addressing such religious praxis, the Dalit theologian Jeremiah describes the existential religious experience of a widowed woman named Sathyamma who belonged to the Arunthathier caste (those who the Pariayars consider to be lower than themselves), she had five children, and was struggling to survive. In the midst of her struggles, Jesus had become a source of strength and comfort, "Sathyamma claimed that it is the motherly nature of god as expressed through

---

49   Wilfred, *On the Banks of the Ganges*, 132.
50   Joseph Prabhakar Dayam "Gonthemma Korika: Reimagining the Divine Feminine in Dalit Christian Theo/alogy", 146
51   M. E. Prabhakar, "Christology in Dalit Perspective", V. Devasayaham (ed.) *Frontiers of Dalit Theology*, (Chennai: ISPCK/Gurukal, 1997), 414
52   Jeremiah, *Community and Worldview*, 78.

Yesusami and experienced by her, which has given her the ability to face the world and carry on with life." She stated:

> When I was a Hindu I used to go to the Mariyamma temple and pour out all my sorrows at her feet. Now that I have become a Christian, I go to Yesusami in the church and pour out all my troubles and he takes care of it. He is like a father to my fatherless children. Yesusami is the reason for the well-being of my children. I have cried and prayed to him every day for them.[53]

Similarly, when I asked Mathamma Kanaganithian of the role Jesus played in her life, she stated:

> Jesus has helped my children, they now receive an education, they will not need to have sex to survive like I did. They will not be treated like I was, because now they are Christians and they can be married.[54]

Jesus like the goddess is received and worshipped as a local deity who expels the current troubles of Mathamma Kanaganithian, whilst the church may not accept her in her entirety, Jesus does. He becomes her god, not the god of the church, or the god of the colonialists or high-caste Christians. Jesus as God is understood as living amongst the people in the community, which as Jeremiah notes "provides a sense of ownership for the worshipper."[55] This is a common expression of religious belonging in the South Indian village, for example, Sasikumar Balasundaram notes how amongst Tamil tea plantation workers in South India and Sri Lanka, the goddess *Mariyamman* is worshipped by all caste groups, and upon asking each caste group on the plantation the caste identity of *Mariyamman,* each caste group claimed the goddess as their own.[56] The embodied religious discourses enable a crossing of caste boundaries as they take ownership of the goddess. Within Dalit village communities Jesus also overcomes caste and class boundaries as he is perceived as Yesusami, "not as Jesus Christ, part man, part divine… It is as though Yesusami is a god, not because he is God incarnate in man, but because he acts similarly to how other

---

53   Ibid, 80.
54   Mathamma Kanagarathinam, interview, Nagalapuram, Andhra Pradesh, December 12, 2014.
55   Ibid, 89.
56   Sasikumar Balasundaram, "An Indentured Tamil Goddess: Mariyamman's Migration to Ceylon's Plantations as a Worker," in *Inventing and Reinventing the Goddess: Contemporary Iterations of Hindu Deities on the Move,* ed. Sree Padma. (London: Lexington Books, 2014), 117.

Paraiyar gods and goddesses function."[57] Yet the feminine aspect of the Dalit *devi* that plays a central role in the lives of Dalit women in the community is missing from the narratives of the Indian church teachings on Christ. As one dedicated woman remarked, *"how can I believe in a god that is a man, when it is men who force me to suffer. This god man will not know my pain – so how can he be a god to me?"*[58]

In contrast Dalit goddesses, like *Masani*, a village goddess in the Kovai District of West Tamil Nadu, share in the pain-pathos that is identity specific to Dalit women, as both their mythology and worship is shaped around a shared narrative of oppression and resistance. The oral mythology behind the goddess *Masani* talks of a Dalit family who came to the village to find work as labourers. One of the young Dalit girls in the family was pregnant. One day she went to offer food to her husband who was working on the land, however upon seeing her walking alone two of the young high-caste men attacked her and tried to rape her. Yet the young girl shouted out in rage and cursed them, in that moment that were turned into stone. Another version of the oral myth talks of a Dalit woman who was pregnant and migrating for work, yet she suffered greatly as she was starving so she begged for food and water, yet nobody came to her aid. In the midst of her great suffering she declared a curse on those who denied her help and then she took her own life.[59] It is based upon these myths that she came to be worshipped as a local village deity who protects the Dalit women from the high-caste men and punishes those who bring harm to her people. As Muthu remarks, the goddess *Masani* knows the needs of women as she is present when they pray for their bodily needs, whether that be for children or when they are menstruating, "they take for this herbal medicine 'uthitamlai' thinking of *Masani*, and after taking it thrice their pain ceases."[60] The Dalit women's prayer to *Masani* outlines the goddesses intimate role in their lives:

> *In thou art dwelling*
> *The one who accepted motherhood*
> *Protect the beautiful lap*
> *With your acts of grace*
> *Protect the thighs of the devotee,*
> *The one coming from the race of justice,*

---

57   Jeremiah, *Community and Worldview*, 153.
58   Village life, fieldnotes, Nagalapuram, Andhra Pradesh, December 11, 2014.
59   Muthu, *Dalit Deities*, 64–65.
60   Ibid, 71.

Protect my knees.
The one makes others happy with auspicious things
Protect the ankle beautifully.
Beautifully protect the breasts Pollachi Mother...
The one who shows justice to the world
Protect me when I stand or walk,
When I breathe in your hand
Protect me graciously
Protect me Oh! Masaniamman,
Driving away all evils.[61]

According to Aloysisus Pieris in the Asian context "religion is life itself rather than a function of it, being the all-pervasive ethos of human existence."[62] This is even more true in the context of the South Indian Dalit village, where the gods and goddesses are very much part of the community. As the mythology, worship, prayers and lived theologies are born out of the Dalit community struggles. The gods and goddesses are conceived in the midst of such existential realities and it is here that the image of Jesus Christ is reborn through the Dalit experience. Jesus becomes a local village deity who is contextually relevant to the needs of the people, the gender of Jesus becomes irrelevant when he functions as the god of the Dalit women who meets their needs and escapes the colonialist missiological lens through which he is preached by the church. As Jeremiah notes, "the feminine nature of Yesusami as expressed by the Paraiyar Christian community undermines the distant, controlling and authoritative image of God the Father, characteristic of Christianity as they have heard it presented in their local church. Their understandings of Yesusami give space for expressing anger, dissent or protest, either individually or communally."[63] A Christian *devadāsī* named Preci captured such praxis of faith when stating: *"Jesus is like a mother to me, one that did not give me away and has never left my side, she is always there for me when I ask, she responds."*[64] The Dalit village Jesus transgresses the fixed genders of the colonial Christ and becomes the God of liberation for the oppressed people as he moves with and amongst them in their community. Althaus-Reid maintains that the feminist theological methodology of reimagining Christ as a female does not sufficiently challenge heterosexual hegemonies, "her indecent approach to Christology challenges

---

61   Ibid, 79.
62   Pieris, *An Asian Theology of Liberation*, 90.
63   Jeremiah, *Community and Worldview*, 153.
64   Prici, interview, Tamil Nadu, Chennai, December, 16, 2014.

feminist theology by pushing feminists to see beyond metaphors of female gendering of the Christ symbol—as, for example, Christa—to the necessity of a more thoroughgoing 'obscene' Christology."[65] Such obscene Christology is apparent in the Dalit village when Jesus is said to be in the brothels of *Mathamma* and by the side of the devotee as she uses her body to feed her children and please her goddess. Locating Jesus in the lives of the sacred sex workers and Dalit villagers enables a true understanding of the incarnation. It is here that Dalit Theology becomes indecent theology.

5   Towards an Indecent Dalit Christology

> Through the teaching of Jesus, we are led to the conclusion that the poor person is Jesus. The prostitute is Jesus. Whoever does not help the prostitute does not help Jesus. Whoever claims to love God who cannot be seen and does not love the prostitute who can be seen is a liar.[66]

In order to construct a Christology that is shaped by the experiences of the Dalit sacred sex workers we must as Althaus-Reid argues be able to "face Jesus' historical shortcomings", noting that he is a male God who has not experienced the sexual discrimination and violation that the dedicated women have, and "who while charitable and compassionate towards individual women, does not concern himself with the reform of harsh laws."[67] Furthermore we must consider how traditional Christological contemplations have been shaped by patriarchal assumptions that have sought to control the bodies of women. Such praxis can be witnessed in the narratives of the *devadāsīs*, where the churches sought to make them "decent." There is a need therefore to reconsider Christ based upon the reality of women's experiences that may challenge notions of "Christ-the-decent-woman" that have been used to justify the bodily subjugation of women. Such Christologies were used by the colonialist missionaries and continue to be used by the patriarchal praxis of the Church that persists in its marginalisation of women who cross the boundaries of the decent heterosexual model of Christian morality. By holding such rigid systematic theologies and traditions with regards to gender, sexuality and human nature, the Church has made "impotent the revolutionary potential of the human/divine

---

65   See, Kamitsuka, *Feminist Theology and the* Challenge, 107.

66   Dom Antonio Batista Fragoso, a Brazilian bishop and a founder of the PMM, as quoted in Margaret Eletta Guider, *Daughters of Rahab: Prostitution and the Church of Liberation in Brazil.* (Minneapolis: Fortress Press, 1995), 73.

67   Althaus-Reid, *From Feminist Theology*, 6.

nature",[68] as it has failed to consider the radicalness of the incarnation of God. In doing so the praxis of the Church has become void of theological honesty and androcentric Christology has dominated the discourses of Christianity in India. There is a need therefore to deconstruct heterosexual and androcentric Christology so that Christ is not only identified with the poor man but also with the most marginalised of women. We can proceed to do so by constructing a Christology from an indecent Dalit perspective and reconsidering Christ in the brothels of *Mathamma*, thereby enabling a theologising that goes beyond the limitations of the historical Jesus. As contemplating Christ in the communities of sacred sex workers challenges hegemonic Christology by enabling the sexual stories of the dedicated women to be prophetic as they expose the inadequacies of the systems that have violated their bodies.

Western patriarchy has taught that moral judgment born out of the voices or experiences of women is dangerous and capable of causing spiritual corruption and social disorder.[69] Women have as a result been taught to hide, control, hate and be ashamed of their body. This is because as Isherwood argues "we live in a phallocentric world where even the language we use and the concepts that shape us are based on the biological realities of the male body, a body quite unlike the female body, yet a body against which women are designated."[70] Such phallocentric ideologies are reinforced by traditions and doctrines that vilify the sexuality of women whilst making the symbol of the Virgin into a Divinely idealised universalising construction of womanhood. [71]

---

68   Isherwood and Althaus-Reid describe the radical implications of the incarnation through a queer theologising that describes the "dynamic life-force" of the divine made human. The incarnation challenges the human and divine identities as "the divine immersed itself in flesh, and that flesh in now divine, is queer theology at its peak." Such a theology cannot strip itself of the humanness that is fundamental to the lives of the poor and marginalised. See, *The Sexual Theologian: Essays on Sex, God and Politics*, eds. Marcella Althaus-Reid and Lisa Isherwood (London: T&T Clark, 2004), 7.

69   See, Melissa Raphael, *Thealogy and Embodiment: The Post-Patriarchal Reconstruction of Female Sacrality* (Sheffield: Sheffield Academic Press, 1996), 187.

70   Lisa Isherwood, "Indecent Theology: What F-ing Difference Does it Make?": 142.

71   Althaus-Reid suggests that the mythology of the Virgin Mary presents a woman without a vagina and that "the Virgin Mary is not a woman but a simulacra in which the process of making ideologies and what Marx calls 'mystical connections' is exemplified." Such Virgin mythology is dangerous as it does not reflect the reality of womanhood and yet is used as an authoritative religious narrative that is reflected in the political and social life of the church. Just as Althaus-Reid notes how many girls and women in Latin America who worship the Virgin Mary are also "forced to marry very young and become pregnant with their first child when they are barely past childhood themselves," the same can be said for the Dalit *devadāsī* girls who are forced into marriages with the goddess and whose virginity is considered sacred and yet available. When the sacred feminine is defined through the hegemonic gaze of patriarchy, heterosexuality, racism or casteism, the Divine feminine

Contemplating a Dalit Christology therefore requires the unmasking of such ideologies and deeply ingrained beliefs and moving beyond the heterosexual imagination that has produced dominant theologies in order to repeat and reinforce discourses of hetero-normativity. Traditional Christian theologies have "been informed by an ideologically constructed love-knowing and a particular understanding of human and divine truth, but this knowledge is also constitutive of a way of thinking/acting theology."[72] The lived reality of the dedicated women challenge such ways of doing theology as their sexual stories expose the inadequacy of church doctrines that focus on controlling the bodies of women. By turning the bodies of women inside out in theological discourse it allows the invisibility of silenced bodies to challenge centuries of religious rhetoric and patriarchal abuse.

> *Say you bury me alive.*
> *I will become a green grass-field*
> *and lie outspread, a fertile land.*
>
> *You may set me on fire;*
> *I will become a flaming bird*
> *and fly about in the wide, wide space...*
>
> *You may dissolve me into the wind*
> *like water immersed into water;*
> *from its every direction*
> *I will emerge, like blown breath.*
>
> *You may frame me, like a picture,*
> *And hang me on your wall;*
> *I will pour down, away past you,*
> *Like a river in sudden flood...*

---

becomes a dangerous tool used by the powerful. We need to therefore challenge Mariologies and other traditions and doctrines that are not born out of the experiences of the oppressed and marginalised, as they have the capacity to produce false consciousness "concerned with the perpetuation of capitalist models of marriage, biological sexual definitions and universal faith constructions of women believers, submissive or courageous..." See, Althaus-Reid, *Indecent Theology*, 39–41.

72 Lisa Isherwood and Marcella Althaus-Reid, "Queering Theology," in *The Sexual Theologian: Essays on Sex, God and Politics* (London: T&T Clark, 2002), 2.

The more you confine me, the more I will spill over.[73]

Sakirtharani's poem captures the Dalit feminist fight to be heard and responds to the call of Indecent Theology that suggests that the more confined the lives of the marginalised are, the more they will "spill over" and in doing so expose all of the unpleasant truths. A Christology born out of the spilling over of crushed, broken, raped, and abused bodies enables us to witness the Jesus who as Isherwood writes, walked "down the vaginal aisle and arrived in a world of shit, blood and weeping..."[74] In doing so we witness the Jesus who is herself a Dalit *devadāsī*. Because an Indecent Dalit Christology "may say: 'God, the Faggot; God, the Drag Queen; God, the Lesbian; God, the heterosexual woman who does not accept the constructions of ideal heterosexuality; God, the ambivalent, not easily classified sexually."[75] Dalit Theology has been comfortable in calling God Dalit, and perceiving Christ as oppressed, but it must also come to see Christ as a prostitute, or a *devadāsī*, in order take the issue of sex and oppression in our societies seriously.[76] As it is the dangerous purity in Christianity and its obsessive need to convert all into a hegemonic "singleness of desire"[77] that denies the lived religiosity of the masses.

Dalit Christology must therefore become more uncomfortable and transgressive in order to witness the indecent Dalit Christ in the Dalit village acting as a local village deity and responding to the needs of the community. It must also recognise the indecency of the multiple religious belonging of the Dalit masses and enter into a genuine dialogue that finds hope in the goddess. It is only by doing so that it will challenge the Christologies that are based on immobile notions and theologies that are purposefully shaped to preserve dogma.[78]Brahminical patriarchy has taken the form of neo-liberal capitalism, colonialism, Christian patriarchal missiology, corrupt landlords, reform programmes and political propaganda. It is through an indecent theological gaze that the bodies of the *devadāsīs* expose the failures of systematic and male-centric theologies, as through their "impure" status and carrying their sexually transmitted diseases they expose the truth of the God made incarnate. Without such indecent obscenities in Dalit theological discourses the ultimate

---

73   Sukirtharani, "Nature's Fountainhead" quoted in *Wild Words: Four Tamil Poets*, ed. Lakshmi Holmstrom (New Delhi: HarperCollins, 2015), 36.

74   Isherwood, "Indecent Theology: What F-ing Difference Does it Make?,"145.

75   Althaus-Reid, *Indecent Theology*, 85.

76   Ibid, 122.

77   Althaus-Reid also questions if feminist theologians are also guilty of having a quest for purity, and singleness of desire...See, Althaus-Reid, *Indecent Theology*, 103.

78   See, Althaus-Reid, *Indecent Theology*, 108.

grace of the Divine cannot be realised. Just as the Black Christ of Black theology exposes the obscenities of racism "under the guise of a white Jesus"[79], the *Devi* Christ of the Dalit village, who is worshipped as a local deity, reveals the inadequacies of the phallocentric Christ of male Dalit theology.

Althaus-Reid talks of *Christa* as another example of obscenity in theology, as *Christa* is the female incarnate God who disrupts the heterosexual gaze. Noting that she "undresses the masculinity of God and produces feelings and questionings which were supressed by centuries of identificatory masculine processes with God." The body of *Christa* reveals the inability of the church to take seriously the torture of the bodies of women. "Why, for instance, is the tortured male body of Christ less offensive and infinitely more divine than a woman's tortured body? Or why does a woman's tortured body become sexy, as in the images of dismembered women found in some pornographic magazines."[80] Yet in the Dalit village the mythology of the Dalit goddesses tells tales of gendered violence, physical and emotional torment and torture inflicted on to the bodies of the women who are marginalised and oppressed and reborn as divine protectors of the village. It does not shy away from the worshipping of women deities who had their heads chopped off, their body stripped and the dismembered head of another woman attached to their own body. *Christa* is not simply about reimagining Christ as female but as *Christa* she must "uncover the contradiction and difficulties of a female Christ if construed as 'the other side of the coin' of Christ."[81] *Christa* in the Dalit village becomes disruptive to the heterosexual gaze of dominant theologies because she lives inside the brothels of another goddess and becomes shaped by Dalit village identity, mythology and religiosity. *Christa* exposes the bodily torment of the women who are marginalised for their ritualised sexuality, and with her "obscene vagina" uncovers the patriarchal systems that have justified the bodily oppression of the sacred sex workers. Re-imagining Christ as the Dalit village *Christa* also transforms the journey to the cross, as it challenges the decency of the torture of Jesus. The torture of the Dalit *Christa* involves gang rape, slut shaming, branding, name calling, manual scavenging and honour killing.

---

79   Ibid, 111.
80   Ibid, 111.
81   Ibid, 111.

6   The Dalit *Christa's* Kin-dom to Come

Truly I tell you, the tax collectors and the prostitutes are going into the kin-dom of God ahead of you. (Matthew 21:31)

Indecency as a methodology in Dalit Theology reveals the God who goes beyond being a friend of sinners and sex workers by suggesting that "Jesus must have had something of the sinner and the prostitute too within himself if he enjoyed their company."[82] As such the Dalit *Christa* interrupts earthly forces of oppression by challenging notions of decency, she extends her solidarity with the promise of liberation for the oppressed to the Kingdom of God, a place where the prostitutes and other socially marginalised groups will be welcomed and liberated from all earthly oppressions. The *mujerista* theologian, Ada María Isasi-Díaz uses the term "Kin-dom of God" in her theologising as a means of moving away from the male-centric imagery of God that is evoked by the term "Kingdom." The notion of a "Kin-dom" theology adheres to the Dalit community call for resistance and solidarity. Focusing instead on the "Kin-dom" transforms the heavenly realm into a space of kin-ship, solidarity, equality, and most importantly for the Dalits, a place void of the caste system, a place of belonging for the un-belonged.[83] Isasi-Díaz further highlights that the Bible needs to be used analogically in order to respond to the atrocities of life with the gospel message of justice and peace as oppose to accepting the patriarchal hegemony of scriptures priests.[84] In her argument for a Kin-dom theology, she contemplates the role of Jesus as mediator of the Kin-dom, yet proposes that Jesus as *Jesucristo,* is not the sole mediator. She "insists that a serious Christology needs to consider him as the full expression of what is human. This is what his life and ministry communicated, and therefore it is how he mediated the Kin-dom..." she argues that as a mediator he is part of a community, it is here that he expresses his full humanity, Mary and the disciples are therefore also part of this mediator..."[85] When contemplated from this perspective, the prostitutes are not only welcome in to the Kin-dom of God but also mediators of the Kin-dom to come, because they are part of Christ's community, they are the marginalised and oppressed with whom Christ takes

---

82   Althaus-Reid, *Indecent Theology*, 113.

83   Edwin David Aponte, *Handbook of Latina/o Theologies* (Danvers, MA: Chalice Press, 2006), 119.

84   See, Lisa Isherwood, "An Interview with Ada Maria Isasi-Díaz" *Feminist Theology* Vol. 20 (2011): 8–17.

85   See Miguel. A. De La Torre, *Hispanic American Religious Cultures 2 Volume Set,* (California: Greenwood Publishing Group, 2009), 745.

the side of. It is through their bodily experiences within the community of the oppressed that the God/ess of liberation is revealed.

The Dalit goddesses *Mathamma, Ellaiyamman* and *Yellamma* are the Dalit deities of the marginalised that as Clarke describes are "sent out into the village to live from the gifts of the people. Here she utilises her powers to protect all those who sustain her with food, offerings and worship."[86] The Dalit goddesses are symbolically the protectors of the boundaries who take the side of the oppressed. Like the Dalit *devi,* Jesus as God incarnate journeys into the margins, and is worshipped by the bodies of the excluded whilst seeking their emancipatory liberation from hegemonic structures. The deities of the Dalits function to develop a community of belonging for the un-belonged, the Divine is also the "indwelling spirit who energises and empowers Dalits" whilst working within and amongst them as the divine agency that "inspires, protects, and participates in the Dalit quest for 'being-in-wholeness.' *Dalit(the)os* is about the interrelationality between Dalits and the Divine."[87] The incarnate *Christa* offered the Kin-dom to the prostitutes, sinners and outcastes, and transformed their vulnerabilities into alternative spaces of empowerment and with them became marginalised and downtrodden.

Such "interrelationality" is further addressed by Marcella Althaus-Reid who states: "if as liberationists claim, Christ is neither male nor female in the sense that Christ represents the community of the poor, then Christ should be portrayed as a girl prostituted in Buenos Aires in a public toilet by two men. Obviously such portrayal would be considered indecent, because we are bringing to the surface the hidden face of the sexual oppression of women but for that reason it should be seen as true theology."[88] It is the bodies of the women who are forced into prostitution, who have been consumed by poverty, disease, STDs, AIDs, HIV, control and castigation, that a true Christology is developed. They are the mediators of the Kin-dom of God because they have experienced the absolute oppression of earthly powers and receive the promise of Christ, that they will have a place in the Kin-dom to come. The Kin-dom of Christ on earth is therefore the community of mediators who are the oppressed. It is here that a body theology, that is derived from the pathos and struggles of oppressed communities, and emancipatory protests and resistance movements, can be contemplated. This is because as Anderson-Rajkumar describes, "a Dalit

---

86   Clarke, "Paraiyars Ellaiyamman as an Iconic Symbol," 50.
87   Peniel Jesudason Rufus Rajkumar, "The Diversity and Dialectics of Dalit Dissent and Implications for a Dalit Theology of Liberation," in *Dalit Theology in the Twenty-First Century: Discordant Voices, Discerning Pathways* (New Delhi: Oxford University Press, 2010), 65–66.
88   Althaus-Reid, "On Wearing Skirts Without Underwear," 41.

female body stands therefore at the threshold of justice, challenging us to look beyond the barriers and recognise in the other, a sister and a brother...they speak of the possibility of life and the possible resurrection of new meaning of love."[89] Theologising in the brothels of the sacred "prostitutes" of South India reimagines Christ amidst the struggles of the silenced and exploited sex workers; it presents challenging Christological contemplations where the divine is present in the most indecent of spaces, and it is in the moments of resistance that we can catch glimpses of the Kin-dom to come.

7   From Dalit Theology to Indecent Dalit Theology

Whilst Dalit Theology has focused on the need for Dalit liberation it has at times neglected its desire to be identity-specific, where it has not been shaped by the religious experiences of the Dalit communities. In particular, it has neglected the narratives of the Dalit women who remain committed to the village goddesses through faith and praxis. As a result, the Church in South India has become disconnected from aspects of Dalit village life and appears to remain distracted by the patriarchal agenda of the white, male, Christ of the colonialists. For Althaus-Reid and Isherwood this is the "terrible fate of theologies from the margins when they want to be accepted by the centre."[90] This comes at the expense of the Dalits who are further marginalised for their gender, sexuality and poverty. The contemporary Dalit sacred sex workers therefore offer narratives that enable a more engaged Dalit Theology that is challenged by the reality of their indecent sexuality, poverty, religious hybridity and sacred belonging. Such a theologising is discomforting because it places God in perverse places and the most marginalised of spaces. Through an Indecent Theologising the body of the *devadāsīs* gains macro-political effect as a result of what Althaus-Reid and Isherwood refer to as a "passion for the marginalised". Such a theologising "identifies moments of sexual resistance", and produces discourses of theology that bring about solidarity and require action. [91] In the Dalit village *devadāsī* communities such moments of resistance are found in the mythology of the goddesses and the lives of the sacred sex workers – where their sexuality is used as a means of oppression, resistance and survival. It focuses on what Althaus-Reid refers to as the "divine gaze on the

---

89   Anderson-Rajkumar, "Turning Bodies Inside Out," 200.
90   Althaus-Reid, *Indecent* Theology, 304.
91   The passion for the marginalised requires a commitment for transformation and social justice, Queer and indecent theologising is therefore shaped by agency. See, Isherwood and Althaus-Reid, "Queering Theology " 6.

vulva" as opposed to the womb, because for the *devadāsī*, her vulva is also her sacred spot, it is what makes her one with the goddess.[92] As an incarnate theology that is produced from the bodies of sacred sex workers it rejects dogma and embraces syncretism and is shaped by unmediated personal experiences of the divine.

> Discourses of liberation have a value which comes not from their textual force, but from the realm of human activity, that is from the rebellious people. Such rebellious activity is what interpellates the reader in her struggle against oppression, and gets objectified in the discourse of liberation.[93]

Indecent Theology "is more marginal and perhaps even more messy"[94] then Feminist Theology and Liberation Theology, and when applied to the lived realities of the Dalit *devadāsī* it becomes even more uncomfortable and challenging. Making space for the *devadāsīs* in a Dalit theological discourse is not done so as a means of opening up the debate over the morality of sex work but instead to allow the sexual stories to speak for themselves. Such theologising is unsettling, unfinished and indefinite and yet it opens our eyes to the truth of systematic oppressions. It allows us to witness the extent to which normative principles of the dominant powers have determined what should and should not be tolerated in theologising. This is because "indecent theologies are sexual theologies without pages cut from the books of our sexual experiences."[95] Indecency as a methodology therefore challenges Dalit feminist theological discourse to be free of the heterosexual gaze. As Dalit feminist discourses have to date constructed the woman's body as Dalit but 'decent'. In doing so it has further marginalised the women who break the conventional models of sexuality. Whilst it presents women's bodies as prophetic through a Dalit feminist hermeneutic that re-reads scripture and exposes moments of resistance and liberation, it does not delve into "hidden spaces of theological struggles"[96] shaped by the sexuality and village religiosity of Dalit women.

An Indecent Dalit Feminist Theology defies the hegemonic theologies that force the prostitutes to bear the stigma of sexual violation and ruin, whilst praising the wife as honourable and sexually respectable.[97] It does so by ena-

---

92   Althaus-Reid, *Indecent Theology*, 56.
93   Ibid, 21
94   Althaus-Reid, *From Feminist Theology*, 146.
95   Althaus-Reid, *Indecent Theology*, 146.
96   Althaus-Reid, *From Feminist Theology*, 100.
97   Ramberg, *Given to the Goddess*, 177.

bling the narratives of the most marginalised and oppressed Dalit women to be prophetic, by incorporating their alienated and oppressed realities in to theological discourse. Inclusive of their identity-specific Dalit mythology that influences and radicalises Dalit feminist discourse. It remains uncomfortable and fluid as it re-contextualises itself based upon the narratives of the most marginalised and is therefore "a permanent exercise of serious doubting in theology." This "serious doubting" involves "questioning those very hermeneutical principles" which led liberation theologies to be indifferent to the reality of the sexual and indecent narratives of the poor.[98] Yet as Slee outlines, "the paradox continues: even the Christa, the female form of the risen Christ… is no final resting place for the Christological creative symbol or story of the divine, she is incomplete, she is provisional. She must be cherished and assimilated but then released, let go of, lost to her own larger reality, to her own future momentum."[99] Dalit Theology inclusive of Dalit feminist theological discourse must therefore reconnect with the lives of Dalit women, men and children who remain the most marginalised. Not as a means of adapting their narratives for "consumption or profit—spiritual, artistic or otherwise",[100] but in order to address the reality of their suffering and acknowledge how traditional Christian theologies and the praxis of the Church has only furthered the oppression of the Dalit women who remain dedicated to their local village goddesses, or exist outside of homogenised heteronormative relationships.

Take for example the unbound matted hair of the *devadāsīs,* which is symbolic of childbirth, sexual intercourse, the death of a husband, menstruation, pollution and for the *devadāsīs,* a sign of her calling to the goddess *Yellamma.*[101] For the church missionaries, the matted hair was emblematic of a deviant woman who needed shaming and transforming in order to become a decent representative of the Dalit community. Their hair represented their sexual indecency and "immorality" – consequentially the religious mythology in relation to the matted hair is made irrelevant through Christian hegemonic reform initiatives. The sexuality of the *devadāsīs* has been considered impure and offensive, as a result their bodies have become contested sites of state-sponsored reform and rehabilitation programmes. Whilst feminist campaigns have seemingly adhered to such programmes deeming the religious praxis of the *devadāsīs* as a violent expression of patriarchal Hinduism imposed on to

98   Althaus-Reid, *Indecent Theology,* 5.
99   Nicola Slee, *Seeking the Risen Christa* (London: SPCK, 2011), 38.
100   See, Alison Jasper, "Book Review, 'From Feminist Theology to Indecent Theology," *Literature and Theology* (2006): 83.
101   David Kinsley, *Tantric Visions of the Divine Feminine* (Delhi: University of California Press, 2003), 84.

the bodies of Dalit women. Yet such missiology is dehumanising to the women who persist in ritual practices as it denies them of their agency by refusing to recognise the women as persons unless they are remade and reformed. Such praxis succumbs to dangerous epistemological structures that seek to destroy the identities of the marginalised groups. This book has therefore sought to explore the epistemological and ontological significance of Dalit village religiosity as a means of contemplating indigenous and identity-specific mythology, worship and theology in order to counteract the dehumanising aspects of hegemonic systematic theology.

In the Dalit village the gods and goddess live and work among the community of "outcastes," as a result the lived religiosity of the contemporary sacred sex workers offers radical and transformative epistemological beliefs and practices. Ethnographic research exposes how goddess village worship as located in the body – does not focus solely on individual bodily religious praxis but is collective, relational and communal. It is disruptive to systems of oppression because it calls on the divine who is outcaste and marginalised. And whilst the church focuses its missiological efforts on making people "decent" the village *devi* is busy helping the sex worker who is suffering from a sexually transmitted disease or trying to feed and clothe her "illegitimate" children. Engaging with the religious discourse and existential narratives of the sacred sex workers fundamentally requires reflecting on the violence, violation and oppression that the dedicated women suffer as a result of the tyranny of casteism, patriarchy, colonialism and misogyny. Their bodily narratives disrupt normative and naturalised expressions of faith and sexuality and intensify theological reasoning over the presence of God in situations of oppression. Melissa Raphael describes this process as the "idea of the female body as a locus and medium of sacred that informs the the(a)ology and practice of spiritual feminism."[102] The bodies of the contemporary sacred sex workers therefore enable a Dalit indecent theologising that disrupts the "highly sacralised" heterosexual gaze of systematic theologies and the liberation theologies that have ignored the indecent reality of oppression.

Carol Christ outlines how it is sometimes argued that "focusing our attention on changing our images of divine power is the privilege of white women who have the time and energy to deal with so-called 'psychological' issues."[103] Yet for the sexually abused Dalit women, who have been raped by the high caste male landlords from childhood, and had their bodies pushed further into the margins of society by the male authorities of the state and the reform

---

102   Melissa Raphael, *Thealogy and Embodiment*, 22.
103   Christ, "The Road Not Taken:" 22–37.

programmes of the church, for them, transgressing the "decent" male Christ of the colonialists is vital. We encounter such alternatives in the lived religion of the Dalit communities that is shaped by human agency and disrupts the normative and naturalised relationships between the sacred and the living. We witness how oppression is lived in the lives of the 'othered' bodies that are the most marginalised and in the midst of such struggles encounter the Dalit goddess Jesus – who upsets the status quo and responds to the most indecent of needs in the here and now.

In the South Indian village, multiple religious belonging and religious hybridity become accepted norms of religious praxis and experience, as religious beliefs are shaped by and dependent on the suffering of the individual and community as a whole. Theologising with the Dalit sacred sex workers therefore challenges the missiological praxis of the institutional Church and the dogmatics of systematic theology and worship. It involves a theological yātrā that refuses to be repressed by heterosexual and patriarchal norms and instead witnesses the Dalit *Christa* in the brothels of the goddess. It is here that we encounter the God who takes the side of the marginalised because she is herself marginalised, her mythology and the fact that she resists the caste-based oppression confirms this. The indecent bodies of the *devadāsīs* are therefore prophetic as their visible suffering in the here and now exposes the promise of a kin-dom to come. A place where men do not dominate, where Dalits are no longer oppressed, and where women are not forced to have sex to feed their children – a kin-dom of justice.

Bibliography

Aguilar, Mario. I. *Religion, Torture and the Liberation of God*. New York: Routledge, 2015.

Aleaz, K. P. "The Theological Writings of Brahmabandhav Upadhyaya Re-Examined." *IJT* 28, no. 2 (1979): 55–77.

Allen, Jafari S. *Venceremos? The Erotics of Black Self-Making in Cuba*. London: Duke University Press, 2011.

Althaus-Reid, Marcella. *Indecent Theology: Theological Perversions in Sex, Gender and Politics*. New York: Routledge, 2000.

Althaus-Reid, Marcella. *From Feminist Theology to Indecent Theology*. London: SCM Press, 2004.

Althaus-Reid, Marcella. "'A Saint and a Church for Twenty Dollars': Sending Radical Orthodoxy to Ayacucho." In *Interpreting the Postmodern: Responses to "Radical Orthodoxy"*, edited by Rosemary Radford Ruether and Marion Grau, 107–119. New York: T&T Clark, 2006.

Althaus-Reid, Marcella and Isherwood, Lisa. *The Sexual Theologian: Essays on Sex, God and Politics*. London: T&T Clark, 2004.

Althaus-Reid, Marcella. "On Wearing Skirts Without Underwear: 'Indecent Theology Challenging the Liberation Theology of the Pueblo'. Poor Women Contesting," *Feminist Theology* Vol. 7, no. 20 (1999): 39–51. Accessed December 17, 2015. doi: 10.1177/096673509900702004

Althaus-Reid, Marcella. *The Queer God*. London: Routledge, 2003.

Althaus-Reid, Marcella and Isherwood, Lisa. *The Sexual Theologian: Essays on Sex, God and Politics*. London: T&T Clark, 2004.

Althaus-Reid, Marcella. "Searching for a Queer Sophia-Wisdom: The Post-Colonial Rahab." In *Patriarchs, Prophets and Other Villains*, edited by Lisa Isherwood, 128–140. London: Equinox, 2007.

Ambedkar, Bhimrao Ramji. "Castes in India: Their Mechanism, Gender and Development." In *Readings in Indian Government and Politics: Class, Caste, Gender*, edited by Manoranjan Mohanty, 131- 135. New Delhi: Sage Publications, 2004.

Ambedkar, B. R. *Dr. Babasaheb Ambedkar: Writings and Speeches Vol. 9*, edited by Vasant Moon. New Delhi: Ministry of Social Justice,1991.

Ambedkar, B. R. *The Buddha and His Dharma*. Delhi: Siddarth Books, 2006. Ambedkar, Bhimrao Ramji. *The Untouchables*. Delhi: Gautam Book Centre, 1948.

Ambedkar, Bhimaro Ramji. *The Essential Writings of B. R. Ambedkar*. Oxford University Press, 2002.

Amandeep, "Dalit Aesthetics: A Study of the Bhakti Period." *Journal of Literature, Culture and Media Studies*, Vol. II. (2010): 1–7.

Anderson-Rajkumar, Evangeline. "Turning Bodies Inside Out: Contours of Womanist Theology." In *Dalit Theology in the Twenty-first Century: Discordant Voices, Discerning Pathways*, edited by Sathianthan Clarke, Deenabandhu Manchala, and Philip Vinod Peacock, 199–215. New Delhi: Oxford University Press, 2010.

Anderson-Rajkumar, Evangeline. "Politicising the Body: A Feminist Christology." Paper presented at the theological colloquium Asian Faces of Christ, Delhi, March, 20, 2004.

Aponte, Edwin David. *Handbook of Latina/o Theologies*. Danvers, MA: Chalice Press, 2006. Appasamy, A. J. *Christianity as Bhakti Marga: A Study in the Mysticism of the Johannine Writings*. London: Macmillan and Co. ltd, 1927.

Appasamy, A. J. *What is Moksha?* Madras: CLS, 1931.

Appasamy, A. J. *The Gospel and India's Heritage*. London: SPCK, 1942.

Appavoo, J. T. "Communication for Dalit Liberation: A Search for an Appropriate Communication Model." Master of Theology Thesis., Edinburgh University,1993.

Ashanet. "MICDA Mathamma Eradication Project, Chittoor District, Andhra Pradesh." Accessed July 25, 2014. https://www.ashanet.org/projects/project-view.php?p=409.

Ayrookuzhiel, A. M. Abraham. "The Dalits, Religions and Interfaith Dialogue." *Journal of Hindu- Christian Studies:* Vol. 7, Article 6 (1994): 1–18.

Baader SJ, Gerard. "The Depressed Classes of India: Their Struggle for Emancipation." *Studies: An Irish Quarterly Review,* Vol. 26. No. 103. (1937): 399–417.

Bae, Hyunju. "The Moments of Divine Eros in Luke 7:36-50." In *Religion, Ecology & Gender: East- West Perspectives*, edited by, Sigurd Bergmann and Yong-Bock Kim, 35–55. Berlin: LIT Verlag, 2009.

Bagwe, Anjali. *Of Woman Caste: The Experience of Gender in Rural India*. Calcutta: STREE, 1995.

Bakshi, S. R. *B. R. Ambedkar: His Political and Social Ideology*. New Delhi: Deep & Deep Publications, 2000.

Bama, *Sangati*. Translated by Lakshmi Holmström. Delhi: OUP India, 2009.

Balasundaram, Sasikumar."An Indentured Tamil Goddess: Mariyamman's Migration to Ceylon's Plantations as a Worker." In *Inventing and Reinventing the Goddess: Contemporary Iterations of Hindu Deities on the Move*, edited by Sree Padma, 103–121. London: Lexington Books, 2014.

Battersby, Matilda. "Prostitutes of God." *The Independent*, September 20, 2010. Accessed March 17, 2015. http://idsn.org/wp-content/uploads/user_folder/pdf/New_files/India/Prostitutes_of_God_-_press_clippings.pdf.

Belkin, Erika. "Creating Groups Outside the Caste System: The Devadasis and Hijras of India." PhD diss., Wesleyan University: 2008.

Bharati, Sunita Reddy. "'Dalit': A Term Asserting Unity," *Economic and Political Weekly,* Vol. 37. No.32. (2002): 4339–4340.

Black, Maggie. *Women in Ritual Slavery: Devadasi, Jogini, and Mathamma in Karnataka and Andhra Pradesh, Southern India*. London: Anti-Slavery International, 2007.

Blanchard, James F. "Understanding the Social and Cultural Contexts of Female Sex Workers in Karnataka, India: Implications for Prevention of HIV Infection." *The Journal of Infectious Diseases*, Vol. 191, Supplement 1. (2005): S139-S146.

Blunt, Edward. *The Caste System of Northern India*. Delhi: Isha Books, 1931.

Bohm. Robert. *Notes on India*. Boston: South End Press, 1982.

Bouglé, Célestin. *Essays on the Caste* System. Translated by D. F. Pocock. Cambridge: Cambridge University Press, 1971.

Brenner-Idan, Athalya. "Clothing Seduces: Did You Think It Was Naked Flesh That Did It?"In *A Feminist Companion to Tobit and Judith*, edited by Athalya Brenner-Idan and Helen Efthimiasia-Keith, 212–226. London: Bloomsbury, 2015.

Brock, Rita Nakashima. "Marriage Troubles," *Pacific, Asian and North American Asian Women in Theology and Ministry*. Accessed, March 17, 2015. http://www.panaawtm. org/images/BROCK_Marriage_Trouble.doc.

Brubaker, Richard L. "Barbers, Washermen, and their Priests: Servants of the South Indian Village and Its Goddess." *History of Religions* Vol. 19. No. 2 (1979): 128–152.

Calduch-Benages, Nuria. *The Perfume of the Gospel: Jesus' Encounters with Women*. Roma: Pontificio Istituto Biblico, 2012.

Carey, Christopher. and Farao, Eileen. "Galtung's Unified Theory of Violence and Its Implications for Human Trafficking: A Case Study of Sex Workers in West Bengal India." In *Global Perspectives on Prostitution and Sex Trafficking: Africa, Asia, Middle East and Oceania*, edited by, Rochelle L. Dalla, Lynda M. Baker, John DeFrain, and Celia Williamson, 83–105. Plymouth: Lexington Books, 2011.

Cannon, Katie Geneva. Townes, Emilie M. and Sims, Angela D. *Womanist Theological Ethics: A Reader*. Louisville, Kentucky: Westminster John Knox Press, 2011.

Chakravarti, Uma. *Gendering Caste Through a Feminist Lens*. Calcutta, STREE, 2003.

Channa, Subhadra Mitra. "Metaphors of Race and Caste-Based Discriminations against Dalits and Dalit Women in India." In *Resisting Racism and Xenophobia on Race, Gender, and Human Right*, edited by Faye Venetia Harrison, 49–67. CA: AltaMira Press, 2005.

Charsley, Simon R. "Caste, Cultural Resources and Social Mobility." In *Challenging Untouchability: Dalit Initiative and Experience from Karnataka*, edited by Simon R. Charsley, and G. K. Karanth, 44–71. New Delhi: Sage Publications, 1998.

Chatterjee, Partha. *The Nation and its Fragments: Colonial and Postcolonial Histories*. Princeton: Princeton University Press, 1993.

Chatterjee, Partha. "Democracy and Economic Transformation in India." *Economic & Political Weekly* (2008): 53–62.

Chatterji, Saral K. "Why Dalit Theology." In *A Reader in Dalit Theology*, edited by Arvind P. Nirmal, 25–32. Chennai: Gurukal Lutheran Theological College and Research Institute, 1994.

Cheruvillil, Sonia J. "Dalit Women, Sexual Violence and the Geography of Caste: A Journey towards Liberation – An Interview with Asha Kowtal and Thenmozhi Soundararajan." *The Feminist Wire*, May, 1, 2014. Accessed December 17, 2014. http://www .thefeministwire.com/2014/05/dalit-women-sexual-violence/.

Chitkara, Madan Gopal. *Dr. Ambedkar and Social Justice*. New Delhi: A P H Publishing Corporation, 2002.

Chitnis, Rucha. "Meet the Indian Women Trying to Take Down 'Caste Apartheid.'" *Yes! Magazine,* October 26, 2015. Accessed November 26, 2015. http://www.pri.org/ stories/2015-10- 26/meet-indian-women-trying-take-down-caste-apartheid

Christ, Carol. "The Road Not Taken: The Rejection of Goddesses in Judaism and Christianity." In Patriarchs, Prophets and Other Villains, edited by Lisa Isherwood, 22–37. London, Equinox Publishing, 2007.

Clarke, Satianathan. *Dalits and Christianity*: *Subaltern Religion and Liberation Theology in India*. Oxford: Oxford University Press, 1998.

Clarke, Sathianathan. "Dalit Theology: An Introductory and Interpretive Theological Exposition." In *Dalit Theology in the Twenty-First Century: Discordant Voices, Dicerning Pathways*, edited by Satianathan Clarke, Deenabandhu Manchala, and Philip Vinod Peacock, 19–38. New Delhi: Oxford University Press, 2010.

Clarke, Satianathan. "Dalits Overcoming Violation and Violence: A Contest Between Overpowering and Empowering Identities in Changing India." *The Ecumenical Review* Vol. 54, Issue 3 (2002): 278–295.

Clarke, Sathianathan. "Paraiyars Ellaiyamman as an Iconic Symbol of Collective Resistance and Emancipatory Mythography." In *Religions of the Marginalised: Towards a Phenomenology and the Methodology of Study,* edited by Gnana Robinson, 35–53. Delhi: ISPCK, 1998.

Clarke, Sathianathan. "The Task, Method and Content of Asian Theologies." In *Asian Theology on the Way: Christianity, Culture and Context*, edited by Peniel Rajkumar and Rufus Rajkumar. London: SPCK, 2012.

Clarke, Sathianathan. "Subalterns, Identity Politics and Christian Theology in India." In *Christian Theology in Asia* Ed. Sebastian C. H. Kim 271–290. Cambridge: Cambridge University Press, 2008.

Clarke, Sathianathan. "Reviewing the Religion of the Paraiyar: Ellaiyamman as an Iconic Symbol of Collective Resistance and Emancipatory Mythology." In *Religions of the Marginalised: Towards a Phenomenology and the Methodology Study*, edited by, Gnana Robinson. 35–53. Delhi: ISPCK, 1998.

Clooney, S. J. Francis Xavier. "Passionate Comparison: The Intensification of Affect in Interreligious Reading of Hindu and Christian Texts." *The Harvard Theological Review.* Vol. 98 (2005): 367- 390.

Coleman, Monica A. *Making a Way Out of No Way: A Womanist Theology*. Minneapolis: Fortress Press, 2008.

Cone, James H. *God of the Oppressed*. New York: The Seabury Press, 1975.

Cordova Quero, Martin Hugo. "The Prostitutes Also Go into the Kingdom of God: A Queer Reading of Mary of Magdala." In *Liberation Theology and Sexuality*, edited by, Marcella Althaus-Reid and Lisa Isherwood, 81–109. Hampshire: Ashgate Publishing, 2006.

Corley, Kathleen E. *Private Women, Public Meals: Social Conflict in the Synoptic Tradition*. Michigan: Henderickson Publishers, 1993.

Cosgrove, Charles H. "A Woman's Unbound Hair in the Greco-Roman World, with Special Reference to the Story of the 'Sinful Woman,' in Luke 7:36–50." *Journal of Biblical Literature* Vol. 124, No. 4 (2005): 675–692.

Counter Currents. "Untouchability, the Dead-cow and the Brahmin." Accessed October 15, 2014. http://www.countercurrents.org/dalit-ambedkarbeef050703.html.

Counter Currents, "Feminism and Dalit Women in India." Accessed February, 17, 2015. http://www.countercurrents.org/stephen161109.html.

Dalit Freedom Network UK. "Ritual Sex Slavery Increases in India despite Abolition." Accessed January 19, 2014. http://www.dfn.org.uk/news/archive/191-devadasi-increases.

Dalit Freedom Network UK. "Devadasi Increases." Accessed December 12, 2013. http://www.dfn.org.uk/news/archive/191-devadasi-increases.

Derne, Steve. "The (Limited) Effect of Cultural Globalisation in India: Implications for Culture Theory." *Poetics 33* (2005): 33–47.

Deliége, Robert. *The Untouchables of India*. Oxford: Berg, 1999.

Deliége, Robert. "The Myths of Origin of Indian Untouchables." *Man, Royal Anthropological Institute of Great Britain and Ireland,* Vol. 28, No. 3 (1993): 533–549.

Department for Women, Children, Disabled & Senior Citizens, Government of Andhra Pradesh. "Andhra Pradesh Prohibition of Dedication Act 1988." Accessed December, 12, 2013. http://wcdsc.ap.nic.in/entitlement_women.php.

Desai, Pratibha. "Exploitation of Scheduled Caste Women in the Name of Religion." In *Development of Scheduled Castes and Scheduled Tribes in India*, edited by Jagan Karade. Newcastle: Cambridge Scholars Publishing, 2008: 102–114.

Devare, Aparna. *History and the Making of a Modern Hindu Self*. New Delhi: Routledge, 2011.

Dhagamwar, Vasudha. *Law, Power and Justice*. Delhi: Sage, 1992.

Dietrich, Gabrielle. *Reflections on the Women's Movement in India: Religion, Ecology, Development*. New Delhi: Horizon India Books, 1993.

Dirks, Nicholas B. *Castes of Mind: Colonialism and the Making of Modern India*. New Jersey: Princeton University Press, 2001.

D. N. "Gandhi, Ambedkar and Separate Electorates Issue." *Economic and Political Weekly* Vol. 26, No. 1 (1991): 1328–1330.

Dube, Musa W. "Rahab Says Hello to Judith: A Decolonializing Feminist Reading." In *The Postcolonial Biblical Reader,* edited by R. S. Sugirtharajah 142–159. Oxford: Blackwell Publishing, 2006.

Dube, Musa W. "Review of Avaren Ipsen, Sex Working and the Bible, London: Equinox 2009." *Religion and Gender* Vol. 2, No. 2 (2012): 360–362.

Dubois, Abbe J. A. *Hindu Manners, Customs and Ceremonies.* London: Oxford at the Clarendon Press, 1928.

Dumont, Louis. *Homo Hierarchichus: The Caste System and Its Implications, Complete Revised English Edition.* Chicago: The University of Chicago Press, 1980.

Dushkin, Lelah. "Schedules Caste Policy in India: History, Problems, Prospects." *Asian Survey* Vol. 7. No. 9 (1967): 626–636.

Elisha, James. "Liberative Motifs in the Dalit Religion." *Bangalore Theological Forum* Vol. 34, no. 2 (2002): 78–88.

Elmore, Wilber T. *Dravidian Gods in Modern Hinduism A Study of the Local and Village Deities of Southern India.* Madras Christian Literature Society, 1925.

Epp, Linda. "Violating the Sacred?: The Social Reforms of Devadasis among Dalits in Karnataka, India." PhD diss., York University, 1997.

Evans, Kirsti. "Contemporary *Devadāsīs* Empowered Auspicious Women or Exploited Prostitutes?" *Bulletin of the John Rylands Library* Vol. 71–80 (1998): 23–38.

Findly, Ellison Banks. "Reviewed Work: Devi and the Spouse Goddess by Lynn E. Gatwood." *Journal of the American Oriental Society* Vol. 107, No. 4 (1987): 77–89.

Fitzgerald, Timothy. "Ambedkar, Buddhism, and the Concept of Religion." In *Untouchable Dalits in Modern India*, edited by S. M. Michael, 59–60. London: Lynee Rienner Publishers, 1999.

Flood, Gavin. *An Introduction to Hinduism.* Cambridge: Cambridge University Press, 1996.

Foulston, Lynn. and Abbott, Stuart. *Hindu Goddesses: Beliefs and Practices.* Brighton: Sussex Academic Press, 2009.

Frederickson, Kristine Wardle. "Josephine E. Butler and Christianity in the British Victorian Feminist Movement." PhD diss., University of Utah, 2008.

Fuller, C. J. "Gods, Priests and Purity: On the Relation Between Hinduism and the Caste System." *Man, New Series.* Vol. 14, No. 3 (1979): 459–476.

Fuller, C. J. *Servants of the Goddess, the Priests of a South Indian Temple.* Cambridge: Cambridge University Press, 1984.

Fuller, C. J. "The Hindu Pantheon and the Legitimation of Hierarchy." *Man,* Vol. 23, No. 1, (1998): 19–39.

Gandhi, Mohandas Karamchand. *My Religion.* Delhi: MGA, 1977.

Ganesh, Kamala. "Mother Who is Not a Mother: In Search of the Great Indian Goddess." *Economic and Political Weekly* Vol. 25, No. 42/43 (1990): WS-58–64.

Ghose, Sagarika. "The Dalit in India," *Social Research,* Vol. 70, No. 1 (2003): 83–109.

Ghurye, G. S. *Caste, Class and Occupation*. Bombay: Popular Book Depot, 1961.

Glushkova, Irina. "Norms and Values in the Varkari Tradition." In *Intersections: Socio-cultural Trends in Maharashtra*, edited by Meera Kosambi, 47–58. New Delhi: Orient Longman Limited, 2000.

Gorringe, Hugo. *Untouchable Citizens: Dalit Movements and Democratization in Tamil Nadu*. New Delhi: Sage Publications, 2005.

Government of India Ministry of Home Affairs. "Scheduled Castes and Scheduled Tribe Population." Accessed December 14, 2015. http://censusindia.gov.in/Census _Data_2001/India_at_glance/scst.aspx.

Guider, Margaret Eletta. *Daughters of Rahab: Prostitution and the Church of Liberation in Brazil*. Minneapolis: Fortress Press, 1995.

Gupta, Charu. "Representing the Dalit Woman: Reification of Caste and Gender Stereotypes in the Hindi Didactic Literature of Colonial India." *Indian Historical Review* 35 (2008): 101–124.

Gupta, Charu. "The Intimate Desires: Dalit Women and Religious Conversions in Colonial India." *The Journal of Asian Studies*, Vol. 73. No. 3 (2014): 661–687.

Guru, Gopal. "Dalit Women Talk Differently." *Economic and Political Weekly*, Vol. 30. No. 41/42 (1995): 2548–2550.

Gustavo Gutierrez, *A Theology of Liberation*. New York: Orbis Books, 1973.

Hardiman, David. *Gandhi in His Time and Ours: The Global Legacy of His Ideas*. London: C. Hurst & Co. 2003.

Harper, Edward B. *Religion in South Asia*. Seattle: University of Washington Press, 1964.

Hebden, Keith. *Dalit Theology and Christian Anarchism*. Surrey: Ashgate Publishing, 2011.

Hieke, Thomas. "Torah in Judith. Dietary Laws, Purity and Other Torah Issues in the Book of Judith." In *A Pious Seductress: Studies in the Book of Judith*, edited by, Geza G. Xeravits, 97–110. Berlin: Walter de Gruyter, 2012.

Holmstrom, Lakshmi. *Wild Words: Four Tamil Poets*. New Delhi: HarperCollins, 2015.

House of Commons Foreign Affairs Committee, *Human Rights Annual Report 2005: First Report of Session 2005–06*. House of Commons, Great Britain: Parliament, 2006.

Hovell, Laurie. "Namdeo Dhasal: Poet and Panther." *Journal of South Asian Literature*, Vol. 24. No. 2 (1989): 65–82.

Hubel, Teresa. "Tracking obscenities: Dalit women, devadasis, and the linguistically sexual." *The Journal of Commonwealth Literature*, Vol. 54 (2019): 52–69.

Human Rights Watch. "Cleaning Human Waste: 'Manual Scavenging' Caste and Discrimination in India." Accessed December 14, 2014. http://www.hrw.org/reports/ 2014/08/25/cleaning- human-waste-0.

Human Rights Watch. "UN Rights Council: End Caste-Based Rape, Violence." Accessed June, 19 2014. https://www.hrw.org/news/2014/06/17/un-rights-council-end-caste -based-rape-violence.

Human Rights Watch, *Hidden Apartheid Caste Discrimination against India's "Untouch-ables".* CHRC&GJ, 2007.

Hunt, Sarah Beth. *Hindi Dalit Literature and the Politics of Representation.* Oxon: Rout-ledge, 2014.

Institute of Social Sciences, *Trafficking in Women and Children in India.* New Delhi: Orient Longman, 2005.

International Dalit Solidarity Network, "Captured by Cotton: Exploited Dalit girls produce garments in India for European and US markets." Accessed, December 14, 2014. http://idsn.org/fileadmin/user_folder/pdf/New_files/Private_sector/CapturedByCottonRepo rt.pdf.

International Dalit Solidarity Network. "Official Dalit Population Exceeds 200 million." Accessed July 19, 2014. http://idsn.org/news-resources/idsn-news/read/article/india-official-dalit- population-exceeds-200-million/128/.

International Dalit Solidarity Network. "Dalit Women in India Stage Month-Long March for Justice." Accessed, March 19, 2014. http://idsn.org/news-resources/idsn-news/read/article/dalit- women-in-india-stage-month-long-march-for-justice/128/.

Irudayam, S. J. Aloysiuis., Mangubhai, Jayshree P., and Lee. Joel G. *Dalit Women Speak Out: Caste, Class and Gender Violence in India.* New Delhi: Zubaan, 2011.

Isherwood, Lisa. "Indecent Theology: What F–ing Difference Does it Make?" *Feminist Theology* 11/2 (2003): 141–147. Accessed April 15, 2015. doi: 10.1177/096673500301100203.

Isherwood, Lisa. and Althaus-Reid, Marcella. Introduction in *Controversies in Body Theology*, edited by Marcella Althaus-Reid and Lisa Isherwood. London: SCM Press, 2008.

Isherwood, Lisa and Jordan, Mark. *Dancing Theology in Fetish Boots: Essays in Honour of Marcella Althaus-Reid.* London: SCM Press, 2010.

Isherwood, Lisa. *Patriarchs, Prophets and Other Villains.* London, Equinox Publishing, 2007.

Isherwood, Lisa. and Althaus-Reid, Marcella. "Queering Theology." In *The Sexual Theologian: Essays on Sex, God and Politics.* London: T&T Clark, 2002.

Isherwood, Lisa. "An Interview with Ada Maria Isasi-Díaz." *Feminist Theology* Vol. 20 (2011): 8–17. Isherwood, Lisa and Stuart, Elizabeth. *Introductions in Feminist Theology.* Sheffield: Sheffield Academic Press, 1998.

Isherwood, Lisa and Stuart, Elizabeth. *Introducing Body Theology.* Sheffield, Sheffield Academic Press, 1998.

Jaiswal, Tulika. *Indian Arranged Marriages: A Social Psychological Perspective.* New York: Routledge, 2014.

Jaganathan, Arun. "Yellamma Cult and Divine Prostitution: Its Historical and Cultural Background." *International Journal of Scientific and Research Publications.* Volume 3. Issue 4. (2013): 1–5.

Janabai, "Jani Sweeps the Floor." In *Women Writing in India: 600 B.C. to the Early Twentieth Century*, edited by Vilas Sarang, Susie J. Tharu, and K. Lalita, 83–84. New York: The Feminist Press, 1991.

Jasper, Alison, "Book Review, 'From Feminist Theology to Indecent Theology." *Literature and Theology* (2006): 82–84.

Jeremiah, Anderson H. M. "Exploring New Facets of Dalit Christology: Critical Interaction with J. D. Crossan's Portrayal of the Historical Jesus." In *Dalit Theology in the Twenty-first Century: Discordant Voices, Discerning Pathways*, edited by, Sathianathan Clarke, Deenabandhu Manchala, and Philip Vinod Peacock, 150–168. New Delhi: Oxford University Press, 2010.

Jeremiah, Anderson H. M. *Community and Worldview among Paraiyars of South India*. London: Bloomsbury, 2013.

Jorgensen, Jonas Adelin. *Jesus Imandars and Christ Bhaktas: Two Case Studies of Interreligious Hermeneutics and Identity in Global Christianity*. Frankfurt: Peter Lang, 2008.

Joy, David. "Decolonizing the Bible, Church, and Jesus: A Search for an Alternate Reading Space for the Postcolonial Context." In *Decolonizing the Body of Christ: Theology and Theory After Empire?* edited by David Joy and David Duggan, 3–25. New York: Palgrave Macmillan, 2012.

Kahl, Werner. "Growing Together: Challenges and Chances in the Encounter of Critical and Intuitive Interpreters of the Bible." In *Reading Other-wise: Socially Engaged Biblical Scholars Reading with their Local* Communities, edited by Gerald O. West, 147–159. Atlanta: Society of Biblical Literature, 2007.

Kandasamy, Meena. *Ms Militancy*. New Delhi: Navayana Publishing. 2010.

Kandasamy, Meena. *Touch*. New Delhi: Peacock Books, 2006.

Kamitsuka, Margaret D. *Feminist Theology and the Challenge of Difference*. Oxford: Oxford University Press, 2007.

Karanth, G. K. "Replication or dissent: Culture and Institutions amongst 'Untouchable' Scheduled Castes in Karnataka." In *Caste in Question: Identity of Hierarchy?* edited by Dipankar Gupta, 137–165. New Delhi: Sage Publications, 2004.

Katha, Mool Vansh. "Bohistattva Bharat Ratna Baba Saheb Dr Bheem Raoji Ambedkar." In *Multiple Marginalities: An Anthropology of Identified Dalit Writings*, edited by, Badri Narayan and A. Misra, 71–101. New Delhi: Monohar Publishers & Distributors, 2004.

Keller, Catherine. *Apocalypse Now and Then: A Feminist Guide to the End of the World*. Minneapolis: Fortress Press, 2005.

Kent, Eliza. *Converting Women: Gender and Protestant Christianity in Colonial South India*. Oxford, Oxford University Press, 2004.

Kermorgant, Catherine Rubin. *Servants of the Goddess: The Modern Day Devadasis*. London: Random House Group, 2014.

Kersenboom-Story, Saskia. *Nityasumangali: Devadasi Tradition in South India.* Delhi: Motilal Banardsidass Publishers, 1997.

Kim, Jean K. "'Uncovering her Wickedness': An Intercontextual Reading of Revelation 17 From A Postcolonial Feminist Perspective." *Journal for the Study of the New Testament 73* (1999): 61–81.

Kinsley, David. *Tantric Visions of the Divine Feminine.* Delhi: University of California Press, 2003.

Knitter, Paul F. "Theocentric Christology: Defended and Transcended." In *Journal of Ecumenical Studies* 24 (1987): 41–52.

Kotiswaran, Prabha. "Law, Sex Work and Activism in India." In *Routledge Handbook of Gender in South Asia,* edited by Leela Fernandes, 84–96. New York: Routledge, 2014.

Kumar, Praveen. *Communal Crimes and National Integration: A Socio-legal Study.* New Delhi: Readworthy Publications, 2011.

Kumari, B. M. Leela. "The Untouchable "Dalits" of India and their Spiritual Destiny." In *Another World is Possible: Spiritualities and Religions of Global Darker Peoples,* edited by Dwight N Hopkins and Marjorie Lewis, 9–20. London: Routledge, 2014.

Kumran, Timur. *Private Truths, Public Lies: The Social Consequences of Preference Falsification.* Boston: Harvard University Press, 1995.

Kuruvila, K. P. *The Word Became Flesh: A Christological Paradigm for Doing Theology in India.* Delhi: ISPCK, 2002.

Krishnan, Suneeta. "Gender, Caste, and Economic Inequalities and Marital Violence in Rural South India." *Health Care for Women International,* 26 (2005): 87–99.

Kṣetrayya, A courtesan to her lover." In *When God is a Customer: Telegu Courtesan Songs by Ksetrayya and Others.* Edited by Ramanujan, 73–74. Berkley, CA: University of California Press, 1994.

Kwok, Pui-lan. *Postcolonial Imagination and Feminist Theology.* Westminster, John Knox Press, 2005.

Kwok, Pui-lan. "Changing Identities and Narratives: Postcolonial Theologies." In *Complex Identities in a Shifting World: One God, Many Stories,* edited by, Pamela Couture and Robert Mager, 115–127. Zurich: LIT, 2015.

Kwok, Pui-lan, "The Legacy of Cultural Hegemony in the Anglican Church." In *Beyond Colonial Anglican Communion in the Twenty-first Century.* New York: Church Publishing Incorporated, 2001.

Lane, Dermot A. *Stepping Stones to Other Religions: A Christian Theology of Inter-Religious Dialogue.* New York: Orbis Books, 2011.

Lele, Jayant. "The Bhakti Movement in India: A Critical Introduction." *Journal of Asian and African Studies* XV, 1–2 (1980): 1–15.

Liddle, Joanna. and Joshi, Rama. "Gender and Imperialism in British India." *Economic and Political Weekly* Vol. 20, No. 43 (1985): WS72–WS78.

Liddle, Joanna. and Joshi, Rama. *Daughters of Independence: Gender. Caste and Class in India.* New Delhi: Zed Books, 1986.

Lynch, Owen M. "A Review of an Untouchable Community in South India: Structure and Consensus by Michael Moffatt." *Journal of South Asian Studies*, Vol. 39, No. 3 (1980): 642–644.

Machado, Daisy L. "The Unnamed Woman: Justice, Feminists, and the Undocumented Woman." In *A Reader in Latina Feminist Theology: Religion and Justice*, edited by, María Pilar Aquino, Daisy L. Machado, and Jeanette Rodríguez, 161–177. Texas: University of Texas Press, 2002.

Madan, Triloki Nath. "Louis Dumont and the Study of Society in India." In *Caste, Hierarchy, and Individualism: Indian Critiques of Louis Dumont's Contributions*, edited by Ravindra. S. Khare. New Delhi: Oxford University Press, 2006.

Malik, Suratha Kumar. "Analysing Dalit Movement: Interpreting the History." Paper presented at Vidyasagar University, Midnapore, West Bengal, November 17, 2012.

Mani, Lata. "Contentious Traditions: The Debate on Sati in Colonial India." In *Recasting Women: Essays in Colonial History*, edited by Kumkum Sangari and Sudesh Vaid, 88–126. Delhi: Kali for Women, 1989.

Mantin, Ruth. "Carol Christ: Feminist Spirituality and Narrative." In *Contemporary Spiritualities: Social and Religious Contexts,* edited by, Clive Erricker and Jane Erricker, 93–113. London: Continuum, 2001.

Maraschin, Jaci."Worship and the Excluded." In *Liberation Theology and Sexuality*, ed. Marcella Althaus-Reid, 163–179. London: SCM Press, 2009.

Marti, Gerardo. "Found Theologies versus Imposed Theologies: Remarks on Theology and Ethnography from a Sociological Perspective", in *Ecclesial Practices 3, Brill, Leiden* (2016): 157–172.

Mantin, Ruth. "Dealing with a Jealous God: Letting go of Monotheism and 'Doing' Sacrality." In *Patriarchs, Prophets and Other Villains*, edited by, Lisa Isherwood, 37–50. London: Equinox Publishing, 2007.

Massey, James. *Indigenous People: Dalits: Dalit Issues in Today's Theological Debate.* Delhi: ISPCK, 1994.

Massey, James. *Dalits in India: Religion as a Source of Bondage or Liberation with Special Reference to Christians.* New Delhi: Manohar Publishers, 1995.

McLaren, Margaret A. *Feminism, Foucault, and Embodied Subjectivity.* New York: State University of New York Press, 2002.

McGuire, Meredith B. "Lived Religion: Faith and Practice in Everyday Life, Rethinking Religious Identity, Commitment, and Hybridity." *Oxford Scholarship Online* (2008): 1–31.

Melanchthon, Monica Jyotsna. "The Servant in the Book of Judith: Interpreting her Silence, Telling her Story." In *Dalit Theology in the Twenty-first Century: Discordant Voices, Discerning Pathways*, edited by Sathianathan Clarke, Deenabandhu Manchala, and Philip Vinod Peacock, 231–252. New Delhi: Oxford University Press, 2010.

Melanchthon, Monica. "Indian Dalit Women and the Bible: Hermeneutical and Methodological Reflections." In *Gender, Religion and Diversity: Cross-Cultural Perspectives*, edited by Ursula King and Tina Beattie, 212–224. New York: Continuum, 2004.

Melanchthon, Monica Jyotsna, "Unleashing the Power Within: The Bible and Dalits." In *The Future of the Biblical Past: Envisioning Biblical Studies on a Global Key*, edited by, Roland Boer and Fernando Segovia, 47–65. London: Society of Biblical Literature, 2012.

Menon, K. P. Kesava. Foreward to *Christianity in India*, edited by A. C. Perumalil and E. R. Hambye, 5–7. Alleppey: Prakam, 1972.

Michael, S. M. *Untouchable: Dalits in Modern India*. London: Lynne Rienner Publishers, 1999.

Michael, S. M. "Dalit Encounter with Christianity: Change and Continuity" In *Margins of Faith: Dalits and Tribal Christianity in India*, edited by R. Robinson and J. M. Kujur, 51–75. New Delhi: Sage Publications, 2010.

Mill, James. *The History of British India, 2 Vols*. New York: Chelsea House, 1968.

Mishra, Shewta N. *Socio-economic and Political Vision of Dr. B. R. Ambedkar*. New Delhi: Concept Publishing Company, 2010.

Misri, Deepti. *Beyond Partition: Gender, Violence, and Representation in Postcolonial India*. Chicago: University of Illinois Press, 2014.

Misra, Kamal K. and Rao, K. Koteswara. "Theogamy in Rural India: Socio-cultural Dimensions of the Jogini System in Andhra Pradesh." *Indian Anthropologists* Vol. 32 (2002): 1–24.

Minz, Nirmal. "Meaning of Tribal Consciousness." *Religion & Society* 6 (1989),

Mody, Navroz. "Atrocities on Dalit Panthers." *Economic and Political Weekly* Vol. 9, No. 3. (1974): 44– 56

Moffatt, Michael. *An Untouchable Community in South India: Structure and Consensus*. New Jersey: Princeton University Press: 1979.

Mohammada, Malik. *The Foundations of the Composite Culture in India*. Delhi: Aakar Books, 2007.

Mondal, Anshuman. A. *Nationalism and Post-Colonial Identity: Culture and Ideology in India and Egypt*. London: Routledge Curzon, 2003.

Mosse, David. "Caste, Christianity and Hinduism. A Study of Social Organisation and Religion in Rural Ramnad." D. Phil diss., Oxford University, 1985.

Mosse, David. "The Politics of Religious Synthesis: Roman Catholicism and Hindu Village Society in Tamil Nadu, India." In *Sycretism/ Anti-Syncretism: The Politics of Religious Synthesis,* edited by Rosalind Shaw and Charles Stewart, 87–92. London: Routledge, 1994.

Mosse, David. *The Saint in the Banyan Tree: Christianity and Caste Society in India*. California: University of California Press, 2012.

Muesse, Mark. *The Hindu Traditions: A Concise Introduction.* Minneapolis: Fortress Press, 2011.

Mullatti, Leela. *The Bhakti Movement and the Status of Women: A Case Study of Virasaivism.* New Delhi: Abhinav Publications: 1989.

Muthu, K. S. *Dalit Deities.* Madurai: The Dalit Resource Centre, 2005.

Nadella, Raj. "The Motif of Hybridity in the Story of the Canaanite Woman: Its Relevance for Multifaith Relations." In *Many Yet One? Multiple Religious Belonging,* edited by Peniel Jesudason Rufus Rajkumar, and Joseph Prabhakar Dayam, 111–121. Geneva: WCC Publications, 2016.

Nair, Janaki. "The Devadasi, Dharma and the State." *Economic and Political Weekly* Vol. 29, No. 50. (1994): 3157–3167.

Nangelimalil, Jacob. *The Relationship between the Eucharistic Liturgy, the Interior Life and the Social Witness of the Church according to Joseph Cardinal Parecattil.* Rome: Editrice Pontifica Universita Gregoriana, 1996.

Narasu, Pokala Lakshmi. *A Study of Caste.* New Delhi: AES Publications, 1988.

Narayan, R. K. *The Ramayana.* Delhi: Vision Books, 1987.

Naregal, Veena. *Language, Politics, Elites and the Public Sphere: Western India Under Colonialism.* London: Wimbledon Publishing Company, 2002.

Nelavala, Surekha. "Liberation Beyond Borders: Dalit Feminist Hermeneutics and Four Gospel Women." PhD diss., Drew University, 2008.

Nelavala, Surekha "Inclusivity and Distinctions: The Future of Dalit Feminist Biblical Studies." In *New Feminist Christianity: Many Voices, Many Views,* edited by Mary E. Hunt and Diann L. Neu, 100–107. Woodstock, Vermont: Skylight Paths, 2010.

Nelavala, Surekha. "Reading the 'Sinful Woman' in Luke 7:36-50 from a Dalit Feminist Perspective." In *Dalit Theology in the Twenty-first Century: Discordant Voices, Discerning Pathways,* edited by, Sathianathan Clarke, Deenabandhu Manchala, and Philip Vinod Peacock 252–266. New York: Oxford University Press, 2010.

Nielsen, Kenneth Bo. and Valdrop, Anne. *Women, Gender and Everyday Social Transformation in India.* London, Anthem Press, 2014.

Nirmal, Arvind. "A Dialogue with Dalit Literature," in *Towards a Dalit Theology,* edited by M. E. Prabhakar, 64–82. New Delhi: ISPCK, 1988.

Nirmal, Arvind. "Towards a Christian Dalit Theology." In *A Reader in Dalit Theology,* edited by Arvind P. Nirmal, 53–70. Madras: Gurukal Lutheran Theological College and Research Institute, 1991.

Liddle, Joanna and Joshi, Rama. *Daughters of Independence: Gender, Caste and Class in India.* London: Zed Books, 1986.

O'Hanlon, Rosalind. "A Tyranny Against Nature: The Untouchables in Western India." *History Today.* Volume 32: Issue 5 (1982): 22–27.

O'Hanlon, Rosalind. *Caste, Conflict and Ideology: Mahatma Jotirao Phule and Low-Caste Protest in Nineteenth-Century Western* India. Cambridge: Cambridge University Press, 1985.

Okin, Susan Moller. *Women in Western Political Thought.* New York: Princeton University Press, 1979.

Omvedt, Gail. "Jotirao Phule and the Ideology of Social Revolution in India." *Economic and Political Weekly* Vol. 6. No. 37. (1971): 1969–1979.

Oommen, Tharailath Koshy. "Sources of Deprivation and Styles of Protest: The Case of the Dalits in India." *Contributions to Indian Sociology* NS, 18 (1984): 45–61.

Orevillo-Montenegro, Muriel. *The Jesus of Asian Women.* New Delhi: Logos Press, 2009.

Ortmann, Bernhard. "Body Constructions Among Devadasi and Dalit Children." In *Body, Emotion and Mind: Embodying the Experiences in Indo-European Encounters,* edited by Martin Tamcke and Glason Jathanna, 1–27. Berlin: LIT Verlagm, 2013.

Panikkar, R. "Indian Theology. A Theological Mutuation." In *Theologising in India,* edited by M. Amaladoss 24–32. Bangalore: Theological Publications in India, 1981.

Passaro, Angelo. *Family and Kinship in the Deuterocanonical and Cognate Literature.* Berlin: Walter de Gruyter, 2013.

Paswan, Sanjay. *Encyclopaedia of Dalits in India Literature: Education, Literature, Political Science, Sociology, Women Studies.* Delhi: Kalpaz Publications, 2002.

Padma, Sree. *Inventing and Reinventing the Goddess: Contemporary Iterations of Hindu Deities on the Move.* London: Lexington Publishers, 2014.

Parecattil, Joseph. Foreward to *The Missionary Consciousness of the St. Thomas Christians.* Cochin: Viani Publications, 1982.

Parsons, Susan Frank. *The Cambridge Companion to Feminist Theology.* Cambridge: Cambridge University Press, 2002.

Pears, Angie. *Doing Contextual Theology.* London: Routledge, 2010.

Peracullo, Jeanne. "Indecent Theology as Catachrestic Postcolonial Method: Gayatri Spivak and Asian Catholic Women" *The Criterion An International Journal in English, Vol. IV, II* (2013): 1–10.

Perdue, Leo G. *Reconstructing Old Testament Theology: After the Collapse of History.* Minneapolis: Fortrress Press, 2005.

Pieris, Aloysius. *An Asian Theology of Liberation.* Edinburgh: T&T Clark, 1988.

Pocock, David Francis. *Essays on the Caste System by Célestin Bouglé.* London: Cambridge University Press, 1971.

Prabhakar Dayam, Joseph. "Gonthemma Korika: Reimagining the Divine Feminine in Dalit Christian Theo/alogy." In *Dalit Theology in the Twenty-first Century: Discordant Voices, Discerning Pathways,* edited by Sathianathan Clarke, Deenabandhu Manchala, and Philip Vinod Peacock, 137–150. New Delhi: Oxford University Press, 2010.

Prabhakar, M. E. *Towards a Dalit Theology.* Delhi: ISPCK, 1988.

Prasad, Amar Nath. *Dalit Literature: A Critical Exploration*. New Delhi: Sarup & Sons, 2007.

Prentiss, Karen Pechillis. *The Embodiment of Bhakti*. Oxford: Oxford University Press, 1999.

Puniyani, Ram. "Religion: Opium of the Masses or..." In *Religion, Power and Violence: Expression of Politics in Contemporary Times*, edited by, Ram Puniyani, 27–45. New Delhi: Sage Publications, 2005.

Quack, Johannes. *Disenchanting India: Organised Rationalism and Criticism of Religion in India*. New York: Oxford University Press, 2012.

Quigley, Declan. *The Interpretation of Caste*. New Delhi: Oxford University Press, 1999.

Rajkumar, Peniel. *Dalit Theology and Dalit Liberation: Problems, Paradigms and Possibilities*. Surrey: Ashgate, 2010.

Rajkumar, Peniel Jesudason Rufus Rajkumar and Prabhakar Dayam, Joseph. Introduction to *Many Yet One? Multiple Religious Belonging*. Geneva: WCC Publications, 2016.

Rajkumar, Peniel Jesudason. "The Diversity and Dialectics of Dalit Dissent and Implications for a Dalit Theology of Liberation." In *Dalit Theology in the Twenty-First Century: Discordant Voices, Discerning Pathways*, edited by, Sathianathan Clarke, Deenabandhu Manchala, and Philip Vinod Peacock, 55–74. New Delhi: Oxford University Press, 2010.

Ramberg, Lucinda. *Given to the Goddess: South Indian Devadasis and the Sexuality of Religion*. Durham: Duke University Press, 2014.

Rani, Challapalli Swaroopa. "Dalit Women's Writing in Telugu." *Economic and Political Weekly*, Vol. 33, No. 17 (1998): WS22–24.

Rao, Y. Chinna. "Dalits and Tribals Are Not Hindu." *Frontier*, Vol. 32, No. 37 (2000): 156.

Raphael, Melissa. *Introducing Thealogy: Discourse on the Goddess*. Sheffield: Sheffield Academic Press, 1999.

Raphael, Melissa. *Thealogy and Embodiment: The Post-Patriarchal Reconstruction of Female Sacrality*. Sheffield: Sheffield Academic Press, 1996.

Rawat, Hemant. *Dalit and Backward Women*. New Delhi: Lakshay Publications, 2011.

Rawat, Ramnarayan S. *Reconsidering Untouchability: Chamars and Dalit History in North India*. Bloomington: Indiana University Press, 2011.

Razu, John Mohan. "Contours and Trajectories of Dalit Theology." In *Dalit and Minjung Theologies: A* Dialogue, edited by Samson Prabhakar and Jinkwan Kwon. Bangalore: BTESSC/SATHRI, 2008.

Reddy, K. Rajesekhara. "Fertility and Mortality Amongst the Scheduled Caste Mādigas of Andhra Pradesh, India." *Current Science* Vol. 88. No. 10 (2005): 1664–1668.

Reid, Barbara. *Choosing the Better Part?: Women in the Gospel of Luke*. Minnesota: The Liturgical Press, 1996.

Rege, Sharmila. "Dalit Women Talk Differently: A Critique of 'Difference' and Towards a Dalit Feminist Standpoint Position." *Economic and Political Weekly* (2008): ws-39-ws-46.

Roberts, Yvonne. "India's Daughter: 'I made a film on rape in India. Men's brutal attitudes truly shocked me.' *The Guardian*, March, 1, 2015. Accessed December 20, 2015. http://www.theguardian.com/film/2015/mar/01/indias-daughter-documentary -rape-delhi- women-indian-men-attitudes.

Robinson, Bob. *Christians Meeting Hindus: An Analysis and Theological Critique of Hindu-Christian Encounter in India.* Milton Keynes: Regnum Books, 2004.

Ruether, Rosemary. "Women's Body and Blood: The Sacred and the Impure." In *Through the Devil's Gateway: Women, Religion and Taboo,* edited by A. Joseph, 7–21. London: SPCK, 1990.

Samartha, Stanley J. *Courage for Dialogue: Ecumenical Issues in Interreligious Relationships.* Geneva: WCC, 1981.

Sahu, Sandeep. "Rejoice, Mourn? Sashimani Devi's death brings end to devadasi tradition in Puri Temple," *First Post India.* Accessed March 17, 2015. http://www.firstpost .com/india/rejoice- or-mourn-sashimani-devis-death-brings-end-to-devdasi-tradition -in-puri-temple- 2175219.html.

Saran, Gurusaran Singh. *The Wheel Eternal.* Pennsylvania: Red Lead Press, 2013.

Satyanarayana, Y. B. *My Father Baliah.* New Delhi: Harper Collins Publishers, 2011.

Schüssler Fiorenza, Elizabeth. *Revelation: Vision of a Just World.* Minneapolis: Fortress Press, 1991.

S. D. "Children of God Become Panthers." *Economic and Political Weekly* Vol. 8, No. 31/33. (1973): 1395–1398.

Sebastian, J. Jayakiran, "Creative Exploration: Arvind P. Nirmal's Ongoing Contribution to Christian Theology." *Bangalore Theological Forum* 31:2 (1999): 44–52.

Shah, Ghanshyam. *Dalits and the State.* New Delhi: Concept Publishing Company, 2002.

Shanmugasundara, Anandhi. "Representing Devadasis: 'Dasigal Mosavalai' as Radical Text." *Economic and Political Weekly* Vol. 26. No. 11/12 (1991): 739–746.

Shanmugasundara, Anandhi. "Gender, Caste and the Politics of Intersectionality in Rural Tamil Nadu." *Economic and Political Weekly* Vol. XLVIII No. 18 (2013): 64–71.

Shankar, Subramanian. *Flesh and Blood: Postcolonialism, Translation, and the Vernacular.* London: University of California Press, 2012.

Shastree, Uttara. *Religious Converts in India: Socio-Political Study on Neo-Buddhists.* New Delhi: Mittal Publications, 1995.

Shenouda II, H. H. Pope. *The Life of Repentance and Purity.* Sydney, Australia: C.O.P.T, 1990.

Sherinian, Zoe. *Tamil Folk Music as Dalit Liberation Theology.* Bloomington, Indiana: Indiana University Press, 2014.

Siddiqui, Faiz Rahman. "Dalit Girl Mutilated for Resisting Rape in UP." *The Times of India*, February 7, 2011. Accessed April, 15, 2015. http://timesofindia.indiatimes.com/india/Dalit-girl- mutilated-for-resisting-rape-in-UP/articleshow/7439907.cms.

Siker, Jeffrey S. *Jesus, Sin and Perfection in Early Christianity.* New York: Cambridge University Press, 2015.

Singh, Ivy. "Eco-feminism as a Paradigm Shift in Theology." *Indian Journal of Theology* 45/1&2 (2003): 15–29.

Singh, Roja. "Bama's Critical-Constructive Narratives: Interweaving Resisting Visible Bodies and Emanicipatory Audacious Voice as TEXTure for Dalit Women's Freedom." In *Dalit Theology in the Twenty-First Century: Discordant Voices, Dicerning Pathways*, edited by Satianathan Clarke, Deenabandhu Manchala, and Philip Vinod Peacock, 215–231. New Delhi: Oxford University Press, 2010.

Skutsch, Carl. *Encyclopaedia of World's Minorities.* New York: Routledge, 2005.

Slee, Nicola. *Seeking the Risen Christa.* London: SPCK, 2011.

Smita Narula. *Broken People: Caste Violence Against India's "Untouchables".* New York: Human Rights Watch, 1999.

Srinivasan, Amrit. "Reform or Conformity? Temple 'Prostitution' and the Community in the Madras Presidency." In *Structures of Patriarchy: State, Community and Household in Modernising Asia*, edited by, Bina Agarwal, 175–198. London: Zed Press, 1988.

Srinivas, M. N. *The Cohesive Role of Sanskritization and Other Essays.* New Delhi: Oxford University Press, 1977.

Stephen, Cynthia. "A Name of Our Own: Subaltern Women's Perspectives on Gender and Religion." *Journal of Dharma* 36, 4 (2011): 419–434.

Stephen, M. *A Christian Theology in the Indian Context.* Delhi: ISPCK, 2001.

Stichele, Caroline Vander. "Re-membering the Whore: The Fate of Babylon According to Revelation 17:6." In *A Feminist Companion to the Apocalypse of John,* edited by, Amy-Jill Levine and Maria Mayo Robbins, 106–121. London: T&T Clark, 2009.

Stoddart, Eric. *Advancing Practical Theology: Critical Discipleship for Disturbing Times.* London: SCM Press, 2004.

Streete, Gail Corrington. *The Strange Woman: Power and Sex in the Bible.* Westminster, John Knox Press, 1997.

Sugden, Chris. *Seeking the Asian Face of Jesus: A Critical and Comparative Study: The Practice and Theology of Christian Social Witness in Indonesia and India 1974–1996.* New Delhi: Regnum, 1997.

Swedberg, Richard. *Max Weber and the Idea of Economic Sociology.* New Jersey: Princeton University Press, 1998.

Tambiah, S. J. "From Varna to Caste through Mixed Unions." In *Character of Kinship*, edited by Jack Goody, 191–229. Cambridge: Cambridge University Press, 1973.

Tambe, Anagha. "Reading Devadasi Practice Through Popular Marathi Literature." *Economic and Political Weekly* Vol. XLIV, No. 17. (2009): 85–92.

Taneti, James Elisha. *Caste, Gender, and Christianity in Colonial India: Telugu Women in Mission*. New York: Palgrave Macmillan, 2013.

Tarachand, K. C. *Devadasi Custom: Rural Social Structure and Flesh Markets*. New Delhi: Reliance Publishing House, 1992.

Thekkedath, Joseph. *From the Middle of the Sixteenth Century to the End of the Seventeenth Century 1542–1700*. Bangalore: The Church History Association of India, 1982.

Teltumbde, Anand. *Khairlanji, A Strange and Bitter Crop*. New Delhi: Navayana, 2008.

Thurston, Edgar. *Castes and Tribes of Southern India Vol. VI*. Madras: Government Press, 1909.

Tiemeier, Tracy Sayuki. "Comparative Theology as a Theology of Liberation." In *The New Comparative Theology: Interreligious Insights from the Next Generation*, edited by Francis X. Clooney. S. J. 129–151. London: T&T Clark, 2010.

Torri, Maria-Constanza. "Abuse of the Lower Castes in South India: The Institution of the Devadasi." in *Journal of International Women's Studies* Vol. 11 (2009): 31–48.

Trible, Phyllis. *Texts of Terror: Literary-feminist Readings of Biblical Narratives*. London: SCM Press, 2002.

Turman, Eboni Marshall. *Toward a Womanist Ethic of Incarnation: Black Bodies, the Black Church, and the Council of Chalcedon*. New York: Palgrave Macmillan, 2013.

Ucko, Hans. *The People and the People of God: Minjung and Dalit Theology in Interaction with Jewish Christian Dialogue*. London: Transaction Publishers, 2002.

Upahyaya, Brahmabandhab. "The Hymn of Incarnation." in *An Introduction to Indian Christian Theology*, edited by Robin Boyd, 77–78. Madras: CLS, 1994.

Ussher, Jane M. "The Construction of Female Sexual Problems: Regulating Sex, Regulating Women." In *Psychological Perspectives on Sexual Problems: New Directions in Theory and Practice*, edited by, Jane M. Ussher and Christine D. Baker, 9–31. London: Routledge, 1993.

Vakil, A. K. *Reservation Policy and Scheduled Castes in India*. New Delhi: APH Publishing, 1985.

Van Dijk-Hemmes, Fokkelien. "The Metaphorization of Woman in Prophetic Speech: An Analysis of Ezekiel XXIII." *Vetus Testamentum* Vol. 43, Fasc. 2 (1993): 162–170.

Vijaisri, Priyadarshini. "In Pursuit of the Virgin Whore: Writing Caste/Outcaste Histories." *Economic and Political Weekly* Vol. XLV. No. 44 (2010).

Vijaisri, Priyadarshini. *Recasting the Devadasi: Patterns of Sacred Prostitution in Colonial South India*. New Delhi: Kanishka Publishers, 2004.

Vinayaraj, Y. T. "Dalit body without God: Challenges for epistemology and theology." In *Body, Emotion and Mind 'Embodying': The Experiences in Indi-European Encounters*, edited by Martin Tamcke and Gladson Jathanna, 27–37. Berlin: LIT, 2013.

Vojdik, Valorie K. "Sexual Violence Against Men and Women in War: A Masculinities Approach." *Nevada Law Journal* Vol. 14 (2014): 923–952.

Wasnik, Krupakar Pralhad. *Lost People: An Analysis of Indian Poverty.* Delhi: Isha Books, 2009.

Weber, Max. *The Religion of India: The Sociology of Hinduism and Buddhism.* New York: Free Press, 1962.

Webster, John C. *Hindu-Christian Dialogue: Perspectives and Encounters.* Delhi: Orbis Books, 1993.

Weems, Renita. *Battered Love: Marriage, Sex, and Violence in the Hebrew Prophets.* OBT: Minneapolis: Fortress, 1995.

Wilfred, Felix. *On the Banks of the Ganges: Doing Contextual Theology.* Delhi: ISPCK, 2005.

Wilfred, Felix. *From the Dusty Soil: Contextual Reinterpretation of Christianity.* Chennai: Department of Christian Studies, University of Madras, 1995.

Wilson, Kothapalli. *The Twice-Alienated: Culture of Dalit Christians.* Hyderabad: Booklinks Cooperation, 1982.

Whitehead, Henry. *Indian Problems in Religion Education Politics.* Bombay: Bombay Press, 1921.

Wojciechowski, Michael. "Moral Teaching of the Book of Judith." In *A Pious Seductress: Studies in the Book of Judith,* edited by Geza G. Xeravits, 85–96. Berlin: Walter de Gruyter, 2012.

Wondra, Ellen K. *Humanity has Been A Holy Thing: Toward a Contemporary Feminist Christology.* Maryland: University Press of America, 1994.

Wootton, Janet. "Biblically Slicing Women." In *Controversies in Body Theology,* edited by, Marcella Althuas-Reid and Lisa Isherwood, 158–174. London: SCM Press, 2009.

Wright, N. T. *Luke for Everyone.* London: Society for Promoting Christian Knowledge, 2001.

Yee, Gale A. *Poor Banished Children of Eve: Woman as Evil in the Hebrew Bible.* Minneapolis: Fortress Press, 2003

Younger, Paul. "A Temple Festival of Mariyamman." *The Journal of the American Academy of Religion,* Vol. XLVIII, No. 4. (1980): 493–516.

Yuval-Davis, Nira. *The Situated Politics of Belonging.* London: Sage Publications, 2006.

Zee Media Bureau. "Uttar Pradesh Shocker: Two Sisters Gang-Raped. Hanged from Tree; 4 Arrested." *Zee News India,* May 29, 2014. Accessed February 17, 2015. http://zeenews.india.com/news/uttar-pradesh/uttar-pradesh-shocker-2-sisters-gang-raped- hanged-from-tree-4-arrested_935769.html.

Zelliot, Eleanor. *From Untouchable to Dalit: Essays on the Ambedkar Movement.* New Delhi: Manohar Publications, 1992.

Zene, Cosimo. *The Political Philosophies of Antonio Gramsci and B. R. Ambedkar: Itineraries of Dalits and Subalterns.* New York: Routledge, 2013.

Primary Sources

Bama, interview, Madurai, Tamilnadu, November, 11, 2014.

Church leaders, interview, Nagalapuram, Andhra Pradesh, December 11, 2014. Dalit Women's Self-Repect, interview, Madurai, Dec, 10, 2013.

Mathamma Kanagarathinam, interview, Nagalapuram, Andhra Pradesh, December 12, 2014. Prasu, interview, Chittoor District, Andhra Pradesh, December, 16, 2014.

Prici, interview, Tamil Nadu, Chennai, December, 16, 2014.

Village life, fieldnotes, Nagalapuram, Andhra Pradesh, December 11, 2014.

Index of Subjects

Index of Names